T0339719

FISCAL CRISIS AND WORLD ORDER

FISCAL CRISIS AND WORLD ORDER

Raymond W. Converse

Algora Publishing
New York

Library of Congress Cataloging-in-Publication Data —

Converse, Raymond W.
  Fiscal crisis and world order / Raymond W. Converse.
     p. cm.
     ISBN 978-0-87586-897-4 (soft cover: alk. paper)—ISBN 978-0-87586-898-1 (hard
cover: alk. paper)—ISBN 978-0-87586-899-8 (ebook) 1. Financial crises. 2. International
economic relations. 3. Economic policy—International cooperation. 4. European Union
countries—Foreign economic relations. 5. United States—Foreign economic relations. I.
Title.
  HB3722.C687 2012
  330.9'0511—dc23
                              2012002330

Printed in the United States

TABLE OF CONTENTS

PREFACE

The crisis facing the United States is both economic and political, and its effects are felt both at home and abroad. The following chapters present a detailed look at how the present world order is being or could be affected by a total global economic collapse.

The recession of 2008 and the fiscal crisis that followed brought about a clear recognition of two major themes. First, economic recessions/depressions are not capable of being contained within a single national economy or a small number of national economies. The current state of economic interrelatedness is truly global. Second, as a result of this globalization, economic distress experienced by one or more nation states will rapidly spread throughout the global market. Globalization of economic activities means that international cooperation is imperative to remedy any real problems within the economic structure. Regardless of whether the current fiscal crisis, for example, is the result of mismanagement on the part of national governments or the activities of an unregulated and parasitic financial community, only cooperation on a global scale appears capable of producing a solution.

The current fiscal crisis is being handled by an attempt to return to solutions that were developed when such economic matters could be directly remedied on a national level. The Keynesian approach to stagnant economic growth patterns, high unemployment, etc., pioneered during the Great Depression, was to infuse the economy with massive government spending. Such spending in times past was successful in stimulating both private sector spending and capital investment. This in turn was successful in bringing the economy back to a rather robust rate of growth, lowering unemployment and increasing government revenue to pay for the stimulus. In the current situation, the cost of stimulating the economy in this manner tends to depress the economy even more and to produce the opposite effect, that is, a slowing of economic growth through consumer austerity and withdrawal of capital investment from the economy. This in turn deepens the unemployment problem and tends to make permanent the high levels of budget deficits and long-term debt. This has resulted in a lack of liquidity available to bail out the national economies heading for default or to pay the interest and maintenance of the current private and public debt.

Two schools of thought have developed around the above scenario. One is that the fiscal crisis will result in the forced default of a number of weaker national economies, such as Greece, Ireland, Portugal and Spain among others. This school believes that the national governments of the wealthier nation states will be forced to stop bailing out local financial and industrial communities as has been the practice of the United States and the European Union. A second school believes that the various national economies can be returned to liquidity through a combination of regulation of the financial community on a global basis, a reduction in the burden of social welfare transfer payments in the industrialized economies, and a series of austerity programs designed to reduce budget deficits and national long-term debt. If the first group is correct, the current economic problems will deepen into either a recession equivalent to the one that broke in 2008 or in the worst case a depression that would equal that of the 1930s. If the second group is correct, the worst effects of a deepening recession/depression could be avoided although large scale economic restructuring might be required. Either result is probably beyond the control of any single nation-state (the US, Japan, etc.) or any group of nation states (the EU, the Russian Federation, China, etc.). The worst case scenario would entail the partial or total dismemberment of the European Union, a significant reduction of economic growth in China and India, and the failure of a large number of weak economies. It would also include a serious reduction of the standard of living globally, including in the United States.

There is growing concern over the seeming impossibility of finding a workable solution. There is also growing recognition that a solution will only be forthcoming if the requisite cooperation is found in the international community. This would in all probability include formation of a supranational organization capable of instituting and enforcing the regulation and discipline needed to end the crisis. The existing international financial organs, such as the International Monetary Fund (IMF), the World Bank and World Trade Organization (WTO) have been tried but are not structurally capable of independent actions and enforcement. The US and the EU have over the last several years attempted to bail out the bankrupt financial community, as well as the equally bankrupt industrial sector, and have failed to stem the problem in that manner. Even the US is beginning to realize that its budget deficits and long-term debt may have already reached a stage that will prove unsustainable even in the short term.

For the above reasons it is slowly becoming clear that the solution will have to be global and will require the cooperation of a significant number of nation-states led by the efforts of the US and the European Union. The solution will undoubtedly require the delegation of a significant level of sovereignty from the participating nation-states to a supranational organization created for the sole purpose of dealing with the fiscal crisis. It is most likely to be structured as an intergovernmental organization similar to the European Council (EC). This organization, unlike the EC, will need to have the power to pass legislation, regulations and edicts that can be directly enforced by it.

The EU represents the most likely source of any approach that is attempted along the lines of intergovermentalism. The EU has consistently taken the position that a system of financial regulation on a global scale is necessary to get at the root of the current fiscal crisis. They have also had experience at finding the methods needed to bring about unanimous consensus on economic issues. The problem that faces even the attempt to establish some type of intergovernmental solution is that it will take a considerable amount of time. It may in fact be true that the amount of time necessary is not currently available. Some experts believe that short term remedies, or at least stop gap measures, can be instituted to delay the impending collapse until more permanent solutions can be applied. Such measures would probably include a determined effort to continue the bailout of the financial community (largely banking institutions) and weak national economies, particularly those found in the European Union. Should a large nation-state, such as Italy, the Russia Federation or India go into default there would be no stop gap measures that could be applied and the effort would be futile. Should the stop gap measures be successful the result would be the need to restructure the current economic environment in such a manner that the financial community would be brought under control and the individual nation states be returned to fiscally sound policies. The latter would need to be allowed to happen voluntarily in all cases where it is possible, but enforced where necessary.

The first chapters of this work will be devoted to an analysis of whether or not a voluntary solution can be obtained or even if it is feasible. A look will be taken at what must be done by the US and the EU, along with the other highly industrialized nations, to provide the necessary stop gaps to gain the time for permanent solutions. A look will also be taken at what the consequences might be if the short term stop gap measures should fail to buy the necessary time. We will also consider several alternative projections that have been made as to the existing world order and where it may be headed. In this vein a look will be taken at the collection of essays written by Robert Cox and the book written by George Friedman entitled *The Next Decade Where We've Been...And Where We're Going.*

The remaining chapters will be devoted to the question of what type of international organization would obtain if the EU model is used. A look will be taken at the possible response if the EU should be forced to enter a partial or total dismemberment; or in case of the disintegration of either the Indian or Chinese nation-states.

CHAPTER 1. THE GLOBAL REPERCUSSIONS OF THE RECESSION AND FISCAL CRISIS

The end of World War II and its predecessors, i.e., the Roaring Twenties and the Great Depression, unnerved the world. Some far-seeing men such as Bertrand Russell and F.A. Hayek had warned of the upcoming perils. The rising totalitarian governments in a few nations such as Germany, Russia, Italy and Japan were being widely hailed as the harbingers of a better future. Capitalism (or the Democratic tradition generally) was being denigrated as responsible for the First World War and for the irresponsibility of the Roaring Twenties and the suffering of the Great Depression. This made it easier to believe the propaganda that was pouring out of Germany and the Soviet Union.

Russell, and especially F.A. Hayek, realized the danger in this intellectual game. They both clearly saw that the Communist and Nazi systems were much crueler and more impotent than the capitalist system even at its worst. They warned that the terrible suffering related to the operation of the Soviet and German governments was an integral part of the system itself. They clearly expressed their fear that the Second World War was just around the corner and would be brought about by the global designs of the totalitarian governments. They could not, of course, foresee the even more terrible cruelty that would attend the establishment of dictatorships and totalitarian-style governments in Latin America, Africa and Asia.

The Second World War came as predicted with a vengeance that shocked even the most knowledgeable. Millions upon millions of people, both combatants and non-combatants, were to die or be maimed in the war. The whole of the European continent, as well as much of Asia, was to be devastated economically. Only the US and a few other nation states would escape relatively untouched. The Soviet Union through the forced incorporation of Eastern Europe was able to maintain its position as a premier military power, but was seriously crippled economically and socially by the war. Western Europe, in particular Germany, Italy, France and the UK lost their status as world powers and were relegated to the rank of secondary peripheral powers. As individual nation states they were unable to recover from this loss of status.

The aftermath of the war quickly evolved into a balance of power between the US and the Soviet Union, at least in the military arena. Although not clearly recognized by the US at the time the US was uniquely placed at the time to win this military balance of power game. The US had lost relatively few casualties during the war and inconsequential amounts of material wealth. The war had opened up the tremendous industrial capacity of the US which was carried forward after the war. In addition, the war had left the US in total control of the world's oceans. These two factors quickly consolidated into an economic hegemony in the US in connection with the manufacture of goods, trade and finance globally. The other half of the balance of power could only hope to maintain its position through military parity with the United States. For whatever reasons, the world generally accepted that the Soviet Union was the equal of the US in terms of military capability. The equality was quickly converted into the so-called Cold War in which the US and the Soviet Union entered into severe competition. This competition in the end boiled down first to a race in the field of military weapons, especially atomic and nuclear weapons; a somewhat later race for clients to support them in world opinion clashes; and lastly, a race to command the use of outer space as a military base of action. In the long run this competition was labeled MAD or mutually assured destruction. This parity, however, was a fantasy right from the beginning. As proof of this statement one needs only consider what was actually done by the two sides. The US instituted the Marshall Plan which was instrumental in the recovery of Western Europe from the war. In order to insure the time needed for this recover the US instituted the North Atlantic Treaty Organization (NATO) to insure that a military umbrella was in place to protect Western Europe from Soviet intentions. The same program was followed in the rebuilding and protection of Japan and Southeast Asia generally under foreign aid programs and the South East Asian Treaty Organization

(SEATO). Indeed the US quickly surrounded the Soviet Union with its string of military and economic aid treaties. The Soviet Union in reality was limited to maintaining enough military strength to destroy the US if attacked, that is to say, to a defensive posture.

The Cold War was to last for some five decades but by the end of the 1980s it was apparent that the Soviet Union would be unable to hang onto its satellites in Eastern Europe and would in the end dissolve in 1992. Without going into any great detail; with hindsight it is possible to see that the Soviet Union was never in a position to challenge the US hegemony in the global market.

The paranoia produced by the cold war caused the US to ignore to some degree its hegemonic status. This allowed two other political entities to infringe on this hegemony, that is, the Japanese and West Germany, at least in the economic arena. Both were able within the first five decades after World War II to obtain a significant share of the global total in manufactured goods and trade. The German success came because of its own efforts but was also a major part of the growth of the European Union (EU). As the influence of the EU and Japan grew in the economic arena they were also able to become more influential in the global political arena, especially in relation to foreign aid, participation in international organizations and in global financial decisions. The adjustments that are taking place in the global market to compensate for these changes are part of the reason that the global economic structure is in its present state of crisis.

With the fall of the Soviet Union the US found itself the "sole superpower". In a rather ironic twist the classification as a superpower in 1992 was somewhat different than was the case prior to this point in time. During the period 1948 to 1992, although faced with the military challenge of the Soviet Union, the US was without question the "sole superpower" economically and politically. This dominance included not only the areas of global manufacturing of goods, global trade, and global finance; but also dominance in the construction and operation of multiple international organizations. This latter dominance was often misused as was the case of the US handling of the Suez crisis in 1956, the US involvement in the Viet Nam action during the 1960s and 70s, the Iran-Contra affair in the 1980s, and the manner in which some Latin American countries were handled during the 1980s. In addition the US failed to maintain its partnership with the EU and Japan in its decision to unilaterally face the dangers of terrorism and the invasion of Iraq in 2003. This political mismanagement over the last two decades has resulted in a serious loss of influence in the EU, Japan, and generally in the eyes of world opinion. This loss of influence has also resulted in somewhat less confidence in the US in relation to its foreign policy.

The rapid and unexpected deconstruction of the Soviet Union brought with it a greater degree of confusion within the foreign policy of the US in relation to its role in the "new world order". In particular the US was uncertain of how to use its massive superiority in military power. Once again the US seems to have mismanaged the opportunities that lay before it. The early use of US military power in the removal of Iraq from Kuwait was done in a manner consistent with the demands of the former Cold War. Sanctions against Iraq were sought by the US from the United Nations (UN); as was the mandate to use force in Kuwait. Both were granted by the UN and the US further solidified its position in world opinion by soliciting and obtaining a rather wide coalition to help fight and pay for the operation in Kuwait. This was the last time that the US would be successful in approaching the use of military power in this fashion. Although the actual military action was short-lived the US found itself facing a united world opinion against taking the war into Iraq and unseating the dictator Saddam Hussein. The US, faced by adverse world opinion, in this case backed down and did not take action against Iraq directly. The leadership of the US however was never fully reconciled to this outcome. The military policy of the US as a result became significantly more aggressive.

During the first decade after the demise of the Soviet Union it became clear, especially in the US and the EU that the US was no longer the sole economic superpower globally. The global economic hegemony remained but was being distinctly challenged by the economic clout of both the EU and Japan. In addition, there was a growing recognition of the economic power of several fast growing economies, such as those of India, China and S. Korea (Southeast Asia generally). The US remained the largest National economy globally particularly in the areas of manufactured goods and finance. This position was being challenged by the EU by the end of the decade with its close second in relation to both trade and manufacturing on the global scale. The EU was now beginning to flex its economic muscle internationally, sometimes in direct opposition to the wishes of the United States. As a result the US was forced, in some areas, to share its political power globally with that of the EU and Japan. These facts do not seem to have been internalized within the US foreign policy decision making process even as late as 2001.

The whole complex of global power was to shift dramatically after the 2001 attack on the US by Al Qaeda. From the very beginning the US response was emotional and to a large degree irrational. The US announced that it was going to launch a war against terrorism and would not only conduct this war against individual terrorist organizations but would also include any nation state that aided or harbored such organizations. This decision was unilateral on the part of the US and definitely displeased the EU, the Russian Federation, China and others. This approach was mitigated to some degree by the US obtaining a UN mandate to use force in Afghanistan to remove Al Qaeda and the Taliban. This military action was to be led by NATO, which was a definite concession to the EU membership. The US, however, squandered this support by extending the mission beyond the removal of Al Qaeda and the Taliban to one of nation building. Most of the support that the US had garnered slowly dissipated over the next decade. The US, through NATO, has now been in Afghanistan for nearly ten years and has borne the majority of the material costs of the war as well as a significant number of human causalities. As a result the UN has failed to respond for calls for it to take over the peacekeeping mission and the members of NATO have largely withdrawn their forces. As of 2011, the US does not appear to be any closer to establishing a democratically stable government in Afghanistan than it was in 2002. The US goal now is to find a face-saving method by which to withdraw from Afghanistan.

Part of the vision of a "war on terrorism" by the US again turned to its unfinished business in Iraq. In this case, with the exception of the UK and a few other nation states, world opinion was openly critical of the US aims. The US responded by making essentially a unilateral decision to invade Iraq regardless of the consequences. After eight years it is clear that the US has not accomplished any of its stated goals with the sole exception of the capture and execution of the dictator Saddam Hussein. The US has once again saddled itself with the total material cost of the war and a significant number of human losses. The US expects to be fully withdrawn from Iraq by the end of 2011 or shortly thereafter. Even so it appears likely that the US will leave Iraq in a very unstable and vulnerable situation.

In addition to the two wars in the Middle East by 2007 the US was also faced with a rather pronounced economic recession, that is, stagnant economic growth and high levels of unemployment. There also at this time was growing evidence of a looming financial crisis. This latter was first denoted by the fiscal mismanagement of two of the three major automobile corporations and their resulting bankruptcy. The federal government determined that these corporations, if allowed to fail, would greatly deepen the recession. The government, therefore, pumped some 50 to 75 billion dollars into these companies to keep them afloat. The government in relation to the bailout of these corporations also required them to restructure their operations, which they did with the cost of some 70,000 additional jobs. The bailout worked, however, and these companies have recovered to the point where they are beginning to return the money given by the US taxpayers. The recession was declared officially over in the summer of 2009, but the very low growth rate in the US economy, very high levels of unemployment, and lack of confidence in the economy and the federal government would tend to belie this pronouncement. At about the same time the US public became aware of the mismanagement and malfeasance of the financial community. The financial community had through the manipulation of assets, misleading mortgage documents, and risky investments artificially created a housing bubble. When the bubble burst the financial community, including Fanny-Mae and Freddy-Mac, were holding so-called toxic (worthless) assets several hundred times in excess of their real assets. Once again the government decided that the financial community should not be allowed to fail and the government guaranteed some 700 billion dollars in toxic assets. This figure is expected to climb to over 3 trillion dollars before a full restoration of the financial community can be affected in this area. In relation to this problem the federal government attempted to pass legislation that would handle the problem in bulk; this legislation was known as the Troubled Asset Relief Act (TARP). The first attempt at passage in Congress was defeated. This so upset the financial community that the New York Stock Exchange lost over 1.5 trillion dollars in investment value on the first day after the vote. The next day Congress passed the bill and the financial community breathed a sigh of relief. The real problem, however, is that the American Public was forced to stand alone in relation to the loss of assets reflected in the high level of home foreclosures and value losses in 401(k) and other retirement vehicles resulting from the fall in stock values. In short, the financial community was bailed out while the public was allowed to suffer the losses and costs of the bailouts. The result of all of these massive increases in spending on the part of the federal government since 1992 is a 2010 budget that is showing a 1.5 trillion dollar deficit and a national debt that exceeds 14 trillion dollars. The same problems of economic stagnation, excessive spending, and unsustainable national debts are also directly affecting the EU, the Russian Federation, India, Japan, and to a lesser degree China.

As of August of 2011 the world stands poised on the brink of economic chaos. Several nations are set to enter into default on their obligations in the near future. These nation states include Greece, Portugal, Ireland, Italy and Spain. There are others across the globe that are also headed in the same direction but are expected to survive for a longer period of time than those named before entering into default. For example, the economic stagnation affecting both the EU and the US is expected to become evident in India, China, the Russian Federation and Southeast Asia during the next decade leading to serious unrest in these states. The US, although capable of avoiding economic chaos, has become increasing incapable of consistent political action. The stalemate, or gridlock, caused by the growing ideological separation between the major political parties since 1992 has nearly paralyzed the government in 2011. For example, the Congress was unable to pass a bill to fund the remaining six months of the 2010 budget until the day that the US was expected to run out of money to pay its bills. The solution obtained at this last hour crisis only handled the issue of avoiding default and did not speak to the solutions to the problems that brought about this crisis. The game being played is a very dangerous one; but the leadership of the US is accepting the gridlock produced by this ideological battle and is allowing the public to bear the cost of its inaction. In addition, the political subunits of the American Union are also teetering on the brink of default. Three of the largest states are included, that is, California, New York, and Illinois. The default crisis extends down even to the level of county and municipal government. While every state in the Union has a balanced budget law of some type, except Vermont, the laws seem to be universally ignored. Whether or not any of these defaults will take place; or whether the federal government will attempt to bail them out if they do, remains to be seen. There is at least the hope that the states, and lower subdivisions of government, will do what is necessary to restructure their revenue and spending to avoid default. The ideological debate is centered on whether it is the cost of social welfare programs, including government pensions, Social Security, Unemployment benefits, etc. that is causing the fiscal crisis; or the fact that the wealthiest individuals and corporations pay too little in taxes coupled with waste and fraud that is the culprit. In reality the ideological debate is a return to the original debate between the Federalists and Anti-Federalist over a large versus a limited government. Initially as was pointed out in the book *World Government: Utopian*

Dream or Current Reality the argument was won by the Federalists who advocated a proactive federal government.

It is very difficult without access to official records to determine whether or not the US is facing a real fiscal crisis or a serious case of political demagoguery. Even with a current budget deficit of 1.5 trillion dollars, and an expected budget deficit of 2.7 trillion by 2013, the US is still within the limits of safety in relation to the deficits percentage of GDP (less than 9%). Even the expected long-term debt of 21 trillion dollars by 2021 amounts to only 65% of GDP, which is also within the accepted range of safety. The drivers which are escalating the deficits and national debt, however, are quickly reaching a point where they will become unsustainable for any length of time. The UK was in a similar position about 100 years ago and survived a debt ratio of 150% of GDP, but they are the only nation state to ever do so. Although the fiscal crisis may be blown out of proportion as to its "real" importance it is, in fact, necessary that factors which led to it be addressed while there is no real crisis. If delayed the US is expected to be facing a real economic crisis within the next decade unless economic growth recovers substantially. The US has gone from being the world's largest creditor nation to the world's largest debtor nation. This in itself is enough to demand that notice be taken of the warnings of economic crisis.

There are many reasons that have been set forth to explain the conversion of the US from creditor to debtor status. Many see the beginning of this process as the movement of US manufacturing concerns outside the national borders. For example, it is claimed that the globalization of manufacturing has tended to marginalize a significant portion of the labor force within the highly industrialized nations. The result of this marginalization has been a rapid increase in unemployment and underemployment both of which cost the various governments addition funding in relation to social welfare programs, that is, food stamps, unemployment compensation, etc. It also results in both the payment of lower amounts of taxes by those marginalized and a reduction in the amount they consume. Both lead to a lower revenue base for the various governments. The globalization of production was occasioned by the perception that manufactured goods could be produced at lower cost in nation states that had an abundance of cheap labor and lax environmental regulations. Internally, however, the globalization of production has tended to lead to the bi-polarization of labor within national boundaries. One pole is occupied by a relatively small portion of the labor market that is well educated, well paid and in stable employment environments. This pole is normally designated as the core labor force. A much larger segment of the labor force is being relegated to low skill, low paying highly unstable employment. These are generally designated as marginalized employees who take part-time, undesirable or other types of underemployment. This segment of the labor force is increasingly to be found in the service sector, while the core employees are found in the high tech, medical and research fields. The polarization of the labor force has tended to lead to a wider gulf between the highest paid and lowest paid segments of the labor force. The core employees represent about 15% of the total population while the marginalized, unemployed and underemployed represent about 40% of the labor force. As a result many experts feel that the middle class is slowly being squeezed into the lower classes through a decreasing real value in the purchasing power of their income. The same process, when the support offered by social welfare programs are considered, is blamed for the high levels of chronic unemployment and the need for immigration to take the jobs that are either too low paying or undesirable for the native work force. These problems, that is, chronic unemployment, high levels of immigration, especially illegal immigration, have become part of the consciousness of the American public over the last decade. In 2010 this awareness took the form of pushing candidates for mid-term election into facing the issues of unemployment and stimulation of the economy. As we shall see later very little heed has so far been paid to these public demands.

On the other hand, many claim that the problem is the spending committed to social welfare programs and the Keynesian approach to government spending in order to stimulate the economy. This approach sees the spending on social welfare and other entitlement programs as a drag on the ability of the wealthiest individuals and corporations to expand their opportunities and thereby expand employment. They claim that the recession in particular, along with the continued stagnant growth of the economy, is being fueled by spending on welfare programs. They are intent upon reducing the size of all levels of government mainly through the institution of spending controls in the welfare and entitlement arenas. This, they feel, should be accomplished regardless of whether or not it is voluntary or forced. In the long run they would reduce the size of government at all levels by totally restructuring such programs as Social Security, Medicare and Medicaid along with other entitlement programs. This they would accomplish with the additional prohibition against the raising of current tax rates. This they feel will release the potentially huge investment capability of not only large scale businesses but also in the small and medium sized business community. This they claim is the only reliable method by which the economy can be stimulated to long term robust growth. Indeed, the claim being made is that 70% of all new job creation in the most highly industrialized nations is generated by the expansion of small and medium sized business. Both this approach and the one set forth earlier are bound to the view that national economic policy can and will resolve the economic and fiscal problems facing these nations.

Lastly, there are those that feel that the problem is beyond the ability of national economic policy to remedy, that is to say, they see the increasing globalization of the marketplace as responsible for both the recent recession and current fiscal crisis. The fall of the Soviet Union, the expansion of the EU to its current position within the global market, and the challenge of newcomers such as India and China has changed the rules of the game. No longer is it truly possible for one nation state to maintain hegemonic power within the global system. The whole economic system has become so interdependent that any change in policy affected by one nation state automatically affects the economic policy of everyone else. The initial rules of the globalization process were set by the US during the period that ran up to 1992. These rules essentially amounted first, to a free market approach to the global economy, that is, a free flow of goods, capital, people and trade with a minimum of regulation. Second, the rules also required that each nation state maintain a low rate of inflation which incorporated several different factors: one, the nation states were to maintain a relatively high rate of unemployment, two, budget deficits of no more than a small percentage of national GDP, and three, long-term debt not to exceed a reasonable ratio of national GDP. Third, these rules were to be enforced mainly through the military hegemony of the United States. The evolution of the EU and Japan among others has brought these rules into question. The first rule concerning the establishment of a free market led directly to the development of the EU and Japan, and later to the development of India and China as economic powers. The second rule concerning fiscal responsibility allowed for the restructuring of national debts when fiscal integrity broke down. This was the case with the consistent restructuring of the debts of many Latin American and African nation states when they entered into default. The third rule imposing enforcement upon the US is evidenced by the US response to the invasion of N. Korea into S. Korea and the invasion of Iraq into Kuwait. Much of the enforcement power of the global system, however, has been relegated to the system known as "poor relief". Under this system the marginalized nations (similar to the marginalized labor force and for the same reasons) are compensated for the loss of national integrity in relation to the establishment of multi-nationals within their borders for export industrial exploitation. This relief was also expected to be partially used by those in power to control whatever social unrest might arise within these nations, that is, for riot control. The problem with the global market stems from the fact that the US did not follow its own rules. After 1992 the US failed to stop the regulation imposed on the global market by the EU and others, failed to maintain fiscal responsibility and let its duty to enforce the rules slide while it fought the war on terrorism. The result over the last two decades has been the exponential growth of social welfare programs, high levels of immigration from south to north and east to west, declining birth-rates, and the repression of robust economic growth rates in the most highly industrialized nations. The attempt of these nations to adjust to the "new global marketplace" has resulted in the recent recession and the current fiscal crisis. The difference between the recent recession and the current fiscal crisis and those that have gone before, including the depression of the 1930s, is that all nation states are interdependent rather than economically sovereign.

Regardless of the specific factors used to explain the existing levels of economic growth and current spending levels the suggested remedies are of only two types, at least in relation to the US and the European Union. First the so-called conservative position places the solution on a reduction of government spending. A stand is being taken against the continued bailout of failing businesses and failing nation states. The only exception to this policy of no bailouts is the desire to continue to bail out the financial community. The position taken is centered on the spending currently found in the social welfare and entitlement programs. The elimination of these programs, either by dismantling them or converting them into private programs, is seen as capable of reestablishing fiscal responsibility in terms of balanced budgets and no long term national debt. This is to be accomplished with no increase in taxes however additional revenue is expected to result from the stimulation of the economy. This stimulation will occur as the money released from spending cuts is invested in the expansion of business interests. This position places the burden of the restructuring of the economic system on the public generally with due consideration for the needs of the business and financial communities. In the case of the later consideration the tax rate on the wealthiest individuals and corporations are to be reduced. This is in accord with the statement of the conservative position that the amount of economic growth is directly related to the amount of money placed in the hands of the wealthy and business interests. If the existing levels of transfer payments both nationally and in foreign aid are continued it will result in higher budget deficits, higher levels of long-term debt, and higher levels of unemployment resulting in the further repression of economic growth and decreasing amounts of revenue. They call for the replacement of the current programs with some type of privatized programs similar to the 401(k) retirement plans, privatized medical programs, and other forms of private "charity" programs. Large scale social problems, such as unemployment, physical disability, old age security, and health care will be automatically dwelt with at the local level with the increased revenues produced by a robust growth in the economy. The current ideological battle in the US Congress is directly related to the positions taken on this stance and the one to be explained below.

The second position is the so-called liberal approach to the crisis. As with the conservative approach this approach also calls for a program for reducing spending at all levels of government. The difference is to be found in where these spending cuts are to be found. This position holds that the amount of needed spending reductions can be obtained by reducing spending outside of the social welfare and entitlement systems. Most of the spending reductions target the military institution, a restructuring of the federal bureaucracy, elimination of waste and fraud in the welfare systems, i.e., a reform of Social Security, Medicare and Medicaid and the elimination of ear-mark legislation. In addition, this position calls for additional revenue to be obtained by either tax rate hikes on the wealthiest taxpayers and the wealthiest corporations, or the reduction of the allowed loopholes and credits available to the same taxpayers. It would also include immediate (2012) elimination of the Bush era tax cuts on those making over 200,000 per year. Lastly, this position calls for the reform of the health care industry, or the funding of the National Health Care Act in 2012, to provide additional increases in revenue at all governmental levels. The reductions in spending and increases in revenue are claimed to be enough not only to bring about a balanced budget and reduce the national debt over time; but also to fund additional spending on alternative energy sources, a high speed railway system, a refurbishing of the urban transit systems and to fund research in medical science and education. The remaining funds would be used to stimulate the economy through the institution of construction projects to improve the condition of the nation's infrastructure (the creation of an infrastructure bank). Lastly, this position calls for a stronger regulatory system to keep the financial and business community in line and to thwart any chance that another housing bubble or round of fiscal mismanagement could lead to another recession or fiscal crisis. The liberal position has already promised to end the two wars in the Middle East by withdrawing from Iraq by the end of 2011 and Afghanistan by the end of 2013. This alone would, according to the Congressional Budget Office (CBO) reduce federal spending by some 245 billion per year.

In a nut shell the conservative position is seen as putting the burden of the cost of solving the nation's economic problems on the backs of the middle and lower classes, in particular those who are participants in the existing social welfare and entitlement programs. The liberal position is seen as putting the burden mainly on the backs of the wealthiest individuals and business concerns and the military. Neither position is accurately described, or explained, that is, both positions seem to be fully aware of the problems that face the nation and also as to what type of actions would solve the problems, although they refuse to sit down and enact legislation that would deal with these issues. The most likely scenario will be a compromise which leads to a substantial reduction of government spending at all levels of government; as well as several different approaches to the raising of additional revenue. It is apparent to everyone that the current levels of spending on social welfare and entitlement programs are not sustainable over the long term. It is equally apparent to everyone that the current level of revenue is not adequate to fund a Keynesian approach to the stimulation of the economy. The "pay as you go" concept in relation to modern government programs is a thing of the past; however, something equally efficient must be instituted to restructure the way governments do business.

Neither position has yet to approach the concept that the Westphalian system of nationalism may have become obsolete. This concept has resulted from the slow awakening of the US and the EU that the problems they face cannot be resolved on such a small scale. If, in fact, over the long term the US and the EU cannot resolve their economic issues as the two wealthiest nation states it must be accepted that the nation state is too small a scale to deal with the problems. Currently the bets being offered is that the US may be able to avoid falling prey to its economic problems but that the EU is almost certain to fall to theirs. It is feared that if either fails then the other will fail also and if both fail we are back where we were during the 1930s. Both positions are calling for a slow withdrawal of the US and EU from its overall position in the global system. The EU is also attempting to reinstitute some of the pre-

EU trade restrictions in its bid to withdraw from the consequences of global participation. Both are calling for more reliance on Nationalism and less reliance on internationalism. In this they appear to be influencing the other highly industrialized nations into following suit. However, it is likely that the globalization process has already evolved to a stage of interdependency that cannot be walked away from without triggering the economic collapse that all are trying to avoid.

The EU has over the last two years made some half-hearted attempts to bail out the national economies that are the closest to default, that is, Ireland, Greece and Portugal. Even this, however, has met with resistance from the European Central Bank (ECB) and some of the wealthier nations, such as Germany, the Netherlands and the Nordic nations. In addition the treaties of the EU make it illegal for the European level institutions to directly bail out a failing national economy. So far the French and Germans in cooperation with the International Monetary Fund (IMF) have arranged two limited bail outs of Greece. However, it is clearly recognized that there is not enough liquidity in the EU and IMF to bail out the larger economies of Italy and Spain who are also facing immediate default possibilities. It is also clearly seen that austerity measures of a scale needed to forestall default in these economies is both socially unacceptable and fiscally impossible. The time table for the default of either Spain or Italy has been revised to occur near the end of 2011 rather than later. Should either or both default the EU as an entity would be dead and the repercussions of such an event would probably put the US into a serious threat of default also. Whether or not any of this happens is still somewhat a matter of speculation. There are currently signs that the US economy may be poised to begin a robust period of economic growth. If this occurs rapidly enough the repercussions would quickly be felt in the EU also and would to a significant degree resolved the default issues for at least Spain and Italy, although it may be too late to save Greece. Even with this the EU might still be forced into a position where they would have to deconstruct the Euro zone. It is clearly apparent that the concept of a single currency in a confederal union will not work when it is shared by wealthy and poor economic units. The best case scenario that can be imagined is that the EU membership is slowly able to return to the guidelines of the Euro-Zone, that is, budget deficits that do not exceed 3% of GDP and long term debt that does not exceed 60% of GDP. It is still likely, however, that the EU will lose some of its weaker members for a period of time before it will be in a position to begin expanding again, if it ever does.

Meanwhile the reaction of the leadership of the US in relation to economic problems is almost a complete paralysis. The ideological battle has already brought the US unnecessarily to the brink of national default. The damage to confidence in the US economy and political system has already become noticeable both at home and abroad. The consumer confidence index is at the lowest level it has been at since 1978. The loss of confidence in the economic system has resulted in both the financial and business communities being willing to sit on some 6 trillion dollars that should be available for normal lending and capital investment programs. Overseas the loss of confidence, especially in the political system, has caused a movement away from the dollar as a safe reserve for national capital. So far this has not affected the purchase of US treasury bonds as a safe haven internationally. These movements will over time make it much more difficult to resolve the economic and fiscal issues facing the United States. The real crux of the problem, however, is that such lack of confidence is justified by the lack of concern exhibited by the political leadership in the US in relation to the economic stagnation, fiscal irresponsibility and high rates of unemployment. Indeed, after the passage of the band aid solution to the debt ceiling crisis Congress has decided to take the rest of the summer off. This same approach is being taken by the political leadership in the European Union. It is expected in the US that once the Congress returns the ideological battles will resume where they left off once again paralyzing the government and preventing any solutions from hitting the books. It is assured that the ideological battle will continue at least until the results of the 2012 presidential election are returned; and probably will extend even further into the future. Some looking on these warnings are predicting a global economic collapse as early as the beginning of 2012. It may, in fact, be true that the only real hope is that the economy will heal itself and enter into a robust period of economic growth prior to the actual collapse. There are at least some signs that the US economy is poised to make just such a take off in the very near future. Over the long run it will still be necessary to restructure the economy of the US and the EU to defend against a return of the current crisis issues.

It is also true that currently some of the states of the US and some of the individual members of the EU are attempting to institute the necessary restructuring programs that will lead them back to fiscal responsibility. This effort, if successful, either because of the advent of robust economic growth, or internal discipline, would by itself go a long way to restoring both consumer and business confidence in the economy and political system. The decisions made, or more likely not made, at the federal level could, of course, totally negate the efforts of the individual states and EU members. It is at least refreshing that the ideological debate has not stopped some individual efforts to restore fiscal discipline at the lower levels of government.

There is another group who takes the stand that the recent recession was not even as serious as the recession suffered during the 1970s when the unemployment rate was even higher than today and the rate of inflation was very high in comparison to today. This group is the one that is certain that the economy will heal itself in the short term and enter into an extended period of robust growth ending budget deficit problems, long-term debt problems, and even create an employment deficit. They advocate that nothing be done to artificially stimulate the various economies and that nothing be done to rescue those businesses and national economies that fail. This is all part of the natural healing process that the global economy must work its way through. Once the robust growth pattern is in full swing it is then time to look into whatever restructuring is needed to soften any future economic slowdowns that might occur. Only time will tell whether this prediction will turn out to be accurate but if history has any lessons one of them may be that all prior depressions, in particular the one in the 1930s, ended only after all artificial attempts to end it had stopped. The recovery was a natural process aided by the onset of World War II. It is ironic that the same natural processes may be released in this case by the ending of the wars in Iraq and Afghanistan.

What all the experts seem to agree upon is that the recent recession and the current fiscal crisis are unlike any others that have occurred prior to them. First, the time honored traditions that depend on massive government spending to stimulate the economy (Keynesian economics) are not working. On the other hand, the lowering of interest rates, the control of inflation and the maintaining of relatively high rates of unemployment to insure fiscal responsibility also is not working. Lastly, the reliance on the operation of a relatively deregulated economy, or free market system, also does not seem to be stimulating the innovation and investment capital that is expected from such policies. In fact all of these measures when applied are having the opposite effect of what are normal expectations. Overall they have led to a further repression of economic growth; while at the same time necessitating larger and larger budget deficits and significantly increased national debt burdens. One recent anomaly that has arisen is the large amount of cash that is being held in reserve by the business and financial communities even though they were bailed out to provide them the opportunity to start investing in their business and to make loans. This has increased the difficulty in relieving the pressure on the economy and the housing market in particular. As stated earlier this is believed to be a vote of no confidence by the business and financial communities in the economy and the US political system. The same pessimism is invading the general public in relation to consumer spending and the overseas interest in holding US currency as security. Added to all this is the rapidly increasing cost of necessities such as gasoline, home heating fuel, food, health care and education. This should be enough to stimulate the political leadership into action, but instead it has created an even deeper gridlock.

There are signs around the globe that people have reached the end of their tolerance for governments they believe are incompetent in terms of political leadership. The "Arab Spring" still under way in Tunisia, Egypt, Bahrain, Syria and Yemen are all examples of people who have tired of the rulers imposed on them by the Western powers after World War II. The West has consistently supported regimes that were corrupt, incompetent and even capable of committing acts amounting to war crimes all for the benefit of the Western powers. It is bantered about that these movements are aimed at establishing democratically-orientated governments, but it is just as likely that the new regimes, when they finally emerge, will be under Shia law. In any case, the new regimes are not likely to be puppets of the Western powers.

In addition, we have the series of riots that erupted in Europe when mild measures of austerity were introduced in Greece, Italy, France and Great Britain. The growing discontent with the EU surrounding the issues of lack of transparency and democratic deficit are another example of the same distaste for political incompetence. It is expected that with the expected downturn of economic growth in both India and China that civil unrest will arise from the lack of unfulfilled expectations in the ruling regimes. Such dissatisfaction has been the commonplace in both Southeast Asia and Africa for the last four or five decades. Such dissatisfaction has occasionally broken out in Latin America; but has so far not been found in North America. However, the paralysis of government now being experienced in the US may over the next couple of years express itself in a peaceful voter revolt such as the one underway currently in Wisconsin through recall elections. There is currently much talk about the dysfunctional nature of national politicians and the need to sweep the Congress clean of those most incompetent in their job. Indeed, it does seem that much more emphasis is being placed on the maneuvers to gain reelection than to handle real political issues in the open light of day. It need not be emphasized that the stakes are very high in relation to the current economic crisis.

The key to resolving the current economic crisis, if it can be resolved, lies in the short term decisions made by the US and the European Union. They represent the two largest economies accounting together for roughly one third of the world's manufactured goods, half of all commercial trading operations, and nearly three quarters of all financial transactions. What is not held by the US and the EU within the global market is largely divided between Japan, India, China, Southeast Asia, S. Korea and the Russian Federation. This, of course, accepts the role played economically by the largest oil producing nations. Both the US and the EU currently appear to be stalling for time in relation to real decisions concerning how to deal with the crisis. Whether they are stalling in order to find a real solution, or stalling because a real solution doesn't exist remains uncertain. One fact that demands notice is that so far no innovative solutions to the problems have been brought forward. Instead the borrowed time is being used to replay the old solutions with the hope that the outcome this time around will be different than the outcome of the last couple of attempts. Most experts feel that this reliance on old solutions is a very dangerous game and may bring the US and the EU to the brink before a real effort is made to find new solutions. Regardless, the world will go on and the real question boils down to how much suffering can be expected and for how long will the suffering that comes last. If the Great Depression of the 1930s and the advent of World War II are any indication of what will appear the suffering and misery may well be beyond the ability to calculate and the length of time involved may approach several decades.

Having established an argument that can plausibly be accepted as accurately displaying the current state of affairs in the economic arena we can move forward. If the fear that nationalism has obtained to its greatest possible influence we can be justified in asking what type of system will replace it. Our answer, of course, will be speculative by the mere fact that no one can predict the future with any degree of confidence. We can, however, be satisfied that our speculations will be no more inaccurate than those already put forth.

A first step will be to locate as accurately as possible where the system of nationalism stands today. This may be accomplished by trying to determine the factors upon which the system was founded and those by which it evolved to its present condition. Initially the system of nationalism was founded as a means of organizing a group of people in such a way as to provide some security against external invasion. This organization was normally centered on the construction of a State whose boundaries contained people who exhibited a high degree of compatibility. Such compatibility was normally based on a common language, a common religion, common customs and history or some other accident of geography or culture. The resulting State was intended to provide protection from those who existed outside the borders of the State, as well as, against aggressions from within the borders. A few of these States were large from the beginning such as France and Spain; others were much smaller such as Belgium, the Netherlands, etc. However, the larger the State formed the more likely it was that the more universally recognized categories, such as religion, language, and geography, would be laced with less universal categories, such as dialects, religious sects, etc. of varying importance. It is obvious that the continent of Europe, the birthplace of the nation state, contained many diverse factors around which a collection of people could be organized. The original foundation of nationalism therefore tended to be around an identity of language, religion and custom contained within an easily identified boundary. These rather natural collections of people were then solidified under some form of government; which at the time tended to be a monarchy. Within the general form of monarchial government other forms were also found and exhibited varying degrees of influence on the monarchy. They included aristocratic nobility formed from service to the monarchy and wealth; a military cast organized around the monarchy; a religious cast of wealthy and powerful priests; and a grouping of semi-independent cities and/or trading complexes. Rather slowly the various monarchies were able to solidify their control of geographical areas and all the various power sources within those boundaries. It was at this point that the system of nationalism as we know it today came into existence. Some of the nation states were well organized, such as France, England, Spain, Portugal, Holland, and the Nordic states, while other areas had not yet begun the journey to nation statehood, such as Italy, Germany and others. A third group had coalesced into an organized whole but had not taken the route to nation statehood, such as the Austro–Hungarian Empire, the Russian Empire, and the Ottoman Empire. Within these empires, however, even at this early date nation states were inherent, such as Poland, Romania, Hungary and many others. The European continent essentially remained the home of nationalism until the end of the 19th century with the exception of the United States, Canada and some few nations in Latin America. The rest of the world existed between 1500 and 1900 under some type of empire system whether native or colonial.

The nation states of Europe throughout this period continued to evolve. As they grew in strength they were able to adopt two very important concepts into their ideological justification for existence, that is, absolute sovereignty and patriotism within their populations. As a result the various nation states found themselves in competition with one another at every level of existence. They were military, colonial, religious, social and economic competitors of the most virulent kind. The onset of wars fought for any number of reasons became the normal means of settling disputes between them. The second stage of evolution was centered on the development of science and technology. During the 18th and 19th centuries this development brought on the industrial revolution, increased the destructive power in military weapons and the awareness that a nation state could now be destroyed completely by war. The last development came with the realization of the possibility of destruction and the attempt to waylay that possibility through the maintenance of a balance of power between them. This attempt failed during the opening decades of the 20th century and led to two world wars, a global economic depression and the establishment of a bi-polar world of superpowers. In addition, the competition between the nation states had led to the colonization of three quarters of the world's land mass and population by a hand full of European nation states and the United States. As of 1940, therefore, the most pronounced aspects of nationalism were the high level of industrialization to be found within them, the ownership of large colonial empires, and a desire to avoid catastrophic wars, absolute sovereignty and patriotism.

The remainder of the 20th century saw three major developments within the system of nationalism. First was the spread of nationalism out of Europe and into Asia, Africa, and the rest of the world. The nation states formed were much different from those formed earlier in Europe. They tended to be less homogenous in nature, less capable of industrial development and less capable of scientific and technological innovation. Second, many of the new nation states were formed from the dissolution of the various colonial empires without regard to their stability as sovereign entities. This tended to divide the nation states into those that were highly industrialized and those that were dependent on the highly industrialized states. This division was supplemented by the policies of client building exercised by the two most powerful nation states the US and the Soviet Union. Third, a movement was beginning to take shape that was intended to reduce the sovereign power of the nation state and to replace it with a pooling of sovereign power in supranational organizations. The whole of the 20th century, therefore, can arguably be seen as a period during which the foundations of the system of nationalism began to be challenged, that is, the homogeneity of the population, the patriotism of the population, the absolute sovereignty of the nation state, and lastly, the integrity of the governments that controlled the nation states. It can justly be held that as of the first decade of the 21st century the concept of nationalism and absolute sovereignty is still the global standard. However, there are also two distinct challenges to this standard. Since 1970 the number of international organizations has ballooned to 25,000. Each of these organizations has a limited amount of sovereign power delegated to it by its members for the completion of a specific task held as common goals by the members. These organizations are not governments in any sense of the word, and their sovereign powers are temporary, that is, they can be revoked at any time by the members; the UN being the stereotypical example of an international organization of this type. There has also come into existence a system that is a hybrid of both international organizations and national statehood. This is, of course, the European Union. It exercises more sovereign power than any international organization but still less sovereign power than a nation state. It still maintains a temporary character with the members being allowed to withdraw from the union at will, and the strongest policy making aspect of the EU still resides with the nation states that are its members. It is, therefore, neither an international organization nor a government. The EU was begun in 1952 with the birth of the European Coal and Steel Community (ECSC). This community was much more like an international organization than the later EU but still held all the later developments of the EU as part of its structure. Between this time and 2011 a new form of governance has essentially taken shape in the European Union. This form of governance is what is at stake in the current fiscal crisis in relation to the European Union. Viewing the EU as a new form of government is still open to debate among the experts; but for the purposes of this work it will be assumed that the EU, in fact, represents a new type of government, that is, something different from the nation state of the system of nationalism. In this capacity it might over the long run, regardless of its survival in relation to the current crisis, be used as a guide for the replacement of the system of nationalism.

Chapter 2. How the Current Crisis Differs from Those of the Past

The nation state in today's world still has pretentions to a hold onto absolute sovereignty and the patriotism of its population. The interdependence that has grown up within continued globalization has tended to reduce these pretentions to a significant degree. It appears to this writer that the problems facing both the nation states and organizations like the EU stem from this interdependence fostered by globalization. It is for this reason that the solutions normally effective in prior recessions and fiscal crisis are not effective today. The interdependence made evident by the current fiscal crisis makes one question whether any nation state is really in control of its destiny economically, politically or socially. Every existing nation state is dependent in some form, and to some degree, upon other nation states and the decisions that they make. The US through its vast military superiority has over the last decade acted as if it could act unilaterally with impunity. However, the two wars in the Middle East, and other saber rattling by the US, has proven that world opinion, coupled with economic muscle, may be as decisive as military power in today's world. The soft power exhibited by Japan, the EU, China and others over the last decade seemingly changed even the rules of military action. It has also become noticeable that the traditional military structure is next to useless in the fight against terrorism and spreading insurrections. The most effective military structure in these cases centers on the use of highly trained, mobile and lightly equipped forces that are involved in limited scopes of action. This is the type of military that the EU, the Russian Federation and others are attempting to develop and rely upon. Because of the wide dispersal across the globe of the various insurrections currently in action a great deal of cooperation between nation states is required to contain them. These new forces are also intended to be available for use in the case of natural or manmade disasters. Once again the unknown place of origin of such disasters, as well as their likely dispersal across the globe requires a great degree of coordination, at least at the regional level, between the nation states to provide an effective response. On a less specific basis such generalized problems as environmental pollution, conservation of natural resources, the use of outer space and the control of pandemic disease also require a pooling of sovereign power by the nation states to insure an effective response to these issues. It may in the short term also prove to be true that the same type of cooperation is needed to control the effects of recession and fiscal crisis.

It is for the above reason that some can argue that the age of nationalism has come to an end. However, it may be more accurate to argue that the age of absolute sovereign power within the nation states has come to an end. The EU and the UN, for example, have established a system under which nation states can delegate, on a temporary basis, a larger or smaller amount of their sovereign power to a supranational organization for limited purposes. The US, however, is an example of a system whereby thirteen originally sovereign entities delegated almost all of their sovereign powers to a supranational government. In this sense the concept of federalism or confederalism can be used to preserve the essence of the nation states while at the same time removing some of their sovereign powers on a permanent basis. Whether or not such a delegation of power in the future will encompass a true government such as that of the US or an intergovernmental system such as that of the EU remains to be seen. In the case of the EU it must be remembered that the overall trend since inception has been towards greater and greater integration politically; drawing the EU closer to a true government status. Indeed, some experts feel that the only practical way for the EU to avoid disaster in the current crisis is to increase the amount of political integration. If we assume that the age of nationalism is at an end can we determine what might happen to its remaining foundational structure? One of these foundations was the use of industrialization to enhance the standard of living within the national population. Others include the development of a professional military to insure the security of the national population, political structures intended to improve the general welfare of the national population and an educational system intended to promote the feeling of patriotism within the national population.

It is clear that many of the traditional supports of the nation state are breaking down. There is a growing disbursement of traditional religious views, customary behaviors, and language even in the most closely bonded nation states. In many ways the traditional nation state seems to be suffering the same fate as the Greek city-state, that is, the nation state has become too small a forum for the solution of the large generalized problems that face them. However, there are no established empires such as those of Alexander, the Persians or the Romans on hand to replace the system of nationalism. There are, however, several large federated states that could act as a guide to what could replace the system of nationalism. In *World Government: Utopian Dream or Current Reality* an attempt was made to indicate how the federal system of the US could be expanded to incorporate the entire globe into a federal system. In this work an attempt will be made to indicate how an intergovernmental organization (the EU) could be used to initiate a system of governance on a global scale without necessarily establishing a true world government. There are other federal type systems that could be looked at such as the Indian, Chinese, and the Russian Federation but in the end there appears to be only the two viable options as these are truly only variations of the US model.

The point being made is that, if the observation that the system of nationalism is in crisis and due to pass away into history is true, something will need to arise to take its place. As stated above the US and the EU represent two separate types of governance that could be used as a guide to establish this replacement system. There may be other such guides in existence, or a new type of governance may be created to fill the gap, should the system of nationalism implode in the short term, as did the Soviet Union. Although, as stated earlier, it seems to be true that the system of nationalism still remains alive and well for at least the short and mid-term it is not a foregone conclusion. Prior to 1985 it couldn't have been surmised that the Soviet Union was close to the brink of implosion, nor could most people believe that it actually happened when it was a fact. The current fiscal crisis may be the same situation but in this case in relation to the system of nationalism. Regardless of whether or not the system of nationalism is in danger of imploding in the short term; or will survive into the relatively distant future does not prohibit the theory that it will eventually reach the end of its existence and be replaced. It does no harm to contemplate what the form of government might be that will replace it in either case. Indeed, under either scenario set forth above the system of nationalism would continue to exist but in a much altered condition. It is likely if the EU is used as a guide that the nation states will retain more sovereign powers than is true of the states of the US or the autonomous regions of India and China. The intention behind the founding of the EU was initially the dream that it would develop into a sort of United States of Europe, however, the political integration needed to produce this result has proceeded much slower than envisioned. On the other hand, the states of the US have over time given up much more sovereign power to the federal government than was ever envisioned by the founders of the Republic.

It is true under current conditions that it is hard to imagine the system of 200+ sovereign entities voluntarily giving up that sovereignty to a supranational government. This sentiment could change rapidly under the right conditions, e.g. total global economic collapse. The question that must be asked is how likely this collapse is to happen. No real solid prediction can be offered along these lines but it is possible to hypothesize that it is very well within the realm of possibilities. It might be possible in any case to outline what conditions would have to exist for such a collapse to take place. In the case of the EU, for example, it would, at the very least, entail the default of several smaller economies such as Greece and Portugal; as well as, one or two of the larger economies such as Italy and Spain. It is almost a foregone conclusion on the part of economic experts that Greece will enter into default in the short term regardless of the intended bailouts being offered. It is also considered by the same experts that either Italy or Spain could enter into default in the very near term. The EU would be unable, even with the aid of the IMF, to bail out such a large economy. This would entail the quick dissolution of the Euro zone, the collapse of the euro, and the partial or total dismemberment of the European Union. This, in turn, would in all probability bring the US back into a serious recession and again to the brink of default. There is, of course, no system on hand that could even contemplate bailing out the US economy. In the case of the US, the failure of the state governments is not as likely as the failure of the weaker members of the EU, but it is possible that some of the smaller states may default in the near term. In the case of the US federal government, a default is more likely to occur from outside pressure, such as the failure of the EU, but it could occur independently through the failure of political leadership, that is, political incompetence.

The failure of the political leadership to seriously address the budget deficit and debt problems over time could lead to a situation in which the fiscal crisis cannot be overcome except by the gratuitous tendency of an economy to enter into a growth cycle. The political incompetence already displayed by the political elite of the US has further depressed the economy and deepened the lack of public confidence both at home and abroad. The US as a result continues to erode its leadership of the globalization process and its status as the premier national economy. It is unlikely that even a total global economic collapse will lead to the dismemberment of the US union, but it might force the US into a position where it has no choice but to enter into serious international cooperative arrangements to end the crisis. Other large nation states are facing exactly the same options, i.e., the Russian Federation, India, China, Japan and the Asian Rim nations. In addition, the withdrawal of the US and the EU from the system of poor relief (now standing as foreign development funding) would have a devastating effect on those who are receiving that aid. This is already apparent from the reduction of such funding by both the US and the EU in reaction to the current crisis.

There is no place on earth that would not be adversely affected by the collapse of either the US or the European Union. The result would likely over time be a significant increase in starvation, famine, pandemic disease and poverty across the globe. This in turn would undoubtedly lead to an increase in the amount of violent civil unrest. It is not a picture that one would gladly see put in place. If these considerations are not enough to trigger serious contemplation of global solutions, then it is unlikely that any global-level solution is possible.

If global solutions are out of reach then the most likely replacement for nationalism would be a return to a governance system based on subnational levels of government. This is, of course, not out of the question as the recent demise of the Soviet Union clearly shows. It is, however, difficult to see the dismemberment of the US union, Canada and Japan among a few others. Even in the case of the Soviet Union the dismemberment led to the creation of new nation states rather than entities less than nation states. This option would, therefore, appear to be one that will not occur without the total collapse of all economic, political and social attachments. The lack of global solutions does not change the fact that in the long run nationalism as a form of governance may be nearing the end of its history. It is still likely that an event such as the dismemberment of the EU would lead to the restructuring of the existing nation states to adjust to the unsolved problems now facing them. Some level of international cooperation due to the dependence created by global-ization would still be needed and might find expression in several ways. Within the system of nationalism a global empire such as the one advo-cated by George Friedman could evolve under favorable circumstances. In such a case nationalism would then be a system under which one na-tion would have a preponderance of power while the remaining nations would be played off against one another in a network of global power balances. On the other hand, within the nationalist system a group of re-gional economic arrangements could be made either as free trade agree-ments, or as regional systems of economic control. They might or might not be subject to political integration. One such regional unit could be envisioned with the expansion of the North American Free Trade Agree-ment (NAFTA) to include all of the nations in the Western Hemisphere. They might, because of the control of the Pacific Ocean by US military power, also include the far Pacific Islands, including New Zealand and Australia. Another regional unit might be put together between the for-mer members of the EU and the Russian Federation, either as a western and eastern regional unit or as all one unit. A third might consist of all the Islamic nations of North and Eastern Africa, the Middle East and Western Central Asia. Some participation in this unit, if viable, might be expected from both India and Southeast Asia, especially the segments of these nations that are Islamic in religion. A last unit might be con-structed with the remaining nations of Asia and the near Pacific Islands (primarily Indonesia, Java and Japan). Under even the most favorable conditions it is difficult to see sub-Saharan African nations included in any of these regional trade agreements. It is also possible that such loose confederations over time would also suffer a trend towards political inte-gration that eventually would lead them to become true governments, at least as powerful as the existing EU, if not more so. A more detailed look at this type of arrangement will be made later.

An alternative if only the Euro zone system fails in relation to the EU one might expect an immediate retrenchment of the EU through a deeper political integration. This would result in the EU adapting its current institutions to form a federal system much like the one that is in existence in the United States. This was the intention of the founders of the EU from the very beginning and a great deal of political integra-tion has already taken place. It would in this case become a very large nation state on the order of the US, India, the Russian Federation and China. If this political integration were to occur quickly and successfully while the US is still reeling from the confusion caused by its political paralysis the global influence of the EU would be greatly enhanced. In fact it is difficult to imagine under the conditions that prevail today just how much clout might be found in a rejuvenated EU, especially if it was capable of making free trade arrangements with the Russian Federation, the Middle East and India. Indeed, what Mr. Friedman forecasts for the envisioned American Empire would be more likely to fall into the hands of an EU Empire.

The EU already has considerable political weight in relation to both the continent of Africa and the Middle East stemming from its economic power and the colonial experience of many of those nations. It is currently developing, especially through the efforts of Germany, a much stronger relationship with the Russian Federation and Latin America. In addition, mainly through the offices of the UK, good relations between the EU and India, Singapore, Hong Kong, Indonesia and the Pacific Islands have formed. These political ties may in fact be stronger than the political ties of the US with the same nations. It is for these reasons that some experts feel the EU would be actually strengthened by the failure of the Euro zone. Many financial experts believe that the euro and the Euro zone was a poorly thought out and executed attempt and that they have weakened the stronger aspects of the European Union. The failure of the euro and the Euro zone would force the EU to reevaluate its position both as a Union and in relation to its relations throughout the globe. One probably cannot devalue the analysis of Mr. Friedman in relation to the ambitions of both Germany and the Russian Federation. The only real question is whether under current circumstances either of them could gain more by establishing détente between them than could be obtained by the development of a strong free trade agreement. Either way the goal would be for the Russian Federation to obtain technology and capital investment and for the EU, especially Germany, to obtain natural resources such as oil and natural gas and access to a strong labor market. Mr. Friedman's analysis, in this writer's opinion, appears to be much too dependent on the traditional factors involved in nationalism rather than on a more international approach. Either way that this situation might develop it would increase the strength of the EU and weaken the political influence of the United States.

Another shock that could push the global system of nationalism towards collapse is one that is seldom followed in detail in today's environment. This shock centers on the short term results of the two wars in the Middle East being conducted by the US and their aftermath; and second, by the aftermath of the insurrections now being carried on in relation to the Arab spring. Once the US withdraws from both Iraq and Afghanistan a power shift of significant proportions is going to become evident. It is a foregone conclusion that Iraq will be left in so unstable a position politically that Iran will automatically become the premier power in the Persian Gulf. This position would make it possible for Iran to cut off the Arabian Peninsulas oil supply to the industrialized nations bringing them to their knees. This could be done in one of two ways, that is, either through the political influence Iran would then wield in the Arabian Peninsula or through the control of the Strait of Hormuz. The US withdrawal from Afghanistan is likely to have just as lethal results with the likely return to power of the Taliban and Al Qaeda in that country. In addition, should the aftermath of the Arab spring lead to the establishment of fundamental Islamic regimes, rather than democratically orientated regimes, the influence of Iran would be greatly increased over the whole of the Middle East. As a result Israel may be forced to see its survival dependent on a preemptive attack against Iran's nuclear facilities. This could easily lead to a wider war, or more likely, the destruction of Israel. In this case the Middle East could become capable of united action in the field of international relations and control of a majority of the world's oil supply through the control of OPEC (Organization of Petroleum Exporting Countries). The US would not be found to have much political influence in this area under those conditions. The EU would probably have more influence, but most influence in the area would be found to have shifted to Russia, Western Central Asia, India and possibly China. Even under the best of conditions Islam can be considered to be anti-capitalistic and therefore capable of connection with China and others who have little attachment to capitalism. At the very least this type of scenario would leave nations such as Turkey, Armenia, Georgia and India without much power to resist Iranian influence over the long run, at least individually. Over the long run, however, it is to the advantage of all the nations of the Middle East and North Africa to maintain at least a working relationship with the industrialized world to assure a market for their only source of revenue, that is natural resources, in particular oil. If the EU is successful in assuring itself access to Russian oil it will be less affected by dominant Iranian influence in the Middle East and probably be capable of avoiding the worst effects of an oil blockade. The US, however, should expect to be the main target of such tactics, as will be Japan. The nation states that would be the most affected would be the US, Japan and China but through an irony of history it may be the combined political influence of these three nations that would soften the blow of predominant political influence in Iran in relation to the Middle East. However, if China was to opt into a type of third world coalition that would involve the Middle East (including North and Northeastern Africa) and Western Central Asia the US and Japan would be left very few options. Japan would be totally devastated by the loss of access to Middle Eastern oil and quickly forced to capitulate to the dominant power. The US might be capable of withstanding even a complete blockade of Middle Eastern oil but the economic damage caused while alternative sources of energy were cultivated might be irrevocable. If this prediction were to prove accurate it is likely that the US would find a way in which it could use its military power to break the strangle hold. There can be little doubt that the use of military force in this case would not include the use of nuclear weapons, especially if Russia, the EU and China remained on the sidelines. A defensive attack by the US to prevent the use of weapons of mass destruction by Iran, especially if initiated through Israel, would probably not invoke a response from any nation states with the possible exception of China. Its geographical position, however, is unfavorable for it to react easily to a US attack on the Middle East. It is likely that the EU and Russia would both protest against such an attack but neither would wish to provoke a nuclear reaction. In this case the war might be kept within the limits of a conventional war if Iran does not yet have the capability of developing a number of nuclear weapons or have the capability of delivering them.

Under the conditions set forth above it is doubtful that a US military action in the Middle East, if conducted with intent, would meet any major military resistance. However, the US would need to be wise enough to withdraw immediately after accomplishing the mission of removing the ruling regime from control of Iran. It would need to immediately bring the UN, or other forms of international cooperation, into play to stabilize the area. The problem would center without question on the ability to bring peace and prosperous relations back into play once the military action was concluded. The US has already shown in both Iraq and Afghanistan that it is not capable of creating the conditions that would lead to a lasting peace in the area. This could probably be more easily accomplished through the efforts of the EU, Russia, or some combination of non-combatant nation states. Indeed, the US has already lost most of whatever political influence it once had in the area. The wars conducted by the US in the Middle East have also squandered much of the political influence exercised by the US in Western Europe, with the exception of the UK. From all that has been said above it is unlikely that even under the best of conditions that the US will be able to restore the level of influence it exercised globally until 1992.

The most effective manner in which the current economic crisis can be avoided is to seek an international solution even though our analysis would indicate that it is a very difficult road indeed. It would be to the advantage of both the US and the EU to spearhead the development of some type of international organization for the sole purpose of bringing fiscal responsibility back to the nation states. This would require an organization that was capable of instituting a plan to prevent the expected defaults by the nations mentioned above; either through a restructuring of their debt or a waiver on the payment of the debt for a period of time. It would also have to have the power to verify and enforce the austerity plans that it would need to institute to insure that no other nations are allowed to enter into default. In order to accomplish these two goals it would need to include in its membership not only the nation's most likely to default but also the nations who are the majority creditors of these nations. The organization would also need the power to enforce a global wide standard that required that budget deficits do not exceed 3%, or whatever percentage is practical, of national GDP; and that national debts do not exceed 60%, or whatever percentage is decided upon, of GDP. Once again the organization would need the power to inspect, audit and conduct whatever investigations were necessary to implement these rules. This would require that a considerable amount of sovereign economic power would be given to the organization by its members. The enforcement powers would need to be of a nature that they would be perceived as a real threat to the continued existence of the affected nation state. The fine system used currently by the EU, if applied might be effective, but the EU has failed to institute the fines that are to be imposed by treaty for violations of the rules. In the long run unsuccessful national economies that cannot maintain fiscal discipline would be allowed to fail with all members sharing the loss on some basis decided upon at the beginning.

The EU level institutions are by treaty prevented from providing bailouts to failing member's economies. The bailouts provided to date for Greece and Ireland have been provided by the Central Banks of individual members, especially Germany and France, in cooperation with the IMF. The Germans are becoming increasingly reluctant to continue the bailout procedures and the French are becoming increasingly unable to provide the funds. The IMF is also finding it difficult to increase the necessary funding from its membership due to the restrictions on US contributions.

Both the central banks and the IMF clearly realize the impossibility of raising enough funds to bail out an economy as large as that of Spain or Italy. In the long run even if a large economy like that of Italy doesn't go into default the short term fixes involved in case by case bailouts will eventually run up to a point where no further funding is available. At that point both the defaulting nation and the mismanaged financial institutions responsible for them will be allowed to fail. Most of the EU membership has recently become serious about attempts to waylay default but so far nothing has been done to touch the major driver of the defaults, that is, the welfare systems of the countries involved. In the US the same process of looking seriously at austerity measures that might be acceptable to the public is being pushed forward but the real driver is being ignored in this case also. There is talk in abundance about the possibility of reforming the welfare system, reforming the health system, reforming the tax code and reforming the retirement system for government employees at all levels of government; but to date little or nothing has actually been done with the exception of actions by a few state governments. Already the tough decisions at the federal level have been postponed at least through the end of 2011 and probably through the end of 2012. Only at the state level, and even here only in a small number of states, has serious action been taken in relation to state pension obligations, state welfare obligations and state infrastructure obligations. Some small measure of success has been achieved by Wisconsin in relation to state pension programs and in California in relation to state welfare outlays, however, with serious resistance from the public. In the EU the emphasis is placed on the reduction of spending outside the welfare structure and the raising of new revenue, i.e., increased taxes. These have been stoutly resisted by the populations affected but any attempt to reduce the welfare burden is likely to draw even stronger resistance from the people. Even so the US and the EU may be capable of buying enough time for the economies of these two giants to heal themselves and put the globe on a track of robust economic growth. However the same policies, especially if enough time cannot be bought in this manner, may end up aggravating the fiscal crisis. As the natural disaster that struck Japan indicates the recovery of an industrial economy is a fragile process. It does not take much to derail it and most of what can derail it is beyond the control of the individual nation. For example, the expected downturn in economic growth expected to hit India and China in the near term may be enough to derail any economic growth that may have begun within the US and EU economies. In truth the economic recovery that is expected by many experts may not appear due to the fact that the factors necessary for it to appear do not exist under current circumstances. This would include not only the needed economic tools but the repression of innovation and confidence in those most active in the promotion of economic growth. The current liquidity retention in both the industrial and financial community may be the result of just such a lack of economic confidence. In the US most experts feel that the drop in consumer spending over the last couple of years is directly related to the lack of confidence the public has in both the economy and the political leadership; rather than just as a result of the drop in the real value of consumer income. All of this is aggravated by what can be seen as hidden inflation, that is, the rapid rise in the cost of energy, food, housing, and education. The middle classes in both the US and EU are being squeezed into an existence that allows for very little discretionary spending. Lastly, the drying up of lending and capital investment is also related directly to a lack of confidence in both the economy and the political elite. All of these factors are part of the reason that economic growth remains stagnant and will probably remain so as long as the lack of confidence remains. One aspect of this is the fact that big business in both the EU and US are currently investing their capital to a great degree outside their national boundaries and most of the profit they take is also earned outside the national boundaries. As a result most of their job creation aptitude is also outside the national boundaries while they were responsible initially for the onset of high unemployment at home. Big business has therefore become a negative factor in relation to the national economies. No doubt the loss of revenue within the nation states represented by loss of revenue in foreign income is substantial by any measurement. In the end shrinking revenues coupled to increases in spending is a formula for economic disaster. Today it is being touted that the EU and the US economies will both grow, at best, at a rate under or at 2% of GDP. This is much too low to offer much in the way of alleviating the existing crisis.

In the US the current mood even though the debt ceiling crisis was avoided until sometime after 2013 is gridlock and the fact that nothing has really changed. The debate on the 2011 budget will come up during the holiday season of 2011 and it is expected that the same debate which paralyzed action on the debt ceiling debate will again be front stage. In addition a so-called super-committee is to be appointed to find 1.5 trillion dollars in additional spending cuts by the first part of November 2011. If the Congress cannot agree on the recommended cuts, if any are suggested, a procedure is in place to automatically put in effect across the board cuts in at least the amount of 1.5 trillion. In short, both of these facts indicate that it will be crisis politics as usual in the US at least until the end of the 2011 and possibly until the presidential election in 2012. One of the most troublesome aspects of the bitter debate over the debt ceiling limit was the complete disregard by the Congress of the demands of the American public for stimulation of the economy and work on the high unemployment level. Even the uneasiness shown abroad for the gridlock displayed by Congress was ignored with the decision delayed until just a few hours before the expected default. The same is expected to happen when Congress returns from its summer break. Although the gridlock is not present in the EU, at least to the same degree as in the US the same disregard for public desires is apparent in the handling of the bailout procedures, as well as disregard for the uneasiness caused by these delays in other parts of the world. In fact, both sets of political elites are responsible for a significant degree of unnecessary concern around the globe, especially if it turns out that the crisis is more easily defused than currently expected. It is, of course, possible that the whole crisis has arisen due to the manipulations and expectations of bailouts within the global financial community. The antics of J.P. Morgan nearly one hundred years ago in capturing the silver market stands as a good example of what type of havoc can be invoked through financial manipulation. It can be hoped that such tactics is not the case in relation to the current economic problems, but the possibility remains. The question has arisen, however, why the EU does not just bail out the financial community and let both the banks in Ireland and the Greek government fail. This would clearly indicate that the financial community is the problem and not the fact that businesses and governments are defaulting on their debts.

The political debate over the debt ceiling and whether or not it would be raised was over the top. The US congress, and the executive branch, wasted nearly three months over an issue that was a foregone conclusion from the very beginning. There was never any question that the debt ceiling would be raised. The debate directly contributed to the drop in approval rating on the job being done by congress by the American public to a paltry 14%. Although the President fared somewhat better than Congress his approval rating did not improve greatly however he lost no further ground. The final bill raised the debt ceiling but did nothing more than that, unless pushing the action on real issues further down the road can be considered an accomplishment. Meanwhile the foreign markets remained very skeptical concerning the ability of the American political elite to face the real problems. Indeed, the same skepticism still invades the operation of the American stock market. The global public is being deeply affected by the seeming dysfunction of the American congress. The public in the EU, for example, seems to be more aware of the interdependency between their economic status and that of the US than the American public. That is to say, the American public is much more willing to focus on domestic issues without concern for its affect on global affairs. The American public immediately after registering its disapproval of the final debt ceiling legislation turned to the issues of high unemployment and stagnant economic growth. The weaknesses in the factors that drive economic growth have weakened since the passage of the debt ceiling legislation. All indicators point to the US entering into a double dip recession within the next six months although the political elite seem to be ignoring this warning. If this prediction proves accurate the rate of unemployment will increase and the economy may well show negative growth figures. The continued rise in prices in the area of food, shelter, health care and education only indicate that there will be an increase in the inability of the lower and middle classes to cope. If the ideological battle for power within the government continues until after the election in 2012 the public will face another year or so of inaction. It can only be guessed what the outcome of such a sterile debate might be as there, at this point, does not seem to be the alternative of a real third party arising. Some predict that there will be a voter revolt and that both houses of Congress will be swept clean; however, under the circumstances controlling elections in the US this is probably no more than an idle dream. In the US discontent tends to be converted to apathy rather than action. So far there has not been a degree of suffering attending the discontent to alter this pattern. The current admixture in the Congress admits of only further gridlock as neither party has enough votes to overcome the other party's opposition as long as the division is along strict party lines. It would appear that only a real crisis will bring enough votes across the aisle to pass any legislation of any kind. The ideological battle is essentially a battle for control of the structure of the US federal government. The conservatives have taken a stand on reestablishing a limited government, if one ever existed prior to this time. The liberals are committed to the continuation of big government or to the status quo. In order to establish a limited government the conservatives are looking to eliminate federal control over welfare and entitlement programs, deregulation of the economy, and release of the control over the financial environments. On the other hand, the liberals want more intervention by the federal government in the stimulation of the economy, the control of unemploy-ment, social welfare and entitlement programs. The conservatives would have the problems resolved without raising taxes, especially on the wealthiest individuals and business interests. The liberals would prefer to handle the problems through reform of existing programs and the rais-ing of taxes, especially on the wealthy and business interests. This, of course, is the same battle that raged for the first thirty years after ratifi-cation of the Constitution between the Federalists and Anti-Federalists. As was shown in *World Government: Utopian Dream or Current Reality* the Federalists (strong federal government advocates) clearly won that con-test. Whether or not the limited government advocates have a stronger case this time around remains to be seen. However, it is difficult to see how they will be able to eliminate such existing federal programs as So-cial Security, Medicare and Medicaid and replace them with something as comprehensive in the private sector. The reason that these programs were instituted in the first place was to eliminate the needs of the public that arose during the Great Depression. Trying to eliminate them when the US may be facing another depression of equal extent, or at the very least is faced with a continuing stagnant economic growth pattern, is asking for the seemingly impossible. The real battle, however, is current-ly being fought at the state level rather than the federal level and the lim-ited government advocates are finding a large base of support among the public. Should the limited government advocates win the battle at the state level over the next year and one half, which currently looks feasible, it will greatly strengthen their chance of winning the same concessions in the 2012 election and its aftermath. The importance of the outcome of the Wisconsin recall elections is of prime importance in this respect.

All of the above factors and the amount of time necessary to restruc-ture both the economic, especially the single currency issue in the EU; and the size of the federal government in the US once again points to the inability of nation states to address the problems that face them ef-fectively. It is, of course, possible that the EU will be capable of reforming the single currency project without entering into fiscal collapse and that the US will be capable of instituting a more limited federal government without fiscal collapse; but it is equally likely that the attempt by either, or both, will result in a reappearance of recession conditions or fiscal collapse. It is still possible to wonder whether the effort to accomplish either goal is worth the effort prior to stabilizing the current economic crisis. Once again it is suggested that the most effective way to end the current crisis is to temporarily pool enough economic power to deal front on with the crisis. If this can be accomplished and it is felt best to disband the international organization created to handle that limited issue, if successful, the time would then be right for restructuring the status quo globally. Currently, however, the betting is in favor of the US entering into a second recession within six months to a year; and that the EU will be unable to prevent the default of Greece and possibly Italy and will see the collapse of the Euro zone and probably the partial dismemberment of the Union; and lastly that no international solution will be forthcoming to step in and take over when the US and EU fail to resolve the issues.

As we have seen there are those that believe that neither side of the ideological debate will be successful. The result will be a substantial increase in unemployment, a negative growth rate in the economy, a renewal of the financial crisis in the near term, and the probability that the 2012 election will be unpredictable; but more than likely ineffective in resolving the current gridlock. As stated earlier, the ideological debate is a renewal of the initial debate between the federalists (Alexander Hamilton, John Adams and George Washington) and the Anti-Federalists (Thomas Jefferson and other states rights advocates). The Anti-Federalist program of limited government, an unregulated free market system, and individual self reliance (the society envisioned by Thomas Jefferson consisting of independent yeoman, mom and pop businesses and private property rights that were sovereign) has only existed within the US during the period when the US was ruled by the Articles of Confederation, if it has ever existed. The federalist call for a strong federal government, a free market regulated by the federal government, and a big business sector protected by the federal government has been in full operation since the ratification of the Constitution or at the latest some 30 years later. It can be argued, however, that until the advent of the 20th century, or a little earlier, there was some balance between the two positions. The federalist position was consistently dominant but not to the point that it could not be controlled to some degree by the anti-federalist position. After the turn of the 20th century this began to change with federal government intervention in many areas of the economy and society of the United States. After the advent of the Great Depression and the New Deal, coupled with the start of World War II, the federalist position became so dominant that it could not effectively be challenged by the anti-federalist position. It is this shift in emphasis over the last eighty years or so that has brought about the resurgence of the anti-federalist approach. It can, of course, be argued that the federalist position pushed to its extreme limits is what is responsible for the current global crisis; and that the solution to the crisis is dependent upon at least a return to balance between the two positions. In particular it remains to be seen whether the population of the US and the EU can be weaned off of its dependence on social welfare and entitlement programs. History clearly points to the inability of the Roman Empire and the British Empire to resolve the same issues and portends the failure in this case also. It would seem to be very difficult to bring dependent people back to self-reliance without creating violent social unrest i.e. revolution.

In the US the problem revolves around the fact that both positions have tended to take a stand at the extreme end of their respective positions. Those who seek the middle road as a compromise have yet to be capable of offering a program for consideration. The President is calling for a balanced approach, that is, an approach that would consider some shrinkage in the size of government but yet raise taxes; but at the same time attempts to take social welfare and entitlement programs off the table. In short, neither the legislative branch nor the executive branch has endorsed the balanced approach. The third branch of the government has not yet found a case that will allow them to take a position; but the construction of the current court would indicate they would support the anti-federalist position. Most experts believe that it is unlikely in the current environment that the US will return to a system in which the federal government is neither to powerful or too limited. Under this system, the one that had essentially prevailed in the US until the Great Depression the federal government was powerful enough to intervene when it was necessary but was prevented from intervening beyond the point necessary to resolve the issue. On the other hand, the federal government was prevented from intervening in areas that were best handled, and were handled, at the state level. All of this arguably has been changed by the process of increasing globalization and the interdependence that it brings with it.

The aftermath of World War II brought not only an increased tendency for the US federal government to intervene in domestic affairs, especially on the economic and social (civil rights) front but also on the international front. The Marshall Plan; the creation of military umbrellas under the NATO and SEATO treaties among others; the participation of the US in the Korean police action, the Viet Nam police action and other military adventures; coupled with the US sponsorship of the globalization process guaranteed the US intervention into all aspects of international affairs. The only prohibition against the exercise of this power initially was the military status of the Soviet Union. Later the use of this power, at least the unrestricted ability to intervene in global economic affairs, was limited to some degree by the growth of both Japan and the EU economically. As we have seen these new restrictions on the power of the US to intervene successfully in international affairs is one cause of the need to restructure the federal government. The EU since 1952 has at the European level obtained to the same degree of intervention capability on the economic level domestically in relation to its individual members; and has to some extent also extended their intervention powers in the social arena (civil rights, security and defense). In the latter area, however, the EU institutions are less capable than the federal government in the United States. The EU is only recently coming into the power that would allow it the ability to intervene in international economic affairs on a par with the United States. The US, with the demise of the Soviet Union, lost much of the rational for its use of the power to intervene, that is, the EU, Japan and others no longer needed to rely on the military power of the US for their security. This allowed them to become more independent in decisions involving their involvement in global economics and politics. The initial reaction of the US was to act as the global bully which only deepened the resolve of others to exercise their independence in the international arena. It has also reduced the likelihood that the US will be able to lead in the creation of an international organization to resolve the current crisis.

After World War II the foreign policy environment changed rapidly. The Soviet Union took full advantage of the geographical position it occupied at the end of the war and absorbed Eastern Europe, including a significant share of Germany. Western Europe was devastated economically, politically and socially by the losses incurred during the war. As a result Western Europe was suffering from a group paranoia involving the fear of Soviet invasion. The only power at the end of the war capable, in the minds of Europe, of preventing this invasion was the United States. Early on the US accepted the role pushed on it by the existing environment in Western Europe. The US quickly became the guarantor of Western European security from attack and the benefactor funding the economic and political revival of the nation states of Western Europe. As we have seen the immediate result was the institution of the Marshall Plan to insure economic revival and NATO to provide the requested security umbrella. The latter contained the unspoken promise of the use of atomic and nuclear weapons if necessary to withstand Soviet ambitions. In a somewhat less dramatic fashion the same position was taken in East

Asia with the rebuilding of the Japanese economy and political structure and a similar military umbrella in SEATO. This became particularly evident after the communist takeover of mainland China in 1949. The role of the US intensified with the knowledge that both the Soviet Union and China had become capable of nuclear weapons and the systems needed to deliver them. This knowledge was followed almost immediately by the invasion of N. Korea into S. Korea.

The cost of the cold war once fully in place (sometime after 1955) was responsible for the growing tendency of the US to run budget deficits and to accumulate long term national debt. The police action in Korea was expensive both in terms of material costs and loss of life. However, the growing commitment to the police action in Southeast Asia (Viet Nam War) after 1962 proved much more costly both in material costs and loss of life than Korea. This action also proved to be very costly in terms of domestic political capital. The war had derailed the Great Society initiative of the Johnson administration and led to widespread protests against the US involvement in the war. This in turn lowered the credibility of the Johnson administration, with President Johnson deciding to not seek another term in 1968. Only seven years later the lack of political capitol forced the Nixon administration to end the war in 1975 with a great deal of lost influence for the US internationally. At the end of the Viet Nam action the influence level of the US internationally was at its lowest point since 1900. The US after 1975 was able to recapture much of this influence due to the position that it still maintained as the premier economy globally; the dollar's position as the favored reserve currency; the continued US military superiority and the invasion of Afghanistan by the Soviet Union. It is likely that the effects of the recession that plagued most of the 1970s help focus international attention on the economic superiority of the US globally also. The Soviet Union lost as much in influence, especially in relation to its position with the so-called third world, over its failure in Afghanistan as the US had in Viet Nam. The recession, which many believe to have been more serious than the one in 2007-8, took both Germany (EU) and Japan into an economic slump which delayed their ability to act vigorously in the global market place. By the end of the 1980s it was also becoming obvious that the Soviet Union was not going to prevent the nation states of Eastern Europe from becoming independent of the Soviet Union. More surprising, however, was the demise of the Soviet Union in 1992.

The immediate result of this collapse, at least on the military front, was to leave the US as the sole remaining superpower. A second result was the economic stimulation it gave to the Japanese and the European Union. The US also entered into a sustained period of robust economic growth. In the case of the EU the result was the reunification of the two Germanys, the establishment of a single market, the establishment of a single currency system known as the Euro zone, and the expansion of the Union to 27 members. This all occurred very rapidly and some claim without the benefit of careful planning and research. By 2005 the EU had become the second largest global economy and the euro was challenging the position of the dollar as the reserve currency of choice. In Japan the impact was at first felt in the expansion of its overseas markets, in particular in the auto and high tech industries, which was quickly followed by political scandals and an economic turn down that temporarily removed Japan from active influence in the global market. Japan, however, remained as the third largest global economy if one included Germany in the European Union. In the US the robust economic growth was first felt in the rapid rise of the high tech industry. This exponential growth in the high tech industry was seconded by an equally exponential growth in the housing market. The period after 1992 also saw the slow decline in market share of many of the traditional industrial giants such as the automobile industry. This resulted largely from the failure of the industrial complex to reinvest profits into modernization and development. As a result the industry during this period was overtaken by the automobile industries, at least in the American market, of Europe and Asia, particularly the Japanese. By the end of the 1990s, however, the artificial bubble created by mismanaged evaluation techniques in the high tech industry burst. The result was a derailing of the high levels of economic growth in the US economy and its replacement with a more moderate growth. It then around the turn of the century became evident that the automobile industry, at least in its domestic capacity, was on the verge of bankruptcy. The federal government made the decision that allowing these companies to go bankrupt would further slow economic growth and have a generally adverse affect. The government authorized the bailout of these companies along with a restructuring plan that was to make them competitive in the global market again. The bailout worked in the sense that the bankruptcy was avoided and the restructuring made it possible for them to compete in the global market; however, it failed to stem the rate at which manufacturing jobs were lost domestically or to effect the overall market share held by US companies in the domestic market. In 2007 the artificial bubble created in both the industrial sector and the housing market by creative financing (to be kind) resulted in the collapse of the investment and housing markets. The economy reacted by immediately entering into a recession at least as serious as any slowdown since the 1970s. Once again the federal government decided that the failure of the financial community could not be allowed to occur as it might trigger the onset of a depression rather than a short term recession. Bailouts were once again provided to save the financial industry. The result, however, was that the business community retracted its operations releasing thousands of workers into the unemployment market; as well as, creating an environment favorable to the foreclosure of millions of individual American homes. The financial community had been responsible for its own failure but had been bailed out by the very people who were to lose their jobs and their homes. It made it possible for many corporate businesses to default on their pension obligations, and to weaken the power of the labor unions. On the public side several trillion dollars was spent on purchasing the toxic assets of the financial community (bad loans) without making the community responsible for its mismanagement. As a result of the government bailouts the financial community escaped failure, but nothing was done to heal the underlying problems that brought about that near failure.

The malady quickly spread from the home of its origin to the economies that had copied the American financial process. It was widely felt in the EU with Ireland suffering from a similar burst of the bubble in its housing market and high rates of unemployment throughout the Union. As in the US the nation states in the EU began to suffer high levels of budget deficits and long-term debt in an effort to shore up the failing financial communities within their economies. Japan which had begun a solid economic recovery after a decade long slump prior to 2007 was struck by a natural disaster the size of which quickly derailed its economic recovery. By 2011 all the major industrial economies were suffering the twin blight of high unemployment and stagnant economic growth resulting in growing budget deficits and long-term debt. Many of the up and coming economies were also beginning to show signs of slowdown, most notably India and China. In short, between the middle of 2009 and the beginning of 2011 the global economic slowdown and fiscal crisis had arrived with a vengeance. None of the nation states effected have to date been able to institute any programs capable of resolving the problems. Some believe, as we have seen, that if effective action is not taken in the very near term the result will be a total global economic collapse. Others believe that action must be taken over the longer term, consisting of at most one or two decades, to avoid such a collapse. Those who hold this view also believe that effective solutions will be found well within that window of opportunity. On the other hand, others feel that the global economy will heal itself over the next two years and that the global economy will enter a sustained period of robust growth automatically resolving the issues. Even under the rosiest predictions there are expected to be serious problems, maybe even crisis level problems, before a total resolution is in place. The most positive predictions foresee the EU and the US restructuring their economies, especially in relation to welfare and entitlement programs, allowing for the sustained resolution of budget and debt problems. They even predict that they might come to a dismantling of the current global military structures further reducing the likelihood of budget deficits and long-term debt. It is still open to debate whether or not such a restructuring would be enough to promote robust economic growth on a sustained basis. Such restructuring might, in fact, repress economic growth, increase unemployment and promote high rates of inflation. Only time will tell whether such restructuring actually occurs and what effects it will have on the global economy. This latter result may be restricted to the economies of the so-called third and fourth worlds, but might also include the so-called core periphery nations like China, India, the Russian Federation, Brazil, Indonesia, S. Korea and others as well. If this is true it would result in two major outcomes: first, the further concentration of global wealth into fewer and fewer nation states, and second, the growing concentration of national wealth into fewer and fewer individuals within the nation states. This is a process that has been on-going since at least 1970 and has resulted in the marginalization of fourth world nations and the marginalization of a large segment of the labor market in the most highly industrialized nations. The fear is that this process will be accelerated by a deepening of economic slowdown in the nation states set forth above. Today a large proportion of the global wealth is concentrated in a relatively small number of nation states known as the core nations. Equally a large amount of the national wealth in these core nations is concentrated in the top 15% of their population. The only real exception to this picture is the nations that contain a majority of the world's supply of energy resources. Some of these nations should be included in the marginalized category but are not because of their wealth in natural resources. This wealth, however, is temporary both due to possible development of alternative energy sources and the finite nature of their resources.

The assessment that the system of nationalism that now exists is in crisis is based largely upon those latter considerations set forth above.

There is not any question in the minds of those who are in the best position to know that most of the nation states of Africa and Latin America have failed. The same may be said for many of the nations that are found in the various island chains that dot the globe. The jury is still out concerning the nations that make up the third world in its now more restricted sense. This would include the new nations that were formed from the demise of the Soviet Union; most of the nations of the Middle East including those rich in oil resources and much of Southeast Asia. The real question surrounds those nations that still may be capable of breaking into the circle of core nations. This group would include Russia, China, India, S. Korea, Indonesia, Brazil and a few others. Their potential to enter the core group of nations is seen as being reliant upon the establishment of regional trade empires or balances of power depending on political orientation. The balance of power concept in the current political environment might best be understood by reading George Friedman's book *The Next Decade. Where we've been...where we're going.*

The concept of regional trading blocs may be envisioned by extending the idea of the EU, NAFTA and other such agreements to a larger regional context. In order to remain truly competitive in the global market most experts feel that larger and larger economic units will be the order of the day. This belief is probably justified by the success of the EU in breaking the US monopoly of power in the global market. This use of regional trading blocs may become imperative should the EU resolve its current issues and begin another round of expansion; or should the EU reach a free trade agreement with Russia. Such a recovery or trade treaty could easily lead to the construction of countervailing economic structures. For example, one can envision the conclusion of on-going negotiations between the US and various South American nations to result in a free trade agreement establishing a single market for the whole Western Hemisphere. The same type of arrangement could arise from the already close corporate relations that exist between Japan and the Asian Rim nations. This could be expanded to include Indonesia, New Zealand and Australia simply by expanding already existing trade agreements. As mentioned earlier it is likely the rest of the European continent and Russia would become a part of at least a free trade agreement with the EU, if not actually becoming members of the European Union. India and China are both so populous and geographically isolated as to put them outside most of the contemplated regional trading blocs; however, it is not beyond reason to believe that the Middle East, India and Southeast Asia could become associated in a loose form of free trade agreement, maybe along the line of the older "most favored nation tradition". North Africa would most likely be approached by both the EU and whatever trading bloc was developed to include the Middle East. Only Sub-Saharan Africa would remain outside a formal trading bloc. All of them might continue to trade with these nations, and continue to provide poor relief, but it is unlikely that any would want them formerly included as members. Once again some type of most favored nation status might be accorded one or another of the established trading blocs. Should some form of this prediction become reality it cannot be doubted that all of the trading blocs would find it necessary to conduct treaty relations with the others much in same manner as the current system of nationalism conducts international trade relations. It also is likely that the competition for global market share would be as competitive between regional trading blocs as it is now between nation states. Such competition could conceivably rekindle the political and military competition that led earlier to two World Wars. On the other hand, the installing of rational competition between regional trading blocs might naturally lead to more integrated political environment consisting of some form of federal world government. In either case the development of regional trading blocs would require a considerable amount of sovereign power pooling.

Returning to the balance of power system envisioned by Mr. Friedman we will attempt to place it in relation to the current political environment in the United States. Under the system set forth there would be no pooling of sovereign powers outside of that already in existence in the EU and the wider international organizations. Each nation state outside those systems would remain absolutely sovereign as they have been throughout the history of nationalism. The US would control a system of balanced powers on a global level due to its overwhelming military superiority and the control of the world's oceans that is derived from that superiority. What is lacking currently, according to Mr. Friedman, is the acceptance by the executive branch of the federal government of the existence of this empire, the conduct of a foreign policy consistent with this position, and an American public mature enough to accept it. We can list the most important components of the balance of power system as seen by Mr. Friedman as the following:

1. The need for US foreign policy to defeat any attempt by Germany, in particular, from forming any type of détente with the Russian Federation. This détente would be based upon Germany's need for natural resources and a ready labor force both of which Russia has in abundance; and the Russian need for technology and capital investment both of which Ger-

many has in abundance. Such a détente, in Mr. Friedman's view, would create an economic and political power, not to mention a possible military power that would challenge the US global supremacy. This détente should be defeated by establishing a buffer zone of nations that runs from Poland in the north to Turkey in the south. This he terms as the Intermarium nations which include Poland, Romania, Hungary, Moldova, and Turkey. It might also include Slovakia, Bulgaria and one or two others but they would not be necessary. The buffer is intended to block the direct transfer of German capital and technology to the Russians and to block the direct transfer of natural resources and labor from Russia to Germany. In order to accomplish these goals the US must adopt a foreign policy which backs away from US support of Georgia, Armenia and the new states of western Central Asia. This must be done carefully to avoid misunderstanding in Eastern Europe. This existing support should be transferred to the strengthening of both the economies and military capabilities of the Intermarium nations. The most important aspects of this foreign policy would be to create a balance of power between the EU (including the Intermarium nations) and the Russian Federation to defeat a German–Russian détente.

2. In the Middle East the US probably faces its greatest foreign policy challenge under the envisioned balance of power system. The US has created this problem for itself through its mismanaged war on terrorism. By conducting this war the US has destroyed both Iraq and Pakistan in their role as power balances in relation to Iran and India respectfully. Up until the invasion of Iraq in 2003 Iraq had been the balance to Iranian ambitions to become the premier power source in the Persian Gulf. The balance of power represented by Iraq prevented Iran from becoming capable of disrupting the flow of oil out of the Persian Gulf. Iraq, because of the war, is no longer capable of acting as a balance of power and Iran will automatically become the premier power in the Persian Gulf with American withdrawal. In the weakening of Pakistan in the war against the Taliban in Afghanistan the US has also nearly destroyed the ability of Pakistan to stand as a balance of power in relation to India. In this case, the concern of India with the policies and pressure put on it by Pakistan prevented India from acting on its ambition to control the waters of the Indian Ocean. In order to mend the damage that the US has caused in these areas our foreign policy in the area would need to be altered in the following ways. First, Israel is no longer in need of American economic aid and no longer needs the military umbrella furnished by the United States. This has essentially been true since the treaty between Egypt and

Israel was signed in 1979. Without Egypt Israel is easily a match for Syria, Lebanon, and Jordan. Iran even if it becomes the premier power in the Persian Gulf does not really represent a military threat to Israel due to geographical and logistic considerations. The same is true of Turkey who currently has the strongest economy and military in the region. Therefore to accomplish a balance of power in this region the US must do the following things. First, it must move away from its unconditional support of Israel and seek to institute an immediate support for a Palestinian home state to reduce tensions in the area. Second, the unconditional support of Israel must be replaced by seeking and obtaining a normalized relationship with both Iran and Turkey. In the case of Iran the US should seek to remove all economic sanctions now in place; and should seek to support the reentry of Iranian oil into the world market. This would stabilize the need for Iran to disrupt the flow of oil out of the Persian Gulf and make a positive of the Iranian ability to be the premier power in the Persian Gulf. In relation to Turkey the US must accept the fact that Turkey will be the premier power in the Middle East outside of the Persian Gulf regardless of US policy. This being true the US should do all in its power to support this result including the promotion of Turkish membership in the European Union. Third, the US must do all in its power to promote the strength of Pakistan both economically and politically in relation to both India and Afghanistan. Pakistan has an important level of influence in Afghanistan already and the US should use this influence to help control the activities of the Taliban and Al Qaeda when withdrawal of US and NATO forces is complete. It is in the US interest to prevent India from taking control of the Indian Ocean even though Mr. Friedman does not see that as much of a possibility in the next decade. Fourth, Mr. Friedman realizes that such shifts in US foreign policy in this region would be very unfavorable to the America public and suggests that the President must be something of a Machiavellian politician to accomplish these results.

This is only a brief glimpse at what is involved in Mr. Friedman's vision of an American Empire and what would need to be done to make if operate efficiently. No notice has been taken at this time to the other balances of power that would be desirable or into the reasons that he feels the Empire can be realized. Our point currently is merely to set forth the idea of an American Empire as an alternative to those already set forth. A more detailed look at the concept of an American Empire will be taken later.

In relation to the current political environment in the US; and what can reasonably be proposed for the political environment after the 2012 election, such a foreign policy as that envisioned under the Empire scenario seems improbable. At the very least, the consistency, deviousness, and foresight needed to carry out just the policy projections for Eurasia and the Middle East seem beyond the executive we currently have; as well as beyond any of the candidates so far in the race on the Republican side. In addition, any of the policies advocated would need to break the American public's call for a full return to domestic policies involving the economy and unemployment. This would indicate that the maturity needed in the public does not now exist. The executive branch does have the power to execute the plans put forth by Friedman under the Constitution but in the current environment the executive branch is not likely to find the will to execute it. If anything the current gridlock in the American political system seems to be decreasing the ability of the executive branch to conduct a comprehensive foreign policy of even the traditional brand. Add to this the fact that a continuing economic and fiscal crisis may ensue over the next decade it is even more likely that foreign policy will take a back seat to domestic issues and the global market place. Mr. Friedman, however, does have the reputation of often being right in his geopolitical predictions. If the current economic and fiscal crisis should resolve in the near term, say the next year or so, and the US and the EU enter into a robust period of economic growth anything is possible no matter how improbable it may seem. This recovery is, indeed, a part of the predictions made by Mr. Friedman.

In the end result the balance of power system envisioned in relation to a US Empire and a balance of economic power envisioned in the evolution of regional trading blocs is not all that different from one another other than in emphasis. The operation of a successful American Empire does not offer much confidence under current conditions; but then neither does the concept of a voluntary construction of regional trading blocs. It is equally unlikely that any type of international cooperation will be put in place to resolve the issues at hand during the short term. This leaves us with the fact that the current problems will have be solved under the current system of nationalism, that is, the efforts of 200 or so independent sovereign nation states. This is a depressing prospect given the lack of ability in them to even identify the problems with any consistency and to develop solutions to them. It would, therefore, appear that those who fear a total collapse of the global economy are offering the most likely prediction. At any rate, it is easier to envision this result than to envision any of the alternatives.

This brings us to the point where we can investigate what might be the result of total collapse and what might arise from such a collapse. There cannot be much doubt that one of the most prominent results would be a general lowering of the standard of living globally. The decrease in the standard of living would, of course, be felt differently in different parts of the globe. The most highly developed nations would probably be affected much less than others. That is to say, a much lower percentage of their population would actually suffer from a reduction in their standard of living. Only at the very bottom of these societies would there be any significant level of suffering. At the most it might result in the expansion of the percentage of their population that would be living at or near the poverty level. There might also be a relative increase in homelessness, drug usage, alcoholism and crime as people attempted to cope with the changes. Some of this would be the result of increased levels of unemployment, home mortgage foreclosures and other financial adjustments. In these nations while the decrease in the standard of living would be felt by all the amount of suffering would be minimal in comparison to other areas of the world. In the case of the EU, and Europe generally, such a collapse might result in the failure of the EU as an entity but the amount of actual suffering involved would not be significantly greater than in the United States. A few of the weaker economies involved in the EU might actually fail and in these cases the suffering would be significantly higher than in the wealthier members, but still relatively speaking significantly less than in other areas of the world. A much different fate would await those nations with relatively fragile economic and political systems. This would include such nations as Russia, India, China, Brazil, Indonesia, etc. who have a large population that are already existing at or below the poverty level. This class of people would be increased significantly by the collapse and their standard of living would decrease to the point where real suffering in terms of starvation, lack of health care, sanitation and housing would become acute. In many cases such an extension of suffering would result in civil unrest and probably violent civil unrest. The attempt to control this unrest might actually mean it would take more time to recover. Lastly, those nations already existing at the fringe of nations, that is, the lower part of the so-called third world and the so-called fourth world, would without the aid now furnished by the highly industrialized nations, succumb completely —economically, politically and socially. The situation in Somalia will stand as an example of the type of suffering that would erupt in this part of the world. Therefore, the first result would be the appearance of a general decrease in the global standard of living, meaning starvation, famine, violent civil unrest and pandemic disease in some parts of the world, even if the outcomes are relatively mild in a significant part of the globe.

Second, the global market would essentially cease to exist. Manufacturing, trade and finance would by necessity be returned to a concentration on the various national markets. This would tend to create serious financial problems for big business in the highly industrialized nation states. Many of the international conglomerates and multinational corporations in manufacturing, trade and finance would fail, or at the very least be forced to withdraw from their current global activities. In short, there would be an almost complete dismantlement of the process of globalization.

Third, the disappearance of the globalization process would lead to a sort of rebirth of the system of nationalism. Those nations that currently represent what is known as the core and near core periphery would retrench into the status of absolutely sovereign states. Manufacturing would revert to a concern with the satisfaction of the national market and the state would revert to the protection of domestic business from outside competition. Customs barriers, tariffs and other restrictions on trade would be reinstituted. Although international trade would still exist, especially in relation to luxury and specialty items, most trade would revert to intra-nation trade. In short, we would most likely return to the conditions that prevailed at the end of the evolution of nationalism in the late 19th and early 20th centuries.

Fourth, under the conditions set forth above it is likely that a return to the nationalistic system of militarism would reemerge. Each nation would do what it could to develop a military organization capable of insuring its existence from external invasion. Balance of power systems would again become important — not under the concept of empire but rather in the manner of the balance of power system used in Europe during the 18th and 19th centuries.

If the above predictions concerning the results of total global economic collapse are accurate, it is reasonable to assume that periods of economic bust and boom, periodic warfare, and totalitarian government will once again become the norm. It is also fair to say that such a result would be most to the liking of those in the conservative camp. There is no reason to believe that past mistakes will not be repeated. However, if the past mistakes are avoided and there is broad recognition that a new approach is needed, it is possible that the rebirth of nationalism could also bring about the conditions necessary to institute a world government. As outlined in the book *World Government: Utopian Dream or Current Reality,* such a world government would most likely be some type of federal system. It would include a constitution that in writing would delineate the powers and responsibilities of all levels of government within the federal system. Initially the most power would remain with the nation states, but significant power would be delegated to the general government, with all remaining powers remaining with the sub-national governments or the people. This is essentially the manner in which the United States was created.

An alternative would be to institute a world system of governance based on the system now in use in the European Union. Under this system a confederation, similar to that of the US under the Articles of Confederation, would be created. In this case the powers delegated to the general government would be limited in scope, focusing on the accomplishment of specific common goals, and would be temporary in nature. This type of governance has been variously designated as intergovermentalism or power pooling.

This system has in general worked well for the EU but in retrospect only in relation to the power pooled for economic goals. The system seems to have broken down somewhat in relation to attempts to expand sovereign power pooling into the political and social realms. These areas do not seem to lend themselves to pooling but seem to require that a true general government be in place. Either scenario, however, would be a relatively long-term development in relation to the type of economic collapse being contemplated.

Returning to a more detailed look at the results of total global economic collapse we can attempt to see what the specific results might be in the case of the United States. The US still arguably represents the premier national economy and the most powerful player in the global market. This includes the fact that the US is still the hegemonic power that supports the global market politically and economically. It is for these reasons that the US must be considered in detail as the US response to a total collapse, and the actions it takes relative to that collapse, will determine the depth of what happens to all other nation states. Even the event of a total global collapse leaves the US with some unique advantages. First, the US military supremacy will guarantee the security of the US from external aggression by any other nation or group of nations. This type of advantage may only be found outside the US in the Russian

Federation and China. Second, the US manufacturing and commercial sectors are strong enough to support a quick conversion of these sectors from international to domestic production. The large multi-national corporations (most of the top 100 corporations in the US) will be at risk with the collapse, and many of them may in fact fail. The US labor force, through a stroke of irony, has already absorbed a large share of the effects of such a failure. A significant portion of the operations of these companies have already been moved overseas with the resulting layoffs and lack of capital investment having been absorbed by the economy. A strong development of the remaining actors in the industrial and commercial sectors will quickly absorb those not already returned to the labor force (the 14 million unemployed). In this case the two most serious issues facing the US economy are the bloated nature of both its service and governmental sector, that is, the amount of unneeded labor that now exists in these two areas. Both the government sector and private service sector will contract substantially with the collapse initially swelling the ranks of the unemployed. This will be a rather short term effect if the economy enters a robust growth stage as the small and medium sized businesses will increase both the levels of their capital investment and labor force to serve the domestic consumer market and to replace what remains of the large corporations who fail. Third, the financial industry will once again be put into serious jeopardy. It is expected that the stock market will fall in the same manner as it did in the 1930s, that is, the stock market may fall to levels 75% lower than the current levels. This would produce a situation where most of the existing retirement and pensioned accounts would be depleted of value. Indeed, the current valuations of all assets in the stock market regardless of their nature would take a serious nosedive. As in 1930s, however, the majority of the people would not only survive but would remain above the poverty level. The only real alleviation that can be expected to these problems is the robust growth of the national economy. As the 1930s clearly indicate this would be a rapid occurrence if the various governments did not intervene on any large scale. There would, of course, be some level of need for government to relieve the worse suffering, that is, such things as work projects, soup kitchens, etc. This, however, should not be allowed to grow to the proportions of the New Deal and should be kept on the local level as much as possible. The suffering caused by the collapse of the global market in the US, at least in terms of unemployment, lack of necessities and negative economic growth would be short lived if the economy becomes robust in the near term. The highest levels of the corporate and financial community would likely be at risk but would quickly be replaced by the still relatively healthy small and medium sized corporate and local and regional financial communities. As with the labor force the corporate and financial communities have already borne the brunt of the mismanagement and fraud that brought on the crisis in the first place. Indeed, the healthy segments of these communities are currently holding as much as three trillion dollars in reserve for capital investment and lending. What is missing now is confidence in the economy and government of the United States. Under these conditions it is reasonable to expect the effects in the US of a total collapse to be relatively short in duration. During this period of recovery the problems of budget deficits and long-term debt would remain and could be expected to present some problems, maybe even crisis level problems, but the recovery of the economy can be expected to relieve them and force the government into a restructuring of its long-term debt drivers, that is, Social Security, Medicaid and Medicare as well as the other entitlement programs. The actions taken by the US as outlined above would most likely be adopted by the other highly industrialized nations and any other nation states that could do so.

A significant reduction in the standard of living can be expected, therefore, in the US, but this will not result in any significant deprivation except in relation to the lowest 25% of society. The populations most affected and probably for the longest period will be the chronically unemployable (10 to 15% of the labor population) and those unable to return to the labor market, that is, the aged, disabled, etc. Even this population will be affected at a much less painful level than others, especially in the third and fourth worlds. It is likely that some form of social welfare will continue until restructuring to mollify the effects of the collapse on the most vulnerable in the population.

The federal government will be forced to shrink considerably in terms of spending as its revenues will shrink significantly. As a result, many of the functions that the federal government has assumed from the states will be returned to them. These functions will include social welfare, infrastructure and securing civil rights. The federal government will essentially be returned to its core 19th century duties, that is, security against external invasion or internal insurrection; the conduct of international relations; the control of tariffs and customs; and the regulation of interstate commerce. The states as well as the federal government will be forced to find a way, through the private sector, to replace the pension and retirement plans that will be lost in the collapse. The problems will be serious and require serious attention but are expected to short term in nature if the right steps are taken and quickly enough to promote economic growth.

The results of a total global economic collapse are likely to be much more profound in relation to the European Union. As stated earlier, it is expected that the EU will be dissolved either partially or fully as a result of the collapse. Under prevailing conditions it is most likely that the dissolution will be only partial. The Euro zone, and possibly the euro itself, are likely to disappear. It is likely that the weaker economies including Greece, Portugal, Spain, Italy and Ireland will withdraw from the Union at least temporarily.

One development that might be seen fairly soon is the restructuring of the European Union into two parts, the western part consisting of the nations of France, the UK, the Netherlands, Belgium, Sweden, Finland, Luxembourg, Austria, and Denmark, and an eastern part led by Germany and containing Poland, Hungary, Romania, the Czech Republic, Slovakia and the other existing Eastern European members. This latter half may also include in short order Turkey and a free trade agreement with the Russian Federation. At any rate, the wealthier members of the EU will be affected in much the same manner as the US, that is, the effects will be serious but short lived if the right decisions are made. For the weaker members of the union, the collapse will be much more thorough and will include serious civil unrest and probably violence of varying levels.

All of the current EU members are likely to remain intact as nation states, although in some cases not much better off than the existing third world nations. Even the wealthiest of the members may see such a reduction in their standard of living that many will fall from the rank of core nations; this could include France, the UK and the Nordic nations. Germany, although like the US relatively safe from the worst economic effects, might be driven to restructure its position within the European Union. It might withdraw from the EU and go it alone for awhile, or it might seek the détente spoken of above with the Russian Federation and Turkey.

Germany, whether it reforms the EU through leadership in the eastern half or remains in the EU proper, will undoubtedly seek to remain aloof from any further financial responsibilities. In either case, Germany is likely to seek a looser organization based more on free trade, or a customs union, rather than an EU type of governance. At this point, however, it is most likely that the EU will survive in its present form but on a much reduced scale of economic and political activity and without the Euro zone and the euro. It is also likely that such predictions as a split

EU and or a free trade agreement with the Russian Federation and Turkey will have to wait for economic recovery. This may take us through the next decade. At any rate, the very least that a total collapse would create is the need to restructure the economy away from its commitment to social welfare and entitlements as a method of accomplishing wealth distribution. The US would be in no position to have a hand in shaping the eventual evolution of the European Union. The members of the existing union that were not included in the restructuring, or in the creation of two unions, would be left on their own to fail or succeed, as the case might be.

The results of a total global collapse would for these reasons tend to be more profound and long lasting in its effects upon the EU than the United States. One further consideration that must be made in relation to Europe, that is, should Germany or the EU fail to enter into some type of détente with the Russian Federation that nation state also would be subject to near term failure economically (within the next decade). It also might dissolve into its constituent parts.

Outside of North American and Europe, a total collapse would essentially aggravate what is already going on in some parts of the world and would aggravate the weaknesses now being masked by economic growth in other areas. In Africa, some portions of the Near East, some portions of both Southeast Asia and Latin America, today's problems would worsen. Africa, especially sub-Saharan Africa, would suffer intensified famine, starvation, tribal warfare and violent civil unrest. The Middle East would also be racked by continued insurrections and political upheavals and a further increase of poverty. The same would be true of both portions of Southeast Asia and Latin America. It can be expected that these areas will suffer a significant increase in the number of people living below the poverty level and an increase in civil violence as a result. In areas such as China, India, and Brazil, as stated earlier, the huge populations living at or just below the poverty level would become destitute. This would spark severe civil unrest and in the case of India and China might result in their breakup into their existing regional power blocs. The problems faced by the vast majority of existing nation states will be much greater than that faced by the core or near core nations. The depth of these effects can only be guessed at rather than predicted, but it is likely to take several decades for most of them to find stability and once again establish a growth in their standard of living.

The world that will emerge from such a collapse will be unrecognizable to all but those who are familiar with the history of the first half of the 19th century. Perhaps fewer than 50 nation states will still be viable. Most of these will be found in Europe, North American and Latin America. Both the Middle East and Latin America have been in close contact with the evolving system of nationalism and may include a number of nations that will still be viable. In the Near East it is likely that only Turkey, Iran, Israel and one or two others will remain viable. Turkey and Iran, for example, have already adjusted to the conditions that are likely to arise with a total collapse and they have a leg up to insure their viability. Saudi Arabia may also remain viable due to the strength of its ruling regime and its wealth. In Latin America, nations such as Brazil, Argentina and Venezuela may remain viable but most will not, due to their current lack of economic and political strength. Latin America is in a strange position that might favor them in the sense that Brazil, Argentina, Venezuela, and one or two others may end up having more economic and political influence than they have currently. The reason for this is to be found in the current attempts of the US to include nations in South America in the existing NAFTA arrangement. The need for such inclusion might in fact be greater after the collapse than it is today.

In the short term, therefore, very few nation states will have the capability to contain the damage caused by the total collapse of the global economy and also have the ability to institute the measures necessary to generate a relatively rapid recovery. The number of nations capable of surviving the collapse and capable of generating a recovery within the following fifteen to twenty years may be a much larger. This group may contain some surprises in terms of which nations are capable of this recovery and which are not. Even over the long term the existing fourth-world nations will be forced to find a replacement for their current status as nations.

Regardless of how many (if any) of the above speculations on what might happen in the event of a total global collapse come true, it would seem to behoove the global political elites to do whatever is possible to avoid such a collapse. Whether they will do so is still very much open to debate, but one can say that they have received fair warning from many sources of the possible consequences should they fail.

CHAPTER 3. THE REACTION TO THE FISCAL CRISIS IN THE US

The recession and fiscal crisis which struck the US economy in full force at the end of 2007 remains essentially unresolved (although the recession was officially declared over in the summer of 2009). As seen from the American point of view, the crisis involves stagnant or slow economic growth, high rates of unemployment, falling value in existing homes, drops in the real income of middle class workers, out of control spending at all levels of government, and a lack of consumer and business confidence in the economy and federal government as a whole. Many different culprits have been blamed for the financial crisis, but for the most part attention has been directed to government spending on social welfare programs, especially Social Security, Medicare and Medicaid. Some attention has been given to the cost of maintaining two wars in the Middle East, but in the media this has taken a back seat to government spending. A secondary blame has been placed on the fiscal mismanagement of the financial and industrial communities in their inadequate response to slow economic growth and the housing bubble, but again the attention given to these concerns is very much muted in comparison to government spending.

The first decade of the 21st century has brought some underlying economic problems into clear focus in the United States. In 2008, the financial market in the US essentially collapsed. The housing boom had created an atmosphere in which banks, insurance companies and investment firms felt safe in taking on shaky assets backed by creative asset manipulation to the tune of leveraging equal to several hundred times actual assets. The various levels of government in order to cover their growing budget deficits and long-term debt continued to borrow money beyond their ability to pay bringing some large states to the verge of default. All of these near default conditions were brought about by fiscal mismanagement in both the public and private sectors. The result was budget deficit of 1.5 trillion dollars at the end of the fiscal year of 2010 and a national debt that exceeds 14 trillion dollars at the same time.

By 2010 these problems and their probable causes had become known to, and emotionalized by, the American public and in a large degree through their popularization by the national media and national talk shows. This knowledge sparked a vigorous debate concerning how serious the problems were and what solutions could be found. These debates have fueled a sense of gloom and doom concerning the economy and the place of the US in the global market. Many of these discussions revolved around whether or not the liberal political system (democracy) found in the US could survive the collapse of liberal economics either nationally or globally. There has been a growing fear that the measures being taken, or in some cases not taken, would lead directly to a deepening of the recession and fiscal crisis.

In the US this awakened a grassroots movement that became known as the Tea Party movement. The Tea Party espouses the return to "core American values" as the solution to the economic and financial problems. The values that they wish to see reinstituted include a more limited government, especially on the federal level, a return to rugged individualism, and a reinstatement of a "truly" free market system (in this case a market subject to deregulation). In addition a call was made to consider a return to a more unilateral policy in relation to international affairs. The movement envisioned that the successful institution of these measures would lead over time to a balanced budget, a slow reduction of the national debt to zero, a true stimulation of the economy based on free enterprise principles, the lowering of the unemployment rate and the reestablishment of the housing market on a true value basis. Unilateralism (a return to national protectionist policies) was seen as the tool needed to balance the huge US trade deficit with the rest of the world. This would include the establishment of domestic industrial concerns protected by high tariffs, etc. The above ideals were behind the Tea Party support, or denial of support, for the candidates who ran in the 2010 mid-term election in the United States. The election resulted in a Republican majority in the House of Representatives (87 newly elected members), and a 5-seat gain in the Senate, although the majority in the Senate remained with the Democratic Party. The 2010 mid-term election has been interpreted as a mandate from the voters to reduce the size of government (reduce government spending) substantially, to begin to seriously reduce the national debt, to get on with the job of stimulating the economy, and lastly, to reduce the unemployment rate which currently stands at over nine percent.

Let's take a look at each of these claims in a little more detail. This should not be done necessarily from either the point of view of the Tea Party or the new conservative Republican point of view, or for that matter, from the liberal point of view, that is, the Obama–Pelosi stance taken prior to the 2010 election. The rhetoric that surrounded the 2010 mid-term election distorted the facts in a unique way.

The Obama administration was accused of spending huge sums of money in the bailout of manufacturing and financial institutions (through the TARP program) when in fact all of the large spending programs had been initiated by President George W. Bush before he left office. Just for the record it should be pointed out that the Bush Administration, with the blessing of a Republican Congress, had put in force the following programs during the last two years of service.

1. The program for the government to buy all of the toxic assets of both Fannie Mae and Freddie Mac; these government sponsored organizations were not backed by a governmental guarantee, however, the decision was made that if the federal government did not back the assets it would bring on a global depression equivalent to the 1930s depression. A total of 153 billion has already been spent on this program and the estimate is that the program will cost over 300 billion before it is ended with the transfer of these agencies to the private sector.

2. At about the same time the bankruptcy of the investment firm Bears Stearns became apparent. This was avoided by the government finding a buyer for the firm. As part of the deal the government guaranteed Bear Stearns toxic assets. This was done at the cost of several billion dollars.

3. The failure of financial institutions continued with the failure of Lehman Brothers, for whom the federal government could not find a buyer, and the near failure of The American Investment Group (AIG), the largest insurance company in the world. Again a buyer was not found and the federal government nationalized the insurance company and put in 150 billion to support its return to the market.

4. The financial crisis quickly spread throughout the industry prompting the federal government to take a new approach. Instead of handling the crisis on a case by case basis the federal government would guarantee all of the industries toxic assets in relation to the housing mortgage market to the tune of 700 billion dollars under the Troubled Asset Relief Program or TARP. This was the largest intervention of the federal government in the private market since 1932 and the New Deal.

5. It lastly became apparent that the American auto industry was about to go bankrupt. Congress failed to authorize the auto company bailout, so the government used some of the TARP money. Both General Motors and Chrysler took advantage of the offer and borrowed some 50 billion dollars or more.

6. In addition the federal government was fighting a two-front war in Afghanistan and Iraq which was costing some 250 billion per year and took on the cost of the devastation of the Texas coast by hurricane Ike.

7. Congress on the first try rejected the government proposal for TARP, to which the stock market responded with the largest drop since 1987. The loss in the first day after the failure of the bill amounted to roughly 1.2 trillion dollars in stock market evaluations, which prompted the quick passage of the bill on the second try.

It must, however, be added, that by the time the Bush Administration left office the auto and financial industries had begun to pay back the monies furnished by the government with interest. In fact, if all of the monies are returned, the programs initiated by the Bush Administration may end up making a little money for the taxpayers. This does not, however, speak to the loss of assets suffered in relation to foreclosed homes, decreases in retirement programs, loss of jobs, and loss of capital assets such as stocks and bonds. It is important that we have a clear idea of where the Obama Administration began its term in office. The one major expenditure offered by the Obama Administration was the so-called stimulus plan which was authorized to spend up to 800 billion dollars.

It will be easiest to use 2008 as our benchmark date even though the problems have a rather substantial historical background. The year 2008 represents the point at which the policies of the Bush Administration were handed over to the Obama team for completion or rejection. It is true that Obama has continued to follow through on the programs begun under the Bush Administration and is directly responsible for much of the actual spending. He has continued to use the money authorized under the programs, but not in relation to the 700 billion in TARP funds. It turned out that the financial industry, as well as the manufacturing sector, did not require that all this money be spent. Obama turned the funds from the purchase of toxic assets to the funding of stimulus programs for the economy. Most of this money was directed to expenditures in infrastructure projects. In this sense the Obama Administration is responsible for an increase in spending as the TARP funds not used could have remained uncommitted. Obama had campaigned on the promise to bring a National Health Program to America. In his first year in office he was able to get this act through congress. It has been analyzed by various sources to either cost an additional 1 trillion a year in spending, or to amount to an equal amount in savings to the budget. The program as passed is not scheduled to be implemented or funded until 2012. It remains budget neutral until funded. On the other hand, the new Republican majority in the House ran during 2010 on the promise that they would repeal the health act. The House of Representatives now under the control of the Republicans did exactly that; while the Senate still under a Democratic majority rejected the repeal. Currently the fate of the bill is undetermined. In addition the recession was officially declared at an end in the summer of 2009. As of early 2011 this determination is still debatable, especially in relation to the unemployment rate and the continued stagnation of the housing market and the economy generally. All told the spending during the last two years of the Bush Administration and the first two years of the Obama administration have resulted in a 1.5 trillion dollar budget deficit for 2010 and a national debt of over 14 trillion at the end of the 2010 budget year.

The size of the US national debt when looked at from the point of view of international finances reveals the following facts. First, the US has gone from being the largest creditor nation only a few decades ago to being the largest debtor nation today. China alone holds some $900 billion of our national debt; with large amounts also held by the EU, Japan, Russia, Brazil and Saudi Arabia. Unless the US gets control over its spending and debt, our credit worthiness will dry up and there could be a call upon our bonds, or significant increases in interest rates.

The federal debt is covered mostly by the sale of treasury bonds guaranteed by the government at a set rate of interest. These bonds are sold to foreign countries, wealthy individuals, and investment organizations.

Should the outstanding bonds be called in or should the US be unable to sell additional bonds, there is little doubt that the US would be forced to default on its national debt.

At this point the bond holders, especially foreign nations, would liquidate all US assets in their realm to pay the bonds. A related problem can be found in the extension of additional credit to the federal government, that is, that the service on this debt will exceed our ability to pay it. For example, it is estimated that by 2021 under current projections the service on the national debt will exceed the entire budget for the US in 1983. This will create a significant drag on economic growth and recovery.

The focus of the 2010 mid-term election was seen to have targeted the following issues in order of importance: first, the recession and the high unemployment that followed it; second, the image of out of control spending on the part of both federal and local governments and the resulting debt. Lastly, the continued gridlock and irresponsibility of Congress in failing to break existing stalemates. This is at least the manner in which the two major parties and the national media have chosen to interpret the election. Actually the public mandate, if one was given, was directly solely to economic stimulus and action on unemployment. As a result the newly elected congressmen and women feel that they have a mandate to slash federal spending substantially and that no spending program is off limits. They have clearly stated that no federal program is beyond reach of such spending cuts, including all social welfare programs. The reduction of spending is seen as the means whereby the economy will again begin to grow at a rate that will eliminate the unemployment problem. To date there have been calls to reduce the 2011 budget deficit by 100 billion dollars and to reduce the 2012 budget deficit by 500 billion dollars. The general consensus at the moment seems to be that the Obama Administration has returned to the centrist position they claimed to represent in the 2008 election. One test of this proposition came when the President gave his State of the Union message on Jan. 25, 2011. It was expected that this message would be long on rhetoric and short on substance. It was also expected that the message would concentrate on the stimulation of the economy and programs that would reduce unemployment with little of substance being said about spending reductions. In the State of the Union message, however, the President surprised the critics a little. In the first part of the speech he spoke of increasing spending in the areas of education, medical research and green technology. These he claimed were areas that could not be neglected if we were serious about stimulating the economy and producing stable, long term, good paying employment within the United States. The surprise came when he suggested that this new spending could be paid for by eliminating the subsidies given to the large oil companies in the form of tax credits. Secondly, he promoted the continuance of programs for the construction of high speed railways in the US; construction and maintenance of existing infrastructure; and the up-dating of urban transit systems. Once again he claimed that these spending programs could in large part be paid for with the voluntary cuts in spending offered by his Secretary of Defense Robert Gates. No specific amount of spending reduction was offered in this area but a general remark left one with the impression that it amounted to tens of billions of dollars of reductions in the military budget. In relation to spending cuts specifically the President offered the following suggestions. He indicated that he will eliminate duplicate services by reorganizing the federal bureaucracy. No specific amount was indicated as probable savings in the reorganization but it would undoubtedly be substantial. Lastly, he stated that he would veto any bill that reached his desk that contained ear mark provisions for discretionary spending. This has been estimated by the budget office to produce more than $100 billion per year.

Assuming the spending programs suggested by the President were accepted as offered, and in addition the oil subsidies were eliminated and the bureaucracy was reorganized in the manner suggested, the result would be a neutral budget impact with the possibility of actual spending cuts. This would allow the military cuts, the elimination of ear mark legislation, and the repeal of the Bush Era tax cuts in 2012 to be used to reduce the budget deficit even further. The latter is expected to return no less than 70 billion dollars a year to federal revenue and probably, if repealed across the board, as much as several hundred billion dollars. In connection with the spending cuts demanded by the electorate, the President stated that he would institute a five year freeze on domestic spending. (That would maintain the spending at 2010 levels rather than reducing them to pre-2008 levels as demanded by the conservative Republicans and supposedly the general public.) He also called on the Congress to act on the reform of the tax code with a reevaluation of the structure of credits and loopholes for the wealthy and corporations in particular. He estimated this could result in addition revenue of some 100 billion dollars a year. He did not suggest that this revenue be limited to use as a sinking fund to reduce the national debt but it could in fact be used for this purpose if the appropriate legislation was passed by congress.

These were the specific reductions in spending and sources of increased revenue suggested by the President. In a more general view the President suggested that our position in the global market concentrate upon the drawing of foreign manufacturing into the domestic market, much as has happened with the auto industry. It is known that both Japan and Germany will soon face serious manpower shortages and that they are not positioned to deal with large scale immigration. This being the case the US can offer its surplus labor (unemployed labor force) through incentives to German and Japanese manufactures to locate their plants in the United States. This item could easily be made budget neutral by matching costs of incentives with increases in revenue. The President also mentioned further reductions in nuclear weapons and the withdrawal of the US from its two front wars in Afghanistan and Iraq. In addition the President spoke in relation to the American health care system and its reform. He ask that the Congress not repeal the whole of the Health Care Act, but merely work on repealing the sections that have been ruled unnecessary or flawed in some way. He indicated he would be open to any suggestions that Congress might make along the lines of reforming the health care system. As an aside the money saved by ending the wars in the Middle East, estimated to be something in the range of 100 billion dollars per year, could also be limited to use in the reduction of the national debt through the creation of a sinking fund. If the two items mentioned for use as a sinking fund were actually used in that manner the national debt would be reduced to zero in a decade or a little longer. This was the sum of the President's suggestion for reducing spending, increasing revenue, stimulating the economy and reducing unemployment. Contrary to expectations, the President's message was long on substance and short on rhetoric.

The Republican response was offered by Senator Paul Ryan of Wisconsin. He gave a flat statement that the programs offered in the President's message were totally dedicated to increased spending, increased growth in the size of the federal government, and an increase in the government's attempt "to do too much". By contrast, he called for a more limited federal government, a return to "self-reliance" on the part of the American public, and a return to a "true free enterprise economy". He did not offer a single specific program to support his call for the above items or as a substitute for the programs offered by the administration. In short, the Republican response was long on rhetoric and short on substance, although there is no lack of programs that could be offered. This response did prefigure the upcoming battle over the funding of the remaining portion of the 2010 budget (raising the debt ceiling) and the items to be included in the 2011 budget.

Since Jan. 25, 2011, there has been very little discussion of the programs suggested during the State of the Union message. The following morning Senate Majority leader Democrat Harry Reid totally dismissed the idea of presenting legislation free of earmarks. The media accepted that the idea of eliminating the oil subsidies would never fly, and the rhetoric continued concerning the increase in spending offered by the administration. There doesn't seem to be much interest in a serious reform of the tax code, and so far no one is talking about what might happen to the money that will be realized with the end of the wars in the Middle East and the repeal of the Bush Era Tax cuts, if such repeal happens at all. All the congressional focus has shifted to means of reducing spending and the public resistance to any tax increases. In short, the approach so far is to allow the status quo to stand until the new conservative Republican members become accustomed to business as usual in Washington.

Putting aside the reluctance of politicians to make any specific commitments; what can be done to substantially reduce spending in both Washington and the state capitals? First, and probably most importantly, the American people and the various interest groups must be prepared to accept that all spending cuts affect someone. Everyone, if the spending cuts are justly distributed, will be required to endure some level of austerity, that is, the public, interest groups, and the private business sector. Second, the fastest way to reach the goal that is being touted by the Republicans is to pass a law that mandates a balanced budget. All states except Vermont have already opted for this type of solution and some are now finding themselves in the enviable position of budget surpluses; however, the majority of states have for one reason or another ignored their balanced budget laws. Both the military and entitlement budgets would need to be reduced significantly in order to reach a balanced budget. This must be understood to mean not the total dismantling of these programs but rather the reduction of the spending in each of them over a couple of decades. As we have already seen, the elimination of the wars in the Middle East would reduce military spending by over 100 billion dollars per year. Furthermore, if the manpower needed for the wars were returned to the private sector, another sum equal to the one mentioned above could be realized. In addition, all non essential military contracts for equipment, or for development of new equipment, should be cancelled. This, according to the CBO, would save an additional 100 billion dollars per year. This is a total of approximately 300 billion dollars a year or a little more. In relation to Social Security and Medicare, if the benefits were reinstated on the basis of need, which was the original intention of the Act, a substantial reduction could be realized over time. For example, if the law were changed so that only individuals with yearly incomes (from other retirement sources, savings, etc.) of less than $50,000 or couples with incomes less than $100,000 could qualify for benefits, another 100 billion dollars could be saved both from SS payments and from Medicare payments. Medicare could even be used in the fashion that is now the province of Medicaid, i.e., as protection against catastrophic illness or injury. The Medicaid program could be eliminated and the Medicare program would no longer be available for everyday medical expenses, except in cases of demonstrated personal need. In short, 400 billion dollars in reduced spending have already been identified.

If we include the bill that has been introduced by Republican Rand Paul of Kentucky to eliminate the federal farm subsidies, the federal Food Stamp Program, federal programs for housing assistance and federal programs for urban transit systems, Mr. Paul claims that another 500 billion dollars per year would be slashed from current spending. So far this is a reduction in spending totaling 900 billion dollars per year. The remaining 600 billion dollars could be found in the complete repeal of the Bush Era tax cuts, the elimination of oil company subsidies, tax code reform, and other non-entitlement or military programs. This would over time undoubtedly result in very large budget surpluses that could be mandated to a sinking fund to reduce the national debt to zero.

Although the above ideas may be the quickest way to obtain both a balanced budget and to eliminate the national debt, they may not be the most practical. Indeed, it is unlikely for the following reason that any of them will even be seriously discussed. No politician, in either party, is likely to be willing to commit to such severe austerity programs. To do so would be political suicide, and everyone knows it. The only way for such programs to be put into law would be for a unanimous vote in both houses of Congress and a complete agreement within the entire federal bureaucracy. Even with such unanimity in Congress, which in itself is hardly thinkable, extreme pressure would still be applied to defeat the legislation or to allow a loophole to exist for one or another interest group. There is no doubt that all the major interest groups would be looking to protect their constituents from such austerity measures. In the end the only large group that would be unrepresented in this debate over spending cuts, balanced budgets, the national debt, etc. would be the unrepresented American public, that is to say, those who can least afford the austerity program.

If the programs listed above are not likely to be approached by the administration and Congress, what type of spending cuts are likely? One suggestion that has come up consistently during the last forty years is the line item veto. This would allow the president to veto any portion of the budget he chose, for instance earmarks, without vetoing the entire budget. As it stands right now the president can only veto the whole budget if the Congress changes his budget request in ways he finds unacceptable. With the deficit projected to be 3.5 trillion dollars in 2012, some effort would be needed for sure. The problem with the line item veto is two-fold, first, that the Congress does not want the president to have the power to veto specific pork barrel items forcing a two-thirds vote to override the veto. Such a vote needless to say would be extremely difficult to manage in most cases of pork barrel earmarks. Second, the line item veto does not appear to be a way to create the amount of spending cuts that are needed to significantly reduce the deficit or to balance the budget. The line item budget, however, remains one means by which earmark legislation could be controlled. A second approach could be looked at in the executive orders for each department within the bureaucracy. These orders would require that each department submit a budget that reflected a set percent of spending reductions from the prior year. This would include the departments in charge of the entitlement programs, the military, as well as all the regulation agencies, etc. This would result in substantial savings across the budget. Lastly, a plan was put in place with the passage of the debt ceiling legislation. Under this plan a congressional committee will be appointed to find at least 1.5 trillion dollars in spending cuts by November 1 2011. If they cannot agree, or the Congress should fail to act on their recommendations automatic procedures for across the budget cuts in the amount of 1.5 trillion dollars would be activated.

The states, of course, are more limited in the areas where they can find spending reductions than is the federal government. In state government the cuts are usually taken in education, employment, social services (such as state health programs), and infrastructure expenditures. The latter have been the largest area of spending reduction as they are in the short run the least visible to the people. Over the long run, however, reduced spending on infrastructure may be the form of spending reduction most dangerous to the people, as illustrated by the bridge collapse in Minnesota. Such spending reductions over the long term may also be the most expensive to address when the day comes to make up for lost time. Even with these cuts, however, the largest states are still facing immediate threat of bankruptcy. In fact where there is some talk about allowing states to declare bankruptcy and to repudiate their debt (in particular their pension obligations). This would include California (the 8th largest economy in the world), New York (equal in size to California, if not a little larger), and Illinois. Should these three states be allowed to repudiate their existing debt and "reorganize" it is predicted that the US economy would immediately enter into a serious recession/depression. It would also mean that those states allowed to go bankrupt would not be able to meet their promises in relation to state pensions and welfare payments, as well as defaulting completely on their outstanding bond issues. On the other hand, allowing a reorganization of the current revenue (hopefully, subject to a mandatory balanced budget legislation) would permit funds to be allocated to employment, education, infrastructure and ordinary spending requirements. It would also be necessary that the states involved be legally unable to reestablish any welfare programs or tax-funded pension plans. Any new pension programs would be required to be set up on the basis of a 401(k)-type program, as is now true of most major corporations. This option, however, is still not seriously being considered, largely due to the unknown consequences of allowing it to happen. This, however, does not change the fact that these states are indeed bankrupt and that the federal government will have to bail them out if they are to be prevented from entering bankruptcy (at least, that is the current probability). This, of course, over time could add tens of trillions of dollars to the federal deficit and national debt.

The same option is available to the federal government, that is, it could declare itself bankrupt and repudiate its national debt. This, however, is not being considered at all due to the prediction that the whole world would be plunged into a recession/depression even more serious than in the 1930s. It is unlikely that this approach will be taken at any level of government over the next decade or so unless there is no other choice. Even if the federal and state governments are not allowed to go bankrupt, they could apply the above approach in a modified form. This would initially require that Congress and the administration to bite the bullet and put in place legislation requiring a balanced budget. This could be done in stages, that is, the actual balanced budget would only be obtained at the end of a certain number of years. Between the passage of the legislation and the first balanced budget the Congress and executive branches would be required each year to reduce the budget deficit by whatever amount was needed to end up with a balanced budget on the time line legislated. This modified program might also include a temporary halt in the payment of the national debt with only the interest being paid until a balanced budget is reached. In addition any spending cuts that produced a surplus over the required deficit reduction should be limited to deposit in a sinking fund to be used to resume the payment of the national debt. At any rate, the resumption of payment on the national debt would resume at the point where a balanced budget was obtained. Most of the savings needed to realize the mandatory budget deficit reductions would come from a reform of Social Security, Medicare, Medicaid, and the Military. It is very likely that these reforms, if carried out on a less stringent manner than set forth above, could produce a very substantial surplus over the mandatory reduction amount in the budget deficit. This money would be required by legislation to be placed in the sinking fund. This program would also require a reform of the tax code along with the possible repeal of the Bush Era Tax cuts. If the reform of the welfare and military programs produced the required cuts, any surpluses produced by tax code reform or the repeal of the current tax cuts would also be required to be applied to the sinking fund. Other internal measures could also be taken, such as the elimination of farm subsidies, oil company subsidies and tax credits, and any other programs that would not affect the quality of life of those least able to support such cuts. Republican Bob Corker has co-sponsored a bill that would place mandatory caps on federal spending which could be tied to the required budget cuts outlined above. Currently they are merely offered as a means of controlling spending on off budget items. It is likely that in combination these various cuts and reforms would not only produce the required yearly reduction in budget deficits but also over a period of time surpluses equal to the existing national debt. This might take as long as a decade or a little more, especially if the national economy remains sluggish during this period of time, but in the end the budget would be balanced and remain balanced and the national debt would be zero. At this point a reevaluation would need to be made concerning the remaining welfare programs, the military, and other spending to bring the US back to the point it had reached in 1992 economically.

It is likely that if the US took the above approach on a unilateral basis that the other highly industrialized nations who hold a significant portion of our debt would be forced to either go along with receiving interest only for a number of years, or to call in our outstanding debt. If they called in the debt we could then consider default or the liquidation of our assets in those nations as payment in full on our debt. It would in the end force all nations that are currently trying to sustain unsustainable welfare programs to find another way of providing a minimum standard of living (it should be kept in mind that the minimum standard of living that was the goal of the original programs now has swelled to the point where an equal standard of living is provided in relation to those who fund the welfare programs). The readjustment of national economies to current realities will also force the adjustment of the global economy to these realities. One question that arises is whether or not such overall adjustment of national economies can be accomplished without the loss of the core Democratic political values. The adjustments that will be required appear on a superficial basis to require the institution of very high levels of centralized planning. This appears to be true even at the level of state governments in the United States. It is possible that such adjustments would be followed by such a reduction of the national standard of living that they would create civil unrest and even violent revolutions. If so, of course, a scale of force necessary to restore peace would need to be applied. It is for this reason that the modified method is recommended above, that is, this program can be sold as one that is the result of the demands of the people themselves. The rhetoric of the Tea Party, for example, could be used for just such a purpose in the United States. If the austerity imposed on the people due to the necessity of a balanced budget and a payment of the national debt is seen as their idea much more will be sacrificed than if it appears to be crammed down their throats. This, of course, must be coupled to the attempt to reduce the severity of the austerity programs as much as possible which is the goal of the modified program set forth above.

It would appear from the above that the solution will in one way or another require the slow limitation of the federal government and the services it provides. How would these existing federal services be returned to the states, or better yet to the private sector? Let's look at just one such service, i.e., the infrastructure system. (This proposal is definitely on the fringe and probably will be considered utopian but may be worthy of thought.) How, through the private sector, does one provide for bridges, roads, school buildings, canals, sanitation facilities, clean water facilities and other infrastructure needs? One solution immediately comes to mind, e.g., private ownership. Most of the hospitals in the US are owned and operated on a private basis, with the VA hospitals being the major exception. There is no reason why schools, sanitation facilities, and clean water facilities should not be owned and operated privately and operated on a profit basis. The expected drawback is the amount of money that would need to be paid by those using the service to allow a rea-sonable profit. One of the major complaints about hospitals is their high costs. However, there has been no attempt known to this author to show that government ownership and operation of these facilities results in lower costs to the customer. If the market is effective in controlling other aspects of the economy, it would seem reasonable that it could also op-erate efficiently in these areas. The same could be true of bridges, roads, railways, canals and other means of communication. Private ownership might, of course, result in tolls being charged for use of these facilities, as is the case today in some areas of the country for highways under public ownership. Once again there has never been an attempt to show that the cost of construction, maintenance, and use of these facilities is lower be-cause the government is involved. It may be, and likely is, that highways, bridges, etc. could be constructed and maintained less expensively under private ownership and with these costs being borne by those who use them. In the end some combination of private and public participation may be the most effective way to control such services, but privatization seems a reasonable avenue to explore in the case of all public services now provided by the various levels of government. A factor to consider in this area would be the large number of current federal, state and local employees that would lose their jobs. Some of these people, maybe the majority, would be able to find the same work in the private sector as companies ramped up to take over the government services. One plus factor here would be the decrease in government contracts for pensions as millions of public employees are converted to the private sector. With government waste and inefficiency being what it is, it may turn out that less than half the employees will find the same jobs in the private sector. In the end, with early retirement programs and with expanding job op-portunities in the private sector for semi-skilled and skilled labor, a huge labor pool is predicted to be the result of such policies.

This brings us to a consideration of the persistent modern problem of unemployment. Several factors are usually cited as contributing to this problem. In the highly industrialized nations the first one is the loss of low skill jobs in the manufacturing sector. This has been the result of both a use of robots for low skill repetitive jobs and the relocation of manufacturing facilities to areas of the world that provide abundant sources of cheap labor. Second, we see the saturation of the service sec-tor with low skill, low pay, part-time employees that is referred to as the marginalization of manual labor or underemployment. Third, there has been a slow decline in professional level employment in both public and private arenas. Lastly, we can consider the drying up of available credit for the use of small and medium size businesses, coupled with the economic recession. The latter is the only growth factor that is generally accepted by economists as a positive influence on creating employment. It is estimated that 70 percent of the jobs within any highly industrialized nation are created by the small business sector. Small business, however, only experiences high levels of growth during periods of substantial growth within the general economy coupled with inexpensive available credit. High growth is usually considered to be something in excess of 3.5 percent of GDP per year. Few if any of the highly industrialized nations have experienced economic growth above 3 percent of GDP consistently over any extended period of time during the last decade. Credit also has been largely unavailable and very expensive since the financial crisis of 2008. One must also take into consideration that the labor pool in highly industrialized nations tends to be of two kinds, one, a core set of employees with stable high paying jobs requiring substantial skill and education; and two, rather low skilled undereducated group of employees who tend to be marginalized. Marginalization in this case being regulation to low paying (or part-time) employment that is highly unstable. In the highly industrialized nations a large majority of the available jobs are in the service sector where just such marginalized employment is found. As a result all highly industrialized nations are finding that a growing share of their annual GDP is being concentrated in a shrinking percentage of their population. In addition the so-called middle class that has always been seen as the main support for a democratic political system and liberal economics is suffering erosion in the value of its real income. This over time will result in the middle class sinking into the lower classes. In order for high levels of unemployment to be reduced over a long period of time, this trend would have to be reversed. This would, at the very least, require a mandatory moratorium in the short term on the manufacturing jobs expected to be transferred away from the core economy. The globalization of the market system may have already arrived at a point where the jobs that have been transferred cannot be returned. If so, some really creative innovations in the economy will be needed to absorb the excess labor.

A more realistic approach might be to take the programs offered by the President in the State of the Union address and determine how they can draw bi-partisan support. First, the call made for the elimination of oil company subsidies has yet to receive any congressional debate by either party. As may be remembered, these funds were to be used to meet the requests for increased spending on research, education, high speed trains and alternative energy and to make these requests budget neutral. Any approach to eliminating oil subsidies is, of course, going to be dramatically opposed by the oil industry. This industry provides a very significant proportion of all campaign funds for both parties, so that it is unlikely that this project will even be considered. Second, the National Trial Lawyers lobby is likely to respond sharply to the notion of placing caps on personal injury, especially medical mal-practice suits. This program was offered as one very important aspect of any rational attempt to reform the American justice system, and the medical industry in particular, but the trial lawyers' lobby has nearly as much clout as, if not more than, the oil industry lobby. Third, when it comes to military budget cuts, there are two considerations. One, the military may suggest cuts in its budget without congressional input as long as the cuts come prior to the approval of the annual budget; and two, congressional approval will be needed to not fund any item already approved, such as the projected development of the second engine for the F-35 fighter jet. Like all cuts in departmental budgets within the bureaucracy they can be made prior to the president submitting his budget for the year without interference by Congress or interest groups. The president's plan to reorganize and reduce the budgets of the various departments, committees, agencies, etc. can be done under constitutional powers already held by the president and without congressional debate. The plan to consolidate duplicate services, obsolete departments, etc. will also run into heavy resistance from specific congressmen and particular areas of the country that now benefit from the actions of the same departments. Four, it is also a foregone conclusion that powerful interest groups, such as the senior citizens, the public safety lobbies, etc. will stoutly oppose any attempts to freeze spending over any significant periods of time in their areas of concern.

In fact, without overwhelming bi-partisan support coupled with equally overwhelming support from both the general public and the private business sector, none of the above programs is likely to pass through Congress and become law. This leaves only the spending increases asked for by the president as issues for debate in Congress. All increased spending proposals have been promised by the Republican Party to be defeated when submitted. This does not bode well for the president in any meaningful programs that he might wish to initiate during the remaining two years of his first term. This is exactly what the Tea Party has asked the congressional members it supports to accomplish, that is to say, making

Obama a one term president. When one looks at the budget that was submitted by the Administration for the year 2011 it is apparent that some of the above speculation has already come to fruit. The president has included his requests for spending increases but has dropped his requests for cuts in any meaningful areas of the budget, that is, any of the so-called entitlement programs, oil subsidies, farm subsidies, etc. The president has pinned his budget deficit deductions on three major assumptions. First, that over the next ten years 1 trillion dollars will be cut from the budget by means of the ending of the wars in Iraq and Afghanistan. Second, several additional trillions of dollars will result from the continuing growth of the US economy under the gradual recovery from the recession. Three, the reorganization of the bureaucracy will result in a continuing reduction of the budget deficit by amounts of billions of dollars per year. All of these assumptions, although they may develop, they may not also. In the past such assumptions have never panned out as expected or the increase in revenue has been spent on new projects. One does not have to look too hard at what is happening at the moment to see that overwhelming bi-partisan support is lacking on all issues. It is equally clear that the private business sector is not attempting to change its old ways in any meaningful manner. GM, for example, has already announced that its bonus structure will on average increase salaries by 50 percent and the financial community continues to produce a growing list of toxic assets. On the other hand the performance of Congress since its inauguration has been anything but exemplary. Senator Harry Reid as majority leader dismissed the suggestion of no new earmark legislation as a pipe dream without any consideration and he is, of course, one of the leaders of the Democratic Party. The State of the Union address was rejected by the new Tea Party aligned Republicans as a spending program aimed at increasing the size of government and the tasks it undertakes without any consideration of the call for specific spending reductions. Instead they have made suggestions of their own. Senator Rand Paul from Kentucky has submitted a bill for the dismantling of the food stamp program, the dismantling of urban assistance programs, as well as national public broadcasting, Pell grants, and others of the like kind with a claim that it will reduce spending by 500 billion in the first year. Others are asking for the elimination of the student loan program, the heating subsidies to the needy, reductions in foreign aid, and the elimination of other programs aimed at the poor and needy. This type of legislation is probably capable of passing in the House of Representatives but will no doubt be rejected by the Senate and the Administration. What is common to both programs is the lack of concern with attacking the fundamental problem, that is, the time left to produce a workable solution.

There are, however, a couple of possibilities that could in fact awaken congress and the administration to the danger that they are courting. One would be the uneasiness of those who hold the US debt. This uneasiness could arise from the perception that the US is not serious about trying to contain its budget deficits, trade imbalances, or with the rapid growth of the national debt. These sources of credit, if prodded enough, could in essence put the US into a kind of receivership that required a balanced budget or at least serious adjustment of spending patterns and the reduction of growth in the national debt. In short, a drying up of credit would force the Congress to work with the administration to find a way of satisfying the demands of the creditors or watch the credit worthiness of the US disappear. This is exactly what is happening since the debt ceiling debacle and the S&P downgrade of the US credit rating. A second cause would be the actual bankruptcy of several small states, counties or municipalities. This is a real possibility if the new Republican members of the House of Representatives are able to block any appropriation bills that come to it authorizing the federal bailout of these entities. The failure of economies of this size would tend to depress the entire national economy in a very significant manner. In fact, some experts contend that if a large state was to default it would automatically put the US into an economic depression and have the possibility of spreading this depression across the globe. Although this may in fact be true it is also possible that it would have a very beneficial effect on the national economy. It might create the bi-partisan support necessary to take real action on the economic problems we have been discussing. It might also generate the level of support from the public and the private business sector to make the acceptance of such austerity measures possible. Either of these two events could act as the "necessity" it appears will be needed to force real and effective action on the part of the Congress and the executive branch.

As of August 2011 the Congress has passed legislation to raise the debt ceiling, but the manner in which the debate was conducted and concluded seriously reduced confidence in the US economy and federal government both at home and abroad. The Congress has since that time taken their summer vacation (something almost unbelievable in relation to the size of the problems facing them) and it is expected that they will return with the same level of gridlock as they left. In short, it looks as if the US will remain locked in the status quo in relation to its fiscal problems at least until the conclusion of the 2012 election. Lastly, the promised withdrawal from Iraq promised for the summer of 2011 is beginning to look as if it will be concluded more from the demand of Iraqis than from US policy. It is also being predicted that the winding down of the war in Afghanistan may take as long as five more years. These possible outcomes are making a shambles of the three pillars upon which the administration has pinned its hopes for economic recovery, reductions of the budget deficits, trade imbalances, and national debt structure. Revenue sources have continued to shrink, spending has continued to increase and the economy has not grown but may in fact have shrunk. As a result the public has continued to maintain a significant skepticism in relation to the economy.

In summary it looks as if the effort of the US in relation to the recession and fiscal crisis will be limited to an attempt to muddle through without any substantive structural changes during the short term. This, of course, is a dangerous game according to most experts and could result in the US being forced to take action on an involuntary basis as outlined above.

CHAPTER 4. THE FISCAL CRISIS AS IT AFFECTS THE EUROPEAN UNION AND THE REST OF THE WORLD

The recession and fiscal crisis in relation to the EU is a much different proposition than the one faced by the United States. The EU is composed of twenty-seven sovereign nation-states rather than fifty dependent or non-sovereign state governments. The EU has gotten its powers through the use of treaties rather than through a constitution. As a result the EU is looked at as something less than a government but more than an international organization. The powers that have been delegated, or pooled, in the EU institutions tend to be limited in scope and operation when compared to a true government such as the United States. On the other hand, the EU institutions have more sovereign power than the ordinary international organization. The EU over its history has been given more sovereign power in the economic realm than in any other area of governance. This has included the creation of a single European market based upon the concept of free trade, that is to say, the free flow of goods, services, capital and people. In addition the single market has been coupled, in the case of seventeen of the EU members, to a unified currency known as the euro. The Euro zone operates under a separate treaty and requires some specific economic disciplines, that is, the maintenance of budgetary deficits below 3% of national GDP and national debts of no more than 60% of GDP. Within the EU it has also been accepted that the European level banking system (The European Central Bank and the Twenty-seven National Central Banks) will not be allowed to finance member governmental debt. The individual members, however, are allowed to lend money (buy national bonds) to finance the member governments' deficits and long-term debt. The wealthier members of the union are, of course, the ones that have provided most of the funding. This, to date, includes Germany, Belgium and the Netherlands.

The recent recession and fiscal crisis has affected the EU members in much the same way it has affected the United States. In some cases the conversion to the euro system has led to mismanagement of government spending resulting in conditions of default such as in the case of Greece and Portugal. In other cases the use of the "creative" financial documents created in the US has led to housing bubbles such as is the case with Ireland. Currently the EU is faced with the possible default of Greece (probably inevitable and immediate), Portugal (probable and somewhat further down the road than Greece), Ireland (currently the failure of the banking system is a reality), and Italy (also possible in the short term). The problem in Greece and Ireland has to date been handled with bailouts furnished largely by Germany and the two international economic organizations, that is, The IMF and The World Bank. Another bailout in the case of Greece is being worked out between France, Germany and the IMF.

There are two different outlooks that have developed in relation to the EU's handling of the fiscal crisis. The current practice of bailouts is seen on the one hand as a muddle through policy that will only work for the very short run, much as is the case in the United States. The hope is, of course, that enough time can be purchased to prevent the actual default of the Greek and Irish economies. Because of the EU structure, this approach is believed even less likely to succeed than that of the same policy in the United States. On the other hand, there is a position that is being taken that would result in allowing the Greek economy to default and force the Irish to allow their banking system to go into default. Such an approach is believed likely to lead to serious economic ripples throughout the EU and the possibility of a partial dismemberment of the European Union. In all cases it is seen as being the end of the euro system and Euro zone although there is currently no policy for doing so.

The EU, as with the US, has opted to take the course of least resistance for the short term in hope that a more permanent solution can be found in the mid-term. One solution offered by the experts would be for the EU to further integrate on a political basis allowing for the creation of a European level institution capable of enforcing fiscal discipline. Currently there is also no process within the current treaties that would allow this to happen. In short, this solution would take time but is feasible.

Any solution would be defeated if the economies of Portugal and Italy should enter default earlier than expected. As we will see shortly there are a couple of scenarios being offered that include the partial or complete dismemberment of the EU and/or the euro system.

Apparently the EU has looked at the repercussions that can be expected from several different courses of action and has decided to attempt to muddle through in the short term. This, as is the case in the US, may in fact be successful regardless of the gloom and doom predicted by many of the experts in relation to this course of action. It must be kept in mind, however, that the EU and the member nation-states are completely separate entities in relation to each other. The EU per se is required by treaty to maintain a balanced budget and is prohibited from borrowing money or going into debt. The integration of the EU institutions with those of its members, however, makes the EU a non-sustaining entity without the contributions of the member nation-states. As a result of the structure of the EU the weaker economies are placing a large amount of strain on the wealthier members, in addition, to their already difficult economic position in relation to their social welfare programs. The German and French governments, for example, had to seek exemption from the requirements of the Growth and Stability Act to avoid the fines for failure to comply with budget deficit requirements. It should also be remembered that even though there is no process in place that allows for the withdrawal of a member from the euro system, any member whether a member of the Euro zone or not can voluntarily withdraw from the union.

In relation to the fiscal crisis one group of economic experts sees the position of the EU as based on two separate choices as to courses of action; first the abandonment of the euro system and a partial dismemberment of the European Union or the failure of the Euro zone. In this case those members that would be required to leave the union would be those also leaving the euro system. Second, a more aggressive stance in relation to integration; this approach would allow for the transfer of fiscal decision making policy to the European level. The latter would include the creation of European level powers of enforcement in relation to whatever laws or actions were promulgated. A closer look will be taken at this option at a later time. So far the option for greater integration is being put on the back burner as is the option of abandoning the euro system.

Therefore, for somewhat differing reasons both the EU and the US have chosen to take the muddle through approach in the short term, which consists of maintaining the status quo for as long as possible. Only time will tell whether either will be successful in this attempt without bringing on worse economic tensions than a more pro-active approach might bring. If one, or both, should fail, as some predict, then creative innovations in the economic and fiscal fields will be required to bring about stability in the global economy. Without them the persistent problems of high unemployment, stagnant or slow economic growth, and a continued withering of the nation-state system will continue. It appears that the globalization of the market over the last seventy years has reached the point where any viable solutions will be found only at a level beyond the nation-state level. As a result without international cooperation the fiscal problems and economic crisis generally, is likely to be as intractable as those of pollution, natural resource depletion, pandemic disease, etc. etc.

It is of interest to note that the same issue facing the US and EU is also being faced by Russia, China, India and Japan. In Greece, Spain, France and Great Britain although attempted austerity measures were rather mild they resulted in widespread civil unrest and protest. In the case of China and India the recession is expected to lead to a slow downturn of the phenomenal economic growth now being experienced by them. When this occurs they will both be faced with the problem of containing the expected unrest of a billion people who are currently living at or below the poverty level and who will be adversely affected by the economic slowdown. Japan has begun a return to economic growth after suffering through extensive austerity programs for the last decade. However, it appears that the recent earthquake and nuclear disaster that resulted may stop the Japanese recovery in its tracks. The rest of the world is suffering in reality rather than in conjecture. The marginalized nations of Africa, Latin America and portions of the Far East have been impacted disproportionally in relation to the current recession and financial crisis. They are suffering from extensive increases in famine, starvation and pandemic disease. In these nations unemployment can reach as high as 90 percent of the population at times. What aid that is sent in ends up in the hands of the elites that run these nations rather than in being spent in relief of the problems set forth above. In short, the effects of the recession and fiscal crisis outside of the industrial world are much more personal and real. In the same way whatever solutions are adopted by the US or the EU on their behalf will affect every individual living on the planet.

One solution is an agreement of cooperation, essentially a treaty, between all the most developed nations to work towards a joint resolution of the problems. The globalization of the world's economies, along with the development of international organizations, has proceeded to the point at which this is a distinct possibility. Such an agreement would require that a single market, similar to the one now in existence in the EU, be established on a global level. This would allow the free exchange of goods, services, capital and people. Manufacturing operations could be located, or relocated, in such a way as to relieve the high unemployment problems now plaguing the industrialized countries. Financial discipline could be instituted to relieve the effects of the economic defaults that are expected to occur, as well as, to provide the conditions that will stimulate the global economy to stable growth. It is likely that such arrangements would result in a significant fall in the standard of living in the highly developed nations, but the standard of living would still be maintained at an acceptable level. There might, however, be considerable unrest resulting from this fall in the standard of living as would be predicted from the results of the mild austerities attempted by Greece, Spain, France and the UK. This approach might also require that the developed nations liquidate their assets (manufacturing concerns, trade advantages, etc) now located in the third world. The failure of support in these nations would need to be compensated for to some degree by a program of financial aid aimed at the development of consumer industry (as opposed to export industries) and the development of true subsistence agriculture. There can be little doubt that the world would quickly be brought to a realization of what constitutes a luxury and what constitutes a necessity in relation to the global economy. Once again, however, cooperation on this scale is not very likely on a voluntary basis or in the short term. It becomes much easier to envision such cooperation should the world be forced into a depression on the scale of that of the 1930s. The level of civil unrest and the violence associated with this depression could quickly escalate to intolerable levels under conditions of this magnitude.

Assuming that the expectation that nothing will be done voluntarily in any of the highly developed nations to realistically solved the issues; what could be expected from a total collapse of the global economy? This is, of course, almost impossible to predict, but it would certainly include widespread famine, starvation, pandemic disease and much other suffering and misery in some parts of the world as has already been noted. At the very least, such conditions would result in a substantial reduction of the standard of living in the highly developed nations. This decreased standard of living would probably be less severe in relation to the top 50 percent of incomes in the industrialized nations than below that number. At the lower levels, even in the most highly developed nations, a significant increase in food deprivation, homelessness, crime rates, and dissatisfaction would be evident. This could be expected to result in social unrest, possibility even the likelihood of violent protest on the scale of the 1970s war protests. It would also be likely to lead to a high level of innovation within the society and the creation of some very effective solutions to the problems over the mid-term. In the third and fourth worlds such conditions would lead to the total failure of existing economies, political structures, and social structures. The level of suffering and death that would be accompanied by this collapse is beyond the ability to comprehend but could easily exceed anything yet seen in history. In this case what occurred in sub-Saharan Africa from 1960 through 2011 will stand as a model for the suffering caused by economic, political and social collapse. Whatever effects that arise from such a catastrophe the affect would be felt around the globe for several decades into the future.

With such dire predictions facing the various nations it only makes sense that everything that can be done to avoid them should be done. While the actual solutions that might be applied will vary, sometimes to a great degree, from nation to nation the US can be used as one example of how such a unilateral approach could be taken. In the two volume work *World Government: Utopian Dream or Current Reality* a solution was set forth that would require the institution of a world government. This may, in fact, be the most efficient and quickest method to avoid the danger of a total economic collapse. However, the passion currently being displayed for "nationalism" would appear to close off the option of a world government being established, at least, on a peaceful basis. The beginnings of the type of collapse described above, however, might provide the conditions under which a world government could be seriously debated. We will, however, assume for the sake of argument that such a solution has been rejected. This leaves only the possibility of finding solutions within the parameters of a 200 plus nation environment and the likely development of 200 different solutions. We will begin by looking at what is likely to be the result of the current debate in the US in relation to a unilateral solution to its economic and political problems.

A beginning can be made by setting forth what is thought to be the most important problems that need to be faced by the US domestically. The problems determined here can reasonably be extended by analogy to all the highly developed nations globally. The problems that will be set forth are those that were found important during the mid-term election of 2010. First, the public was concerned most highly by the need to stimulate the economy in order to reduce the amount of unemployment found across the country. Second, the public was expressing its concern with the amount of spending exercised by both the federal and state governments and the required cutbacks in services to handle this debt. Third, the public expressed its concern with the rapidly growing national debt. Lastly, the public expressed its concern over the continued lack of action on the part of its congressional leaders in addressing these problems and the stalemate caused by the inflexible political positions adopted by the two parties. The issue of stimulation of the economy and reduction of unemployment has several different facets. For example, there is currently a difference of opinion as to whether or not the economy is best stimulated by additional spending or spending reductions. Increased spending would include such things as increased spending on infrastructure projects, tax credits and additional credit for small and medium sized businesses and the development of alternative energy sources that would produce local jobs. On the other side of the argument are those that favor allowing the free enterprise system to develop by removing the current federal regulatory laws, allowing larger tax credits and deductions for small and medium sized businesses, and encouraging increased availability of credit through tax credits and deductions for the wealthiest of Americans and financial institutions. It is important to note that neither of these has in the past produced a very successful track record in relation to the goals sought. For example, the lack of what is now being called rational regulation has been set forth as a significant part of the reason that poor management decisions, coupled with unreserved use of dangerous investment tools, has led to the financial crisis and the meltdown of the housing market. On the other hand, the spending programs instituted during 2008 to stimulate the economy are being touted as total failures. Meanwhile the leading economic experts are in some cases advocating a do nothing policy to allow the economy to recover on its own. This has been the approach that in the past has had the best track record in relation to the stimulation of the economy and has led to the call for a return to a truly free enterprise system. The government must do nothing to stifle the creative innovation that resides in every society and must produce conditions that allow for such innovation to be put into practice. It would appear therefore that the demands made by the public in this area during the 2010 mid-term election will to a great extent be ignored. In relation to the issues revolving around federal spending and the national debt the debate has developed in the following manner. The first step was to draw the lines concerning what spending was open to being reduced. The line seems to have been drawn, at least for the moment, along two lines. First, a realistic acceptance has been implicitly made that no spending reductions of note would be applied to existing Social Security, Medicare or Medicaid benefits although all of them would be subject to future reform. Second, what spending was reduced would be applied against the programs serving the needy, such as assistance with heating bills, food stamps, school lunch programs, urban housing assistance; or against some liberal darlings, such as the Public Broadcasting Corporation, the Endowment for the Arts and Partners for Progress. In addition calls are being made to cut entitlement programs, such as farm subsidies, oil subsidies, etc. In the former the people upon whom the reductions will have the greatest impact represent those who have the least voice and ability to air their grievances. In the latter there will be resistance from some of the strongest lobbies in the country, that is, the oil and agricultural industries. The same types of resistance to spending reductions are being faced by the EU, Japan and other nations. The new budget as mentioned earlier does not really represent any real reduction in spending but rather a retention of current spending levels for five years and a reduction of the budget deficit through revenue increases that may or may not materialize. Once again if this is the best that can be offered by the "new" Republicans and current democrats then the demands of the public will again be largely ignored prior to 2012. It goes without saying, and without any discussion, that if the budget deficit cannot be brought under control the national debt will continue to grow rather than be reduced. In relation to the budget just submitted by the administration for 2011 the deficit over the next ten years is expected to grow another 7.7 trillion dollars. If this occurs the interest on this debt will amount to a sum greater than the entire federal budget for the year 1983. Under any definition this is not getting the national debt under control.

In the end there is only one way in which the global fiscal crisis can be brought under control. The various governments must spend less than they receive in revenue creating a surplus in the annual budget which then must be applied to reducing the national debts. This would result in the reduction of the national debts over a period of time, maybe years, maybe decades, to zero. The same course must be followed by the subnational and local, especially urban governments, to obtain the same results. This sounds extremely simple and is in fact what every individual should do in relation to their own finances. However, actually accomplishing this feat appears to be extremely difficult. The US, for example, must currently find ways to reduce spending in the amount of at least 2 trillion dollars per year just to produce an annual budget surplus of 300 billion dollars. It can be assumed that the spending reductions within the EU would be in the same range. This could, of course, be realized but the sacrifices required are considered by many to be beyond the tolerance level of the American and European public. For example, an expansive reduction of spending on the Military, Social Security and Medicare and Medicaid programs alone would produce the 2 trillion needed in the United States. Reductions in social welfare in the range of 10% would do the same in the European Union. However, a large number of the 58 million people now receiving Social Security, Medicare and Medicaid would be left without an adequate source of support to maintain their current standard of living; as is also true of a large number of people in the European Union. They would most likely be unable to replace this lost income. Quite literally a large number of them would face a serious reduction of their standard of living and some would suffer actual deprivation in both the US and the EU. The elimination of military spending, especially if it was done unilaterally by the US alone, would create an environment open to abuse by terrorists, opportunists of all kinds, and to criminal elements within the society. Neither of these results could justifiably be allowed to occur. There have, as we have seen above, been suggestions of smaller reductions in lesser programs that would over longer time periods create the same results. This is also very unlikely to occur or to be sustainable for any length of time. It is necessary to prepare the global public to realize that the amount of spending reductions required to achieve the goals they need to institute are impossible of fruition in the short term. They must be prepared to face relative austerities for a significant number of years, possibly amounting to several decades to completely realize their goals with only reductions in spending. There does not really appear to be any likelihood that such severe spending reductions will be enacted.

However, spending is not the only way that budget deficits and national debts can be reduced. This can also be accomplished with increases in revenue. Increased revenue can usually be generated in only one of two ways, that is, by the robust growth of the economy which produces increases in revenue collected even if the rate of taxation remains constant; or by the raising of taxes regardless of whether or not the economy is growing. The demand of the public at the mid-term election in the US, and by the riots in Europe, has been interpreted as saying that they do not approve of any tax increases. This, however, is not necessarily true of the public in all the EU members and in some other nations. In fact, this was the result in the US congressional vote to extend the Bush Era Tax cuts. As an example, the last recession which officially lasted from late in 2007 until the summer of 2009 is estimated to have cost the federal and state governments several trillions of dollars in revenue; mostly in the form of loss tax revenue. The Bush Era tax cuts are also estimated to have cost the federal government about 700 billion a year in lost revenue. This is very close to the 2 trillion dollars mentioned earlier that is needed to balance the federal budget and to generate 300 billion in debt reduction. The economic slowdown in the EU is estimated to also have cost close to two trillion in lost tax revenues. If one accepts the economic forecast of the experts in the field then it can be expected that the US and the EU will over the next decade enter into a period of robust economic growth leading to an employment deficit. In short, the economy would be growing at a rate that would reduce unemployment to a very low rate. This in turn would generate tax revenue in amounts greater than those which are available today. This is one of the assumptions upon which the Obama administration and the political elite in the EU are staking their claims for control of spending and debt reduction. Lastly, in the US environment large amounts of revenue can be generated by a reform of the existing tax code. The reform would in essence eliminate a large number of tax credits and loopholes that are now given mainly to the wealthiest taxpayers and to the largest and wealthiest corporations. These loopholes and credits are estimated to cost the federal government nearly a trillion dollars a year in revenue regardless of whether or not the economy grows at a reasonable rate. In addition the same credits and loopholes given to the lower and middle classes may in fact generate even greater losses of revenue. The culture of avoiding taxes is also rampant in both Greece and Italy and is seen as responsible in large part for these nation's financial problems. Is it possible, if control is maintained over new spending, regardless of the reduction of existing spending, to balance the budget and to produce the surplus necessary to eliminate the national debt? The question, of course, is whether or not the type of financial discipline can be expected without being mandated by law. As we have seen earlier all passed attempts to control government spending and to reduce the national debt by means of increased revenue expectations have failed in all the highly industrialized nations.

It appears, therefore, that the solution in the case of the EU and other highly industrialized nations will be found in some combination of disciplined spending behavior, increased revenue production from a couple of different sources, and a rational program for the stimulation of the economy. For example, a reform in the various welfare systems would result in over 2 trillion in additional revenue. If the economies of the highly industrialized nations are currently headed into a robust period of growth another several of trillions of dollars will be generated that could, if mandated, be applied to the reduction of the national debts. This could be accomplished without the reduction of current spending in significant amounts. It is, however, true without any doubt that the highly industrialized nations must reevaluate the programs that they are currently spending well in excess of 2 trillion per year upon. Although reductions in military spending would help in nearly every case the US must end its commitment to the two wars in the Middle East which would generate at least 100 billion in yearly spending reductions. The increased revenue, or savings, that could be generated from all three programs mentioned above together could provide another trillion dollars. Other areas could be looked into including all kinds of subsidy programs, foreign aid programs and bureaucratic waste. In total there is no doubt that the highly industrialized nations could reach a balanced budget and a zero national debt without all the suffering and misery predicted in the paragraphs above. In order to insure these results, however, the global public must demand and get a law mandating a balanced budget and at least a reasonable ceiling on the national debts. It may also be time for the global public to demand transparency in relation to the donations and demands of interest groups, earmark legislation and other targeted expenditures that have nothing to do with the welfare of society in general. The current tax codes in the industrialized world are riddled with loopholes, subsidies, credits and other income reduction provisions that were originally intended to alleviate specific conditions but which have now become a form of entitlement or welfare. This in turn has made reform of the tax codes imperative. The growth of the various economies when it is robust is most quickly felt by those in the lower and middle classes, but the benefits are most abundant for those in the upper middle and upper classes. A reduction of military personnel would also affect the lowest classes disproportionately due to the fact that the largest segment of those serving come from those classes directly affecting their rate of unemployment. The Democratic Party in the US, for example, has for many decades found its base constituency in the lower middle class and lower classes of society. It can't be doubted that the Democrats will do all in their power to protect this constituency in relation to the proposed spending cuts and tax increases (especially in relation to social programs). On the other hand, the Republican Party, including its new wing, the Tea Party, has been equally dependent on a constituency that consisted of the upper middle class and the upper classes of society, including the donations of the business community. They will do all in their power to protect their constituency from the effects of spending reductions and tax increases (especially tax increases in relation to investment income).

This is true in every industrialized nation, even though the interests are more split up than in the United States. A significant portion of the middle class in every industrial nation makes up what has become known as the "independent" voters. This group is solicited by all parties and often represents the swing vote that ends up being the determining factor in election votes. All parties will at least boast of attempting to protect this class of voters, although for obvious reasons they are not crucial to any party. It is no wonder that it is the Republican Party that is pushing for huge reductions in spending on all programs that represent payments to the lower middle or lower classes. It is also no wonder that the Democratic Party is most interested in solving the problems by increasing the burden of the upper middle and upper classes, as well as the business community. Once again, by analogy, the same considerations can be applied to all highly industrialized nations. There has never been a sustained period of time in which there were no tax increases; and there has also been no sustained period of time that a truly free market system has existed. As for the concept of limited government, it may have reached the end of its history, just like Thomas Jefferson's ideals concerning the agrarian society. The above comments can justly be applied to the whole of the highly developed nation-states, and in a portion of the more highly developed areas of the third world in its most expansive sense.

For all these reasons it is not likely that anything but token gestures will be made by either the Congress or the executive branch in response to the demands of the American public as interpreted from the mid-term election. Most likely, the 2012 election will result in a further shake up in the political environment which will probably include Obama serving only one term as president. It remains for those who wish to rely solely on spending cuts and high levels of economic growth generally to show how this can to be done. Serious consideration to the two most expensive budget items, for all practical purposes, are off the table. The amounts of spending reductions necessary to accomplish the goals of the public have also already been shown to be impractical in the current political environment. The prediction of robust growth in the economy, while possible, has also been shown to be theoretical and unlikely to happen.

Historically, the revenue produced by a growing economy is normally spent in ways other than budget deficit reduction. From the Republican point of view, the only way growth in the economy can be created and sustained is for large amounts of money to be put in the hands of the wealthy and the corporations. Their plan is to institute tax cuts, tax credits, and tax deductions to accomplish this transfer of funds. On the other hand the reduction of government revenue this would represent has to be offset by spending cuts, or the budget deficit and the national debt will continue to grow unless the economy quickly enters into a robust boom. Thus Republicans follow the mantra that it is small business that fuels economic growth. However, the republicans seem to remain blind to the fact that over the last decade the number of small businesses, that is, companies employing between one and one hundred employees, have suffered a net loss in the numbers of people employed. At the same time it is ignored that the wealthiest corporations have largely been responsible for causing the high rate of unemployment through the practice of removing manufacturing concerns overseas. The Democrats, on the other hand, follow the mantra that stimulation of the economy and reduction of unemployment will only be accomplished by governmental stimulation in the form of money. This approach is blind to the fact that without increased revenues such spending acts as a real drag on economic growth and results in larger deficits and debt.

As to the public demand for an end to government gridlock, stalemate, and vicious rhetoric, we can only look at what has transpired up to this point. There has not been any reduction since the 2010 midterm election in the bitterness of the debates or in terms of the relaxation of party positions. A definite wall is being drawn down the middle of the aisle separating the Republicans and Democrats. In addition, there is a battle raging between the "new" Republicans elected in 2010, the so-called Tea Party candidates, and the Republicans already in power. This wall is not going to be torn down any time soon. The administration, while in concert with a portion of the congressional Democrats, is at odds with the more liberal wing led by such representatives as Nancy Pelosi. For the time being, maybe until the results of the 2012 election are known, stalemate and vicious infighting will probably continue. This is less true of the contrasting positions that can be found in the political environment of the EU, China, India, Japan and the Russian Federation among others; but in these cases the political battles of the political elites may be masked by what in the European Union is termed lack of transparency and democratic deficit.

When any of the more dire effects of a failure to act upon the problems facing the world might appear, or even if they will appear, one cannot predict, but one thing does seem certain. It would behoove the governments to allay the fears of the global public. An honest effort to obtain small spending reductions and revenue production would probably be enough to provide breathing room in relation to the public demands and the nervousness of the foreign markets. No one wants to see the world fail economically. Any effort to prevent that could include some efforts aimed at reducing future spending rather than current reductions, and the same would apply to revenue production, such as the reform of the various tax codes. Such efforts might also spur confidence in the economy, allowing the public and the various businesses to get down to the job of innovation and capital production. In the US, the repayment of the government debt to the Social Security Fund might also relieve the immediate fears of the senior generation by extending the expected life of Social Security beyond the 2037 terminal date now expected. The extent to which other nations may have borrowed from their welfare programs is unknown to this author, but the temptation will have been great. In the case of the US, correcting this situation would require the allocation of funds in the amount of 2.5 trillion dollars over some period of time. All of these measures would provide the space needed to come up with compromises that would truly solve the problems that face the US, with a minimum of social unrest and suffering among the population.

In the US, and also in most of the highly developed nations, the concept of retirement must be modified. Currently the drive is for younger and younger retirement ages and larger and larger benefits to be paid out over longer and longer time periods. This is clearly unsustainable, regardless whether the retirement is funded privately or through tax revenues. Whatever other reform is attempted the retirement age must be extended and the benefits must be restricted to those who have a real need for assistance. In short, retirement must be privatized in some way taking the burden off the various governments and the tax payers. Some system similar to the 401(k) used in the private sector appears to be the most viable manner in which to privatize retirement. While reform of the health industry per se does not affect many of the industrial nations, its inclusion as a social welfare program creates many of the same problems as in the United States. Ordinary expenses for medical check-ups, routine medical services, routine dental care, etc. should be handled in the private market. It could be suggested that a private medical savings account be set up, allowing some level of payroll deduction and employer contribution to be made into it. (This approach is already being used by some innovative corporations in the private market in the US). This savings account would then be available to be drawn on by medical providers for these routine services. More serious medical problems could be handled through a combination of private insurance and public assistance. This would return us to the place where all medical expenses would be covered on an individual basis except for serious and catastrophic illnesses. The unemployed, temporality disabled, and aged could be covered in this area by short term government aid. This would require a reevaluation of both the medical industry and the manner in which medical services are provided and paid for; also the insurance industry as to the coverage offered and the cost of the services provided. Lastly, the drug industry should also be held responsible for the costs of the products they provide and be required to operate in a competitive rather than a tightly monopolistic market. These last two factors are not found in public health systems, but if they were reformed on the basis of the above program they would become a factor in the reform. At any rate, in the case of serious or catastrophic illnesses that extended over long periods of time, a combination of individual resources, donated medical care, and donated pharmaceutical services must be looked at. In the end illnesses of this nature may require the institution of some more limited form of public health service.

This would result in a health care system that operated on the following principles. The individual would be responsible for all routine medical expenses for his or her family through the establishment of a savings account funded by his or her contributions and matching funds from the employer. Major illnesses and catastrophic injuries or illnesses would be covered by individual payments, if available, coupled with the provision of medical and pharmaceutical services by the medical and drug industries up to a stated amount, and the remainder being provided by a combination of insurance payments and government assistance. This would break the reliance of the health care system on private insurance and public welfare systems. It would also eliminate many of the unnecessary tests that are now conducted, the inclusion of pre-existing condition clauses, and cancellation procedures based on total risk to the insurance industry. In order to reach this goal the legal industry must also be reformed to prevent the institution of frivolous lawsuits and the awarding of outrageous jury awards against the medical industry. In other places these same problems would have to be prevented from arising when the health systems are privatized. The problem being solved in the above reforms has several dependent factors. First, is the aging of the population with which comes an almost automatic increase in the amount of medical care needed, coupled with the fact that this medical care tends to be the most expensive and of the longest duration. Second, the aging of the population, at least in highly developed nations, is accompanied by a declining birth rate which creates a large population bulge in the older segment of the population. In terms of the current social welfare system, that means less tax payers in relation to those receiving medical care to pay for the services given. Third, the unregulated health industries, including medical practitioners, hospitals and medical clinics, pharmaceutical companies, and insurance companies, have been responsible for costs and charges escalating at astronomical rates. These increases have been justified by the medical industry as necessary to pay for the cost of lawsuits, research, and equipment, as well as the expansion in the type of medical care provided. This assertion is at best debatable and is still largely not supported by documented evidence. There can be no doubt that the medical industry as a whole is one of the most highly compensated segments of the economy, at least in the United States. It still remains to be seen what type of meaningful reform can be made in this industry outside of government regulation and imposed limits on profit margins. Several things are certain: the US public health system is laced with fraud and waste; worker contributions cannot continue to cover the costs at current rates; there is too much borrowing from the fund by the federal government; and the system is not sustainable under current conditions. In the EU the situation is somewhat different as most of the members have instituted public health care systems that are even more expensive and unsustainable than that found in the United States. The need for restructuring however is found in all the most highly developed nation-states.

It might be useful to ponder the possible course of events from two separate viewpoints, that is, the short term and the long term. First, a supranational organization such as the EU is not very likely to be created in the short term. It is even less likely, although still conceivable, that the extension or reform of existing international organizations, such as the International Monetary Fund (IMF), the World Bank or World Trade Organization (WTO), will occur in the short run. Although all of the latter may be used in some fashion to ease the effects of the recession and financial crisis in individual cases it does not seem likely that their functions will be used to create a generalized solution. In the short run, therefore, it is most likely that the problems we have been reviewing will be solved, if they are solved, under the current system of nationalism. This means that there is likely to be 200-plus solutions to the same problems. In the long term it is possible that some international cooperative approach will be taken to coordinate these solutions.

Most of the predictions offered above seem to put very little hope in the system of nationalism to be able to solve these issues in the short term, or possibly even the long term. If these problems are to be settled or resolved on a strictly national level, then the burden will fall most heavily on the most developed nations as it should. These nations will have to address the economic problems, mainly slow economic growth, that has resulted from the recession; and the problems that have resulted from the unregulated mismanagement of the financial community. It is likely that these nations will in fact arrive at various solutions to the individual problems faced in the short term. It is, however, unlikely that in the short term the highly developed nations will return to an economy that is enjoying robust growth, and that a rational way will be found to control the financial community. In the long run the solution of the immediate problems of recession and financial crisis will be replaced by the more chronic problems of environmental pollution; unsustainable consumption of natural resources, in particular oil; the aging and deterioration of national infrastructure systems; the inability to maintain the current public welfare systems and the control of poverty, famine, pandemic disease and social unrest. Almost all of the highly developed nations have side-stepped these issues, although they are a primary cause of the recurring cycles of economic boom and bust. The modern approach has been to postpone the day of reckoning through the use of credit, leaving the problem to future generations. Finite natural resources such as oil, mineral ores, and water, means there is a limit to the amount of time that can be borrowed this way. Similarly, there is a limit to how long one can put off repairing and expanding the national infrastructure, the sustainability of high unemployment and high taxation levels, as well as to the amount of debt that can be sustained over significant periods of time. In short, the recession just past and the current financial crisis may be a wake-up call indicating that time has already run out for postponing solutions. The rather extensive integration of the global economy seems to indicate that the solutions must be global in scope rather than national if they are to be successful. Such global solutions would require a significant degree of cooperation, at least, among the most highly developed nations. Currently such cooperation can only be visualized by the use of such international organizations as the G-8, IMF, World Bank, WTO or some other existing organ. So far, however, the developed nations have opted to look internally for the solutions, at least in the short term. In the US, for example, this opting for internal solutions has led to a very spirited debate about what must be done. The solutions offered by the Republicans and the Democrats have brought about another stalemate concerning concrete solutions.

It seems doubtful that the national solutions will be instituted to resolve even the most basic problems that will be forthcoming in the short term. The same seems to be the case in Greece, Spain, France, Great Britain and Ireland, where rather weak austerities have been attempted. They resulted in widespread social unrest and an immediate retreat on the part of the governments. It is, of course, possible in the US over the next two years that enough bi-partisan support can be generated to at least stir the debate towards the proposal of some rational solutions. Such solutions will undoubtedly be directed at the problems highest in the public mind: that is, federal deficits, the national debt, stimulation of the economy, reducing unemployment and the breaking of government gridlock. There is no sign of such bi-partisanship yet. We must next attempt to determine, at least in the case of the US, what the solutions would look like in the long term. Second, if the short term solutions, or stop gap measures, can only be provided under the auspices of nationalism, of what will the long term response consist? As mentioned earlier many of the problems that are national in character also have an international repercussion due to the integrated nature of the global market. Indeed, the highly developed nations (the only ones we are considering at the moment) are so highly integrated that there is very little done in one that does not affect the others. The balancing of the US budget, for example, deeply affects other nations' abilities to control their finances, especially such nations as China and India. The turning of the US economy inwards to relieve the stress of high unemployment directly affects the global market, especially the economies of the third- and fourth-world nations that have come to depend upon foreign manufacturing concerns being located within their borders. While the US, or the EU, might control its own internal employment problems, the result might be a much more widespread unemployment problems coupled with deeper levels of poverty, famine, social unrest, and immigration outside the developed nations. Likewise the capturing of large amounts of money for the funding of internal development and maintenance of national infrastructure would most likely reduce the amount of money available for use as "poor relief" (what we call foreign aid) and other international expenditures.

The reincorporation of manufacturing within national boundaries would also lead to a reestablishment of protective tariffs and other barriers to protect these industries from foreign competition. This in turn would cause an imbalance in the globalization of trade causing serious damage to economies such as India, China and Japan. At the very least the solutions obtained by the various nations under the system of nationalism would have widespread and in some cases unexpected repercussions across the globe. At the very least a new scramble would begin for the capture of the natural resources needed to create and repair national infrastructure and to capture the necessary manpower when a labor deficit was reached within national boundaries. It is likely that national solutions put into effect in the highly developed nations would lead to a further depression of the third and fourth world economies accompanied by an increase in poverty and social unrest. In these areas without serious restructuring the effects will be long term rather than short or mid-term in duration. The most efficient and less disruptive solutions in the long run, however, would appear to be found at the supranational level rather than at the national level. It is likely that the short term use of international organizations, such as the IMF and World Bank coupled with regional political cooperation at the level of the EU would be needed to provide the stability and time needed to put into operation a truly world system of governance, even if it was a form of intergovermentalism similar to that found in the European Union. Even this may involve a two or three step process but the fact remains that some level of international cooperation will be needed to control the effects of nations dealing with the current problems individually.

Let's return to the question of what can be done by the various nations and how they can limit the collateral damage. We can then look outside the club of most highly developed nations and consider how the rest of the world might add to or detract from the attempt to limit the collateral damage. It must be noted from the outset that a significant number of experts expect that the highly developed nations will do nothing instead of acting quickly to attempt to resolve these issues. It is already apparent, for example, that Greece, Ireland, Spain, Portugal and Italy have waited too long to be able to effectively resolve the issues on their own. Now only the wealthier members of the EU, or the international community, or some combination of the two, can bail them out to prevent their bankruptcy. It is thought that a fairly large number of other nations are also close to being in the same situation. Those nations that are not tied to some alliance of core nations will probably be allowed to fail and forced to reorganize themselves in some manner. With similar problems facing larger nations, such as Russia, India and others, the ability of the core nations and the international community generally will be limited in what they can do to help. Beyond the EU, however, the sovereign debt problem should not need to be faced in the next decade. Even the US will not face this issue within the next decade or two regardless of dire predictions concerning its future. During this period of time many experts say they expect that the national and global economies will enter into a robust boom which will eliminate the problem without effort of any kind. Those who see the crisis bottoming out in less than two years predict there will be at the end of the next decade huge labor deficits in the highly developed countries especially in their service industries. They also predict a substantial increase in the standard of living globally. This will, in the minds of some, result in a world unrecognizable to those living today. Let's take a look at this "new" world and see how much contrast can be drawn between those who predict gloom and doom and those who do not see the current crisis developing into a tragedy.

CHAPTER 5. SOME ALTERNATIVE OUTLOOKS ON THE FISCAL CRISIS

We will start with the alternative view offered by George Friedman in his recent book mentioned above. Mr. Friedman begins with a statement concerning the fiscal crisis and recent recession. In his opinion, neither the slow economic growth related to the recession nor the panic caused by the fiscal crisis will be of much consequence beyond the short term. He predicts that within two years the US and the developed nations generally will enter into a period of robust economic growth resolving the issues of both the recession and the fiscal crisis at the global level. Indeed, he states that the economic growth will quickly lead to a labor deficit in the developed world ending the unemployment problem but possibility aggravating the immigration problem. For a more detailed look at Mr. Friedman's predictions concerning economic growth and the fiscal crisis a close reading of his book is recommended.

What Mr. Friedman does see as a reality that needs to be faced, particularly by the US, is the fact that the US has become an empire. He states that the US became an empire through a natural accumulation of both economic and political power after the conclusion of World War II. He claims the US did not choose to become an empire and indeed does not currently seem to recognize that she is an empire. Like the Romans and the British, the Americans just grew into empire. Now that an empire has been established, however, it requires that America take steps that reflect this fact. In Mr. Friedman's view, this essentially is reflected in foreign policy rather than in domestic policy. If the US acts as an empire, it will be to establish its imperial status as the premier economic power in the world. The key to the economic imperialism of America resides in its control of the oceans. Empire status also requires the US to reconsider its alliances in relation to a new system of balance of power. For instance, the US must arrange its policy to insure that others fight its battles rather than itself as it has done in both Iraq and Afghanistan.

In looking at the foreign policy of the US Mr. Friedman breaks the world up into areas of interest and sets forth the balance of power system for each area that the US should attempt to create and maintain. The emphasis is the reestablishment of an old idea, that is, a balance of power liek the one that was practiced by Great Britain in relation to the European Continent during most of the 19th century. The old idea of a balance of power will now be applied by a new empire, that of the US, and it will be applied on a global scale.

One area of great importance to the balance of power systems envisioned is the area of Eurasia. In this case Eurasia includes the European continent, including Russia and Turkey, coupled with the new nations of Western Central Asia. In this area US policy must be based on preventing an entente between Russia and Germany. In Mr. Friedman's view Germany has already begun to move away from its support of the weaker economies of the EU; and the EU generally. Although it has so far supported EU bailouts in Greece and Ireland it is looking to shift this financial support burden to international organizations such as the IMF. Russia is aware of the German uneasiness with the financial burden of EU membership and is actively courting a relationship with Germany. It has long been known that Russia is in great need of technology which Germany has in abundance; and that Germany is becoming more intimately attached to the natural resources which Russia has in abundance. As icing on the cake, however, Russia still has an excess of labor. Germany is currently facing serious internal opposition to the immigration that is filling its labor deficit. One aspect of the German–Russian entente would be German use of Russian manpower. This use would probably be based upon the movement of German manufacturing concerns into Russia or, if possible, into Eastern Europe, with Russian manpower being imported.

In Mr. Friedman's view, if this were allowed to happen it would have two major results. First, it would so weaken the existing EU that a number of existing member nations would likely voluntarily withdraw from the Union. Some of the Eastern European nations are the prime suspects in this breakdown due to their position in relation to an entente between Germany and Russia. Western Europe would probably survive such a breakdown, unless the economic power of Germany could not be replaced. Second, a German–Russian entente, in particular if it also included some arrangement with the new Eastern European and Western Central Asian nations, would quickly result in a global power equal to or exceeding that of the United States. It is, of course, in the vital interest of the US that this entente is not allowed to develop.

The US, in Mr. Friedman's vision, could avoid this by instituting several alterations in its foreign policy. First, in order to avoid any negative response from Russia, it is in the interest of the US to withdraw from its support of Georgia, Armenia, and the Western Central Asian nations. They are definitely within the sphere of Russian influence and could not be protected from reincorporation into Russia at any rate. The same is true of the Ukraine and the Baltic nations of Latvia, Lithuania and Estonia. Dropping US support for Georgia, in particular, must be done in such a way as to insure that we do not reduce our credibility with Poland. This would require a very finely tuned diplomatic program. At the same time, the US must do all in its power to bring the nations stretching from Poland to Turkey under its control. The nations of most importance to this policy are Poland, Hungary, Romania, Moldavia, Slovakia and Turkey as they would provide a corridor that would block direct German access to Russian natural resources and manpower and also block Russian access to German technology and capital investment. In short, it would establish a balance of power to offset any entente that might be established between Germany and Russia. Here the goal would be to insure that the economies of these nations are allowed to grow and become stable through US aid (possibly a modified Marshall Plan). We should also do all in our power to help revitalize the EU through a combination of international help, particularly through the use of funds from the IMF or World Bank, to guarantee bailouts for the weak economies, and possibly through another form of Marshall Plan. We must also support as strongly as we can the inclusion of Turkey into the European Union.

What is the basis of this new foreign policy for America? Although Mr. Friedman only vaguely alludes to the desire of Russia to reemerge as a world power; in this author's opinion this is what lies behind Mr. Friedman's plan. A question can be raised as to whether or not an entente between Germany and Russia would automatically lead to the creation of a global power directly in competition with the United States. This assumes that Germany would return not only to its old global desires but also to its old militarism. If this assumption is valid the combination of German economic strength with the existing military strength of Russia could certainly result in a military power equal to or exceeding that of the United States. On the other hand, if Germany could accomplish its goal of gaining access to Russia's natural resources and manpower without developing a strong military force it would probably do so, especially considering the current attitude of the German public towards peace. Perhaps the EU would make some type of free trade treaty with Russia, or even better bring Russia into the European Union. The corridor envisioned by Friedman would still exist but would be used in a much different fashion. For example, it is likely that German technology and funding would flow into those Eastern European nations along with Russia. This would probably include the movement of German manufacturing concerns into these nations to make use of their labor surpluses. It would also guarantee the flow of Russian resources on the basis of the single market system now in place in the European Union. Indeed, this is already underway with Germany in the lead in an attempt to reduce dependence on Middle Eastern oil. The benefits sought by both Russia and Germany under Friedman's analysis could also be obtained under this projection.

What would be missing is the element that essentially remains hidden in Friedman's analysis, that is, the revamping of German and Russian military ambitions coupled with the desire to reincorporate the nations of Eastern Europe and Western Central Asia into the entente. Mr. Friedman may, however, be correct in his belief that a true American empire could not survive either the expansion of the EU to include both Russia and Turkey or the creation of a military/economic entente between Germany and Russia.

Here the question boils down to whether or not it is really in the interest of the US to try to maintain its empire. One of the fears that Mr. Friedman expresses is that acceptance of the American role as an empire could entail the loss of its status as a democratic republic. He claims without equivocation that he does not under any circumstances want to see America emerge as anything other than a democratic republic. But retaining that status may only be possible if the US accepts some other role than that of an imperial empire. It is certain that an EU expanded to include the whole of the European continent, as well as the nations of Western Central Asia, would be the economic equal or surpass the US in that category. This, however, may not be a bad thing in the end.

A second area of great importance in the balance of power scheme outlined in Friedman's book is the Middle East. We must begin by noting that the book was written before the current unrest in the Middle East ("Arab Spring") broke out. Only Mr. Friedman can tell us whether or not this unrest alters his view of US foreign policy in the area. He accepts the fact that the US presence in the Middle East is altering the situation for the worse under current conditions. Prior to 2001 the balance of power in the Middle East rested on the control of Iranian and Indian ambitions. Iran's ambitions were seen in light of its desire to become the major regional power in the Persian Gulf and the ability thereby to control the flow of oil from the Persian Gulf. This ambition was blocked by the balance of power exercised by Iraq in concert with the desire of the Arabian Peninsula nations such as Saudi Arabia. India's ambition to expand into Central Asia and to become a naval power in the Indian Ocean was blocked by its need to placate the power of its neighbor Pakistan. With the US decisions after 2001 in its war against terrorism the balance of power system then in place began to fall apart. In Mr. Friedman's view the eight years that the US has been in Iraq have totally eliminated that nation's ability to block Iran's growth as a regional power. In a like manner our invasion of Afghanistan has so weakened the regime in Pakistan that it no longer can act as a balance of power in relation to Indian ambitions. With the current decision on the part of the US to withdraw from Iraq by the end of 2011 and from Afghanistan by the end of 2013 a duty has been laid on the United States. In Mr. Friedman's view there is nothing under the current circumstances that can be done to prevent Iran from becoming the premier power in the Persian Gulf. The US must, therefore, alter its foreign policy from one of opposition to Iran to one that establishes a good working relationship. The goal of US policy in this regard is to make it impossible for Iran to institute any program that would interrupt the flow of oil from the Persian Gulf. This could be done in two ways, that is, by control of OPEC and by blocking access to the Strait of Hormuz. The least likely scenario would be Iranian control of OPEC which has been historically very ineffective in controlling either supply or demand in relation to oil. A more likely scenario would be the ability of the Iranians to mine the Strait of Hormuz preventing its use as the main conduit for Persian Gulf oil. On the other hand, Mr. Friedman believes that it is greatly in the interest of Iran to court a favorable relationship with the United States. This would involve the removal of the sanctions that are currently greatly depressing the Iranian economy; and the opening of the world markets to Iranian oil. These favorable factors would be enough to cause Iran to forgo disruption of the flow of oil and to forgo aggressive sabotage of other Middle Eastern political systems.

This result could also be enhanced by the US support in the continued growth of Turkey both economically and militarily. In Friedman's view Turkey is going to become a regional power whether or not she is supported by the US; and it is in our interest to have Turkey as a balance of power to Iran outside the Persian Gulf. In much the same way it is necessary for the US to give up its commitment to Afghanistan and to reinforce its relationship with Pakistan. In Mr. Friedman's view it is not important who controls either Iraq or Afghanistan. Iraq can fall under the influence of Iranian Islamist law and not be a problem in accomplishing the US goals. The Taliban and Al Qaeda can retake control of Afghanistan and not impede the implementation of the programs that are really in the interest of the United States. In this context the main US interest that needs to be protected is the naval control of the Indian Ocean, especially in relation to the Strait of Malacca. Once again the US Empire is dependent on the control of trade through the Strait and its connection of the Indian Ocean and the South China Sea. Because of land barriers (the Himalayas and the jungles of Southeast Asia) the only practical means of sustaining trade by India is by sea. Currently the US controls the trade between India, Southeast Asia and China through its naval control of the water bodies involved. If Pakistan is removed as a balance to Indian power Mr. Friedman believes that India will take the opportunity to develop its own naval presence in the Indian Ocean. He feels that India over time if allowed to do so would displace the US naval presence in the area. It is, therefore, in the interest of the US to maintain a close and supportive relationship with the Pakistani regime even to the point of encouraging their presence in Afghanistan. Once again Friedman feels that this policy would need to be conducted with a great deal of duplicity to avoid annoying either India or China.

Friedman also believes that currently Israel does not need a close relationship with the United States. He feels that Israel is currently in a very stable situation in relation to its neighbors. The mainstay of this stability is the peace treaty with Egypt that has been in force since 1979. The current unrest in Egypt has brought up doubts about the continuation of the treaty, but all signs seem to indicate that it will remain in effect, at least in the short term. Outside of Egypt, Israel is a match for any of its neighbors militarily, either singly or in concert. Even if Iran becomes a regional power in the Persian Gulf, she is not capable of carrying out and sustaining a hot war with Israel. In effect this would also be blocked by the development of Turkey as a regional power and the unreliability of Jordan, Lebanon and Syria. This situation can be made even more stable by pushing the Israelis into executing the plan to develop an independent Palestinian state now rather than later. It is, therefore, in Mr. Friedman's system necessary for the US to weaken its ties with Israel and to strengthen our ties with the Palestinians and Iranians. Even more here than in the other areas the policy must be executed as if it didn't exist. The power of the Jewish lobby in Washington would need to be placated if such a policy were practiced openly. The best approach therefore would be to keep it on the QT.

The last important area in which the US interest involves the creation of regional balances of power is Asia. In this case, Southeast Asia is seen as incorporating India, China and the two Koreas as a mainland unit, with Japan and the Pacific islands, including New Zealand and Australia, as a balance to mainland power. The key in this area is again US naval control of the Pacific and Indian Oceans as well as the South China Sea. It is extremely difficult to envision any type of entente between the mainland nations of Asia. Their traditional background, coupled with their current diversity in relation to "Westernized modernization" seems to debar this from happening. However, it is easy to see either India or China developing into the premier regional power in Asia, or for that matter, for each of them to develop into a regional power. The two Koreas are currently very closely tied to separate portions of the Asian complex of nations. North Korea is dependent upon China for its very existence. South Korea is very closely tied to Japan economically through the interconnection of corporate ties in manufacturing and finance. Japan, of course, is already a regional power in an economic sense and has developed a substantial commercial naval capacity. Mr. Friedman sees the interest of the US best served by reducing our relationship with China and India and relocating that relationship towards Japan, Southeast Asia, the Pacific Islands, and in particular with New Zealand and Australia. Japan's greatest need is natural resources. She has literally none of her own. It would be in the interest of the US to promote the flow of natural resources from New Zealand and Australia, as well as from the Persian Gulf and Africa, to Japan. It would also be in the interest of the US to promote the maintenance of our naval control of the South China Sea.

Mr. Friedman does not foresee, at least in the next decade, any real threat of China or India replacing Japan as the premier regional economic power in Asia. He predicts that both the economy of India and China will enter into a period of significantly slower growth during the next decade just as the highly developed nations are experiencing robust economic growth. The result will be a withdrawal inward by these two nations to deal with the problems created by each of them having nearly a billion people living at or near the poverty level. A slowdown in their economies would undoubtedly cause serious problems for this population and would likely be expressed in widespread social unrest. This, of course, leaves Japan as the most likely candidate for the position of premier regional power, a position that it already holds currently in the economic arena. In order to balance this power it would be in the interest of the US to court a close relationship with South Korea, Southeast Asia, New Zealand and Australia. Mr. Friedman's vision suggests that some type of interrelationship be developed bringing Indonesia, New Zealand, and Australia in a balance of power relationship with the Japanese. Again he does not feel that Asia represents any real threat to the US Empire, at least within the confines of the next decade.

Mr. Friedman feels strongly that the nations of Africa and Latin America are not of any real interest to the United States. Our goal in Latin America is to maintain our trading relations and to strengthen them whenever possible. If Brazil should become a regional power it would be in the interest of the US to balance this power by developing Venezuela, Paraguay and Uruguay, or Argentina, Paraguay and Uruguay as a counterbalance. In any case this is not likely to happen within the next decade under Friedman's system. Our real interest in Latin America is what it has always been, that is, to prevent any outside power from developing a strong presence there.

Africa is of no interest to anyone, according to Friedman, other than the use that can be made of its resources. He suggests that the US strategy should be to totally disencumber itself from the African nations. The development of Africa, especially sub-Saharan Africa, is best left to India or China who have the cheap manpower and financial resources to pull it off. Once again our interest would be best served by trying to maintain a trading presence only in Africa. Even this, however, is not likely to develop to any appreciable degree during the next decade. Most important to Friedman is the fact that neither of these areas is going to require any degree of intense international policy making by the executive branch of the United States.

The withdrawal of German support for the euro and for its weaker EU partners will create a certain crisis in the European Union. Without German support, or something equally effective to replace it, the likelihood is that members such as Greece, Spain, Portugal, Italy and Ireland will default on their debt. This would further depress the economies of the other members, particularly those in Eastern Europe, and probably lead to the abandonment of the Euro zone. The Eastern European nations, however, in one of the ironies of history may be able to retool with the help of the US in its attempt to stop or delay an entente between Germany and Russia. Great Britain and France will likely have to champion the reorganization of the EU to eliminate the Common Agricultural Program (CAP) which now represents such a large share of the contributions made by the members. They may also have to consider altering the deficit and debt ceilings in relation to GDP. It is likely if the problems become too difficult to solve that some members will either be asked to leave, or voluntarily leave, the EU which is perfectly legal under the current treaties. In the long run, however, it would appear that the EU would survive and probably even revive with the rebound of the global economy that is expected in Friedman's prediction. The entente between Germany and Russia, of course, does not necessarily mean that Germany would leave the European Union. It is in the interest of the US to sponsor in all possible ways the continued membership of Germany in the EU and this might best be accomplished by removing the financial burden Germany feels in saving the weaker members. This might be accomplished by supplying funds from the various international organizations as a form of bailout. It appears that the economic situation within the EU is already becoming much more acute and the euro is struggling to recover its international currency reserve status. If the financial crisis and the effects of the recession are replaced with a boom economy over the next two years, as predicted by Mr. Friedman, then the issues facing the EU become less important and more easily resolved.

Further east it would appear that the US (and the German–Russian entente) would need to face the problem represented by China. China through the use of a command economy on the national level is still able, and does on a regular basis manipulate its currency and the prices on the products it puts on the global market. Such manipulation allows China artificially to make its products and currency immune to the competition normally offered by other nation states. This advantage is believed to be one of the reasons for the spectacular growth of the Chinese economy over the last couple of decades. This growth, however, has taken place at the expense of nearly a billion people who still exist at or below the poverty level. The introduction of a limited market economy on the local level has alleviated to some degree the poverty and famine that has for centuries plagued the Chinese on the regional level. On the other hand, this alleviation has also increased the expectations of this class for the future. Mr. Friedman feels the US in particular will be forced to cut its ties with China and replace them with a stronger reliance on the existing relationships that exist with Japan, South Korea, Australia and New Zealand. The US should also push to strengthen the rather weak relationship it has with the various nations of Southeast Asia, particularly Indonesia; as well as, attempting to bring Australia and New Zealand into some type of free trade agreement with Indonesia. Japan is in a position very similar to that of Israel in the Middle East. There is currently little need for the military umbrella to be continually spread over Japan. It is also certain that Japan is not in need of US economic support outside of continued trade relations. Japan during the next decade is expected to rebound both economically and politically and become the premier regional power. The US interest is to insure that Japan does not develop its already considerable naval presence into naval control of the East China Sea, the Yellow Sea and the Sea of Japan. This would replace the current control of these waters by the US and block US direct access to South Korea, China and portions of Southeast Asia. In order to accomplish the balance of power needed the US must support both South Korea and Indonesia as power balances to Japanese power. In the former case this might be most easily done by resolving the 70-year division of North from South Korea. The age of the current regime in North Korea would indicate that an opportunity to accomplish this will occur during the next decade. During this same period India and China will undergo a slowing of their economic growth and become absorbed in internal affairs, that is, the unrest expected to follow from a slowing of the economy as a billion people in each country begin to suffer.

Africa, under the scenario offered here, would be cut loose to develop on its own without the massive poor relief now given by the EU and the United States. These funds would be redirected to support the economic recoveries needed in both of these organizations. This may force the African nations to end their unsuccessful run at Westernized modernization. This effort has been focused on developing export industries (as opposed to consumer industries) and natural resource support systems with the money provided by poor relief. The actual result has been the failure of industry to take hold due to a lack of technology (infrastructure), lack of education (wide-spread illiteracy) and the lack of skilled labor. The attempt to survive on an export economy has failed, with disastrous results that have been greatly aggravated by the corruption and greed of the ruling elites in Africa who have absorbed a large portion of the funds provided. The nations that are providing the poor relief funds are using the African nations as dumping grounds for their surplus agricultural products (part of the social welfare system of agricultural sub-sidies). This over time has destroyed the ability of these nations to even sustain subsistence agriculture and has resulted in widespread famine, disease and starvation. The African nations will be forced to find new al-liances to replace those with the US and the European Union. The most likely candidates will be India, China, Southeast Asia and possibly New Zealand and Australia. Although the new alliances will not replace the no-strings attached poor relief Africa is now receiving they will give the Africans a chance to establish much more stable economies and political structures — if corruption can be contained.

It is certain that unpredictable changes will occur in the short term. Many of these changes are likely to result in profound reorganization of current political, economic, social and psychological traditions. The cur-rent acceptance of liberal democracy, liberal economics and modern sci-ence as the main tenets of modern life may degrade substantially. Should the worst predictions of gloom and doom prevail it is certain that all three will be challenged. There are already circumstances under which it is realized that the above trilogy may not be the paramount manner in which to approach problems. For example, it is becoming apparent that authoritarian political standards may be more appropriate for the resolving of the problems facing sub-Saharan Africa than is the establish-ment of democracy. The same may be true in some Latin American and Southeast Asian nations for exactly the same reasons. To a lesser extent, and for different reasons, the same may be true for nations like India and China. Here the ancient traditions and cultural aspects of their societies point towards the use of a paternal authoritarianism rather than a true democracy. It may be only in North America and Europe that the above trilogy remains supreme. Modern science has certainly shown its nega-tive side in its ability to produce weapons of mass destruction, global pollution and unsustainable population growth. It has, however, also been largely responsible for the high standard of living found in the more developed nations, although even this may not be sustainable.

From what has been said above it can be expected that major changes are just around the corner — probably within the next decade. These changes will undoubtedly bring significant suffering to some parts of the globe. Others, however, may escape without feeling any real adverse ef-fects. If this is accurate then one can expect that an even sharper line will be drawn between the "have-not" and "have" nations of the world. This can be expected to bring forth a significant amount of social unrest and probably even violent revolt. One can already see this happening in the

Middle East, Africa, Latin America and some Southeast Asian nations. It will soon also probably be very evident in India and China. The violence may be so great as to impel the developed nations to exert a force great enough to control the violence or at least contain it to Africa, Latin America and Southeast Asia. Such a result might be avoided by the reinstitution of a milder form of imperialism as suggested by George Friedman.

A second alternative to the gloom and doom scenario of global economic collapse is to postulate that a group of regional entities will arise. These entities are likely to be something less than a consolidated empire as is envisioned for the US, but rather entities established along the lines of the current European Union. It is likely, at least in the short term, that these regional groupings will be essentially free trade arrangements or customs unions put together to increase the members competitiveness in the global market. They would include the US, Canada, Central and South America as one regional group; the EU, Turkey, Russia and Western Central Asia as a second group; the Far East including the far Pacific Islands of New Zealand and Australia as a third group; Africa and the Middle East would make up the last or fourth group, if only as a response to being left out of all the other groups. The Middle East might in fact be incorporated into either the Eurasian or Asian group, or might stand independent of any grouping. It is difficult in looking at logical regional customs unions or common markets to determine just where the Middle East might fit due to its religious commitments. The same is true of Africa, although it's best fit as set forth above would probably be with the Asian group. The logic behind the first grouping is merely an extension of the already existing agreements such as the North American Free Trade Agreement (NAFTA), MERCOSUR, and the long standing Monroe Doctrine. The logic behind the second group is again the exchange of German technology and EU funding for Russian and Western Central Asian natural resources and manpower. The logic behind the third grouping lies in the extension of the interlocking corporate and financial systems already in place in relation to Japanese and South Korean manufacturing industries and the need for China as a market for their products and vice versa. None of these groupings should be expected to result in anything other than a rather loose economic integration. The wild cards of the Middle East and Africa, although they are unlikely to become major regional powers in the short term, must be accommodated in some manner by the various trading groups, especially in relation to the oil deposits of the Middle East. In the short term this accommodation would probably consist of continuing the current system of trade agreements and economic aid in Africa; and the attempt to stabilize the unrest in the Middle East while maintaining the current trade agreements. The key in the Middle East still seems to center on the creation of a viable Palestinian homeland and the withdrawal of American presence in both Afghanistan and Iraq. The Far East is a different level of problem as far as developing a true free trade system. The whole area has been for millennia developing separate and very diverse cultures. There have been many traditional disagreements between the various components of this area. India has for millennia been at odds with the Middle East, Southeast Asia and China. Recently the Indians have gone to war with China over border disputes, as well as, fighting wars with Pakistan over the fate of Kashmir and Bangladesh. Southeast Asia has been at odds not only within its own cultural diversities but also with both China and India. Japan has constantly been at odds with both China and Korea, and at times with Russia. In short, the cultural aspects found in Asia have created a long standing aura of distrust and dislike across the board in the area. However, if the EU were to expand to include Russia and Turkey, and the US were able to put together a free market consisting of North, Central and South America, and Australia were able to create a free trade system with Indonesia and New Zealand, the rest of Asia would be forced to overcome this distrust and dislike. One of the major stumbling blocks at the moment is the fate of North Korea and Tibet. As mentioned earlier, during the next decade the death of the leading communists in North Korea will open an opportunity to reunite the two Koreas. As with the unification of the two Germanys this will have a profound effect on the area. The establishment of an independent Tibet would ease much of the tension between India and China and would hurt neither of these countries economically or politically. Without these tensions there is no reason why these nations could not join with Japan and the Southeast Asian nations in some type of free market or custom union. In the end, the short term will remain fluid in relation to the development of the first two trading blocs and probably exclude the third for the short term.

As stated before the integration of the economic interests of the trading blocs, if they develop, should not be expected to generate much, if any, movement towards a political integration other than the already existing intergovermentalism of the European Union. The solution to long term problems such as the sustainability of large welfare and military structures, the abuse of natural resources, pollution, pandemic disease, poverty and others will remain at the national level. It may be, however, that if the regional blocs develop that the 200 plus voices now being heard in these areas will be reduced to three to five voices. This would allow for more opportunities to reach agreement on the basis of compromise. Many events or unexpected developments can come about which could alter either of the alternatives presented above in significant ways. The current unrest in the Middle East is a good example of the foregoing statement. The one constant that always remains is that the future cannot be predicted with any hope of accuracy.

Once again a return will be made in order to look at the US in isolation with all that has been offered in the two alternatives in mind. The current mood in the US public seems to be a traditional concern for domestic policies rather than foreign affairs. This type of approach if carried to extremes may be dangerous considering the current interrelation of world politics and economies. However, under the current system of nationalism this approach can also be seen as the normal response inculcated within the nationalistic ideology. Returning from the realm of prediction and overlarge surveys is there any realistic down to earth programs the US can take to resolve its national issues? The national issues most prominent in the US public debate are as follows:

1. The public is demanding that programs be instituted to stimulate the US economy and bring down the high rate of unemployment.

2. The public has demanded the institution of programs that will reduce federal government spending and attempt to reduce the national debt.

3. The public has made the demand that the congressional representatives find a civil way of communicating with one another and to bring the long gridlock between the parties to an end. In short, the public has demanded a return to bi-partisan action in relation to the above problems.

The US economy has, since the recession officially ended in the summer of 2009, entered into a very moderate growth, something less than three percent of GDP. This growth, although welcome, is not enough, according to economic experts, to impact the level of unemployment. It is also not certain whether the steps taken by the federal government, that is, TARP and the stimulus plan had any responsibility for the ending of the recession or for the new growth in the economy. The latter two may have occurred without either program, or may in fact have been more efficiently and effectively resolved without them. At any rate, the public still perceives that the economy needs to be further stimulated and that the high unemployment problems still exist. Some action is being taken within Congress to address the spending issue but to date this is not accompanied with any significant degree of bi-partisanship. Enough time has not elapsed, nor have the programs introduced firmed up enough, to tell whether or not the American public will be satisfied with what is being done. It is also still open to debate whether or not deep spending cuts or increased spending will end the fragile economic growth underway. It has been estimated that the US economy would grow only 1% in fiscal 2011.

The Tea Party attempted to bring these rather vague demands of the public into focus during the mid-term election of 2010. They were successful, at least in terms of being able to claim responsibility for the election of 38 new Republican members of the House of Representatives and 5 new members to the Senate. It is of interest that the new representatives and senators all claim connection to the Tea Party but are registered as Republicans. This would indicate that the Tea Party represents a new conservative wing of the Republican Party rather than a third party. The Tea Party has also been responsible for an impressive attempt to initiate new programs aimed at reducing government spending; however, these attempts have been met with further stalemate. Although not directly called for by the American public, the Tea Party included within its campaign promises to repeal the National Health Care Act passed in 2009. It appears that the American public would accept either a repeal of the act or a more moderate program aimed at reforming the flawed sections of the Act, although even this is uncertain. The Tea Party advocates, however, appear locked into the position that only a repeal of the Act would be acceptable. The Republicans in the House of Representatives were able to pass a bill for the repeal of the act but the democratically controlled Senate voted the bill. The President, of course, has also promised to veto the repeal bill if it reaches his desk. The House Republicans are now focused on not funding the bill when it comes up for appropriation in 2012. This from the Republican standpoint will reduce future spending by a trillion dollars a year or more; while the Democratic take is that if the bill is not funded the cost will be in trillions of dollars in new spending within the provision of current medical system.

In an effort to stimulate the economy the lame duck Congress (the Congress that finished serving before the new representatives were sworn in January 2011) started by extending the Bush Era Tax cuts across the board. This is a major tenet in the Republican philosophy in relation to stimulating the economy. This Congress also passed a bill that

would allow a one year reduction in payroll taxes of 2 percent in relation to Medicare. This also was seen by the Republicans as a measure
to stimulate consumer spending and thereby stimulating the economy.
These measures are also expected to cost the federal government several
billions of dollars in lost revenue. The new Congress has promised to
pass legislation that will promote further tax credits and/or loopholes
in favor of small and medium size businesses. The Republican view is
that the only effective way to stimulate the economy enough to produce
a reduction in unemployment is through relief to small and medium size
businesses. It is claimed by some experts that small and medium sized
businesses represent about 70 percent of the new job creation in the current economy. The result to date has been the postponement of debate on
the reform of the health care act until after the election of 2012. It is also
unlikely that any programs aimed at stimulating the economy will be
placed into effect, if passed at all, prior to the middle of 2012. It appears
that the Democrats have been very effective in shifting the responsibility of creating effective programs to deal with stimulating the economy
and reducing high unemployment into the Republican camp. However
this has caused them to lose the image of leadership. If the public should
believe that their demands have been ignored, the Republicans will face
a good share of the blame and voter anger in the 2012 election.

When it comes to the reduction of spending and the national debt
even less has been accomplished. The extension of the tax cuts and the
institution of a payroll tax break, in fact, are likely to increase the federal
budget deficit and the national debt through at least 2012. An attempt
was made to reduce the appropriations connected with the 2010 budget by 62 billion dollars. This attempt heightened tensions in the debate
over what budget items should be subjected to spending cuts and by
how much. It was also the basis of the stalemate as regards the funding
of the of the 2010 budget (debt ceiling debate). Even the second engine
for the F-35 still faces stiff resistance in the Senate and a possible veto by
the president.

A bill was introduced into the Senate by Senator Rand Paul that
called for the reduction or elimination of The National Endowment for
the Arts, payments to the needy for electrical bills, the School Lunch
Program, financing for urban housing and transit and the food stamp
program among others. Mr. Paul claims that this would reduce the current budget by 500 billion dollars. This bill awaits a hearing and a vote
in the Senate and would then have to go to the House and lastly to the
president where it would almost certainly be vetoed. The Congress had

to face the issue of financing the remainder of the fiscal year which ended Sept. 30, 2011. This had to be done by August 4ᵗʰ 2011. There was no real concern that Congress would fail to pass the spending appropriations necessary to keep the federal government in business, but it was scrambling to find cuts in spending equal to the increased debt ceiling prior to issuing that approval. If Congress had failed to pass the spending bill the government could limp along on the basis of short term loans or print money for a few weeks but in the near term would have defaulted on its obligations. This leaves the public demand for bi-partisan action on current and future spending, as well as consideration of ways to reduce the national debt, in a rather unproductive position. In the short term, that is, prior to the 2012 election, it does not bode well for any significant action to be taken in either of these areas. Whether or not the public will accept the attempts as legitimate remains to be seen in the results of the foresaid election. As it turned out, at the last hour the debt ceiling was raised by 2.2 trillion dollars, enough to get the US through to 2013, while at the same time 900 billion dollars in future spending reductions were passed. A committee was appointed to find another 1.5 trillion dollars in reductions by November 1, 2011. This bill requires automatic reductions in spending in the amount of 1.5 trillion if congress fails to enact their recommendations by the end of 2011. No one is happy with this legislation, including the people, but it is what is on the books and indicates that another crisis will be faced before the 2012 elections.

Another issue is state spending and state debt. Several very large states are on the verge of bankruptcy. These include California, New York, Florida and Illinois. A significant number of smaller states, while not technically bankrupt, are carrying excessive budget deficits and state debts that will later bring them to the same point of default. Most of these states are currently attempting to remedy the problems through mandatory cuts in spending, mostly aimed so far at education, health care, infrastructure and public employment. The biggest issues are state funded pension programs, state funded health care programs, and vital services such as fire protection, police protection, social entitlement programs and the National Guard programs all of which have not been put on the table. As with the federal government, the cuts offered in these areas do not appear to be large enough to offset the current budget deficits nor to reduce the state debt structure. It is also a rather dangerous game to cut funds for infrastructure creation and maintenance. Infrastructure is probably the most important factor in insuring a state's ability to attract new industry and to preserve its old industry base. Also, the failure to fund consistent infrastructure maintenance, although not as noticeable in the short run, requires a massive expenditure in the long run.

The solutions proposed have run the gamut from allowing the states that are in trouble to go bankrupt and to default upon their debt to arranging some sort of federal government bailout for the states. The first solution would in the view of some experts put the US economy into a deep depression and the second would undoubtedly seriously increase both the federal budget deficit and the national debt. It appears likely in the current atmosphere that the states, and smaller governmental institutions (county, urban, etc.) will be left on their own to solve this problem with the worst case scenario being that some states, or smaller government units, will be forced into bankruptcy (currently several states are instituting the necessary measures to bring about balanced budgets and debt reduction in order to avoid default).

Can any realistic predictions be made as to what might occur during the next decade within the US in relation to these problems? The following predictions seem to be fairly safe.

1. That the 2012 election will be another battle between the new Republican (Tea Party) conservatives and the more liberal wing of the Democratic Party. If the public perceives that nothing has been accomplished by the current administration, it is likely that the Republican momentum from the mid-term election will be carried forward. On the other hand, if enough is done to disarm the Tea Party initiative, then it would appear that the Democrats would hold onto the White House and maybe extend its majority in the Senate.

2. If the public decides it is likely that the global economy will rebound in the next couple of years, this will affect the United States. In response to an easing of global economic woes, the US could enter into a robust period of growth, easing unemployment pressure. Although this trend will have been just begun it may have proceeded to the point where it is being felt by the public and would certainly affect the outcome of the election in 2012.

3. The withdrawal of our troops from Afghanistan and Iraq will relieve the federal spending issue to some degree, as will the increase in revenue from the growing economy. The withdrawal, however, may be offset by other international problems created in its wake.

4. The national debt will remain high and in fact will increase over the next decade, but if spending is controlled and robust growth resumes the budget deficits may largely disappear.

5. A lack of bi-partisan action, compromise, and toned-down rhetoric will continue throughout the decade and may even become more pronounced; but with good times such things are largely ignored by the public.

It appears, therefore, that nothing can be done in the short term to relieve the effects of the recent recession or to allay the upcoming effects of the fiscal crisis. The only salvation appears to be a hoped for robust recovery of the economy. This, however, is not expected to kick in during the short term, or at best, at the very end of the next two years.

In the two years that are left to the Obama administration in its first term the most likely prospect of things that could be done to strengthen the changes of a second term are as follows: First, in relation to the stimulation of the economy and production of new jobs the administration could reduce the amount of government regulation concerning the start up of new businesses at lower costs. This the administration could accomplish without the aid or interference of the congress. The relaxation of the EPA rules indicates this option is being given serious consideration. Incentives could also be offered to construction companies involved in infrastructure creation or maintenance to promote the hiring of additional labor to obtain bonuses for completion of projects before schedule. This also could be done without the approval of congress. Lastly, many of the bureaucratic functions now handled by the federal government could be delegated to the state and local governments for execution. For example, the inspection duties of the Food and Drug Administration could be farmed out to state and local agencies responsible for hiring the manpower locally. This function would remain a federal budget item but the manpower and duties would be given to state and local agencies. All of these projects would increase activity in the economy and produce much needed jobs at the state and local level. As a result the public perception of the administration would be enhanced, as would the chances of them winning the election in 2012. (This would appear to be a case in which centralized planning would result in greater efficiencies and cost savings.)

It was contemplated that the troop commitment in Iraq would remain at about 50,000 at the end of 2011. Two additional factors however changed that plan. First, it turned out that the political structure that was in place, including the Iraqi army and state police, were prepared to handle whatever effects followed the American pullout. Second, the new government in place in Iraq did not wish any further US presence and that they requested that we remove the remainder of our troops as promised. The current plan is that the troops in Afghanistan will be withdrawn during 2013. This plan, however, could be altered in several ways. First, the US could realize that it doesn't make any difference who rules that nation. It does not adversely affect the US even if the Taliban and Al Qaeda regain control. The US cannot effectively protect itself against terrorists and it cannot make a self-governing people out of people who do not wish to be self-governing. Actually the US cannot produce a democracy for people who are still ruled for all practical purposes by tribal governments. The most that we can hope is that a continuing relationship with Pakistan will have some influence on how much control the Afghans allow the Taliban and Al Qaeda. In any case, the money that is saved in relation to current budget expenditures by the withdrawal of troops from these two nations could be set aside specifically for national debt reduction, that is to say, Congress must be pressed to pass legislation that creates a sinking fund specifically for the purpose of reducing the national debt and that earmarks savings from the ending of the two wars as funding for the sinking fund. Currently, however, the expectation is that the US will remain in Afghanistan for at least the next five years and that the withdrawal from Iraq will be replaced with other commitments for the funds saved.

If just these programs were established and in effect by the 2012 election, with the exception of withdrawal from Afghanistan, it is possible that not only the American public, but also the foreign creditors, would be satisfied that the US has become serious about controlling its budget deficits and reducing its national debt. This alone would effectively eliminate the risk that the bond market will crash in the short term and should go some way in relieving the fear of the economy failing. Much more would still need to be done but an atmosphere conducive to accomplishing much more would be available. These are short term gains that could be predicted as both reasonable and capable of being achieved prior to the 2012 election.

In relation to the reduction of both federal and state budget deficits and debt a more aggressive program is needed over the long term. If the economy enters into a period of robust growth during the next two years, the most that can be expected from the increased revenues is some of the pressure will be relieved, at least, in the sense of increasing deficits above the current levels. This would to some degree lessen the pain that will come with reducing the deficits to zero over the long haul. There is no question that the following steps must be taken. First, legislation must be passed at the federal level requiring a balanced budget, or at the very least mandatory spending caps, by some specific point in the future. That point could reasonably be assigned to the date 2021. This would put the federal and state governments in the position where each year they would be required to cut the budget deficit by an amount that would result in a balanced budget by 2021. In the case of the federal government, the budget deficit would need to be reduced by 150 billion dollars per year beginning in 2011. Whether or not this could be accomplished remains to be seen; there is no agreement on where the cuts would be applied. The state spending deficits would have to be reduced in the same manner. Once a surplus was obtained in the federal and state budgets, even if this surplus came before the mandated date for a balanced budget, this surplus would have to be earmarked for funding the already proposed sinking fund. It could take as long as two or three decades to entirely eliminate the existing national and state debts, but even so it would prove beneficial long before they were totally eliminated. The same economic discipline should be applied to any local (mainly urban) governments that find themselves in the same condition of budget deficits and long-term debt. Second, a serious attempt should be made to reform the current entitlement programs even if they do not need to be touched to accomplish the necessary reduction of spending deficits and long-term debt. If nothing else a look should be taken at the existing qualifications for benefits. It is likely with the population bulge and continued aging of the population that the minimum age qualification should be raised from 62 to 67. It is also likely that those who have retirement incomes in excess of $100,000 per year should not be eligible to draw Social Security Benefits; although they may still be allowed to qualify for Medicare and Medicaid. A serious look will probably need to be taken in relation to whether or not there is a better way to fund retirement, disability and unemployment needs than social welfare. The federal government by legislative act must be made in a mandatory manner to return the 2.5 trillion dollars it has borrowed from the Social Security Fund in order to insure it's solvency until 2037. The same type of social services offered by the states on a blanket basis must be reformed to fit only those who have a demonstrated need for the service. These long term approaches will be relatively painless and will require no significant amount of austerity on the part of members of the society if they are justly applied. Lastly, and maybe most importantly, the federal and state tax codes must be reformed. The easiest reform would be to scrape the current tax code and replace it with one that imposes a straight tax of 10 percent (or whatever percent is deemed necessary) on all incomes above the poverty level with absolutely no tax credits, deductions, or loopholes. This is by far the most productive method to tax income and is probably also the most rational in that it taxes everyone the same. Some will argue that taxing the person who makes ten billion dollars ten percent of his or her income hurts less than taxing the person who makes 50,000 dollars ten percent of theirs. However, no one has shown that paying one billion in taxes hurts any less than paying five thousand. At any rate, most experts in the area agree that the current taxation system both at the federal and state level is highly riddled with loopholes that are mainly beneficial to the wealthy and corporations. The tax code, however, still remains essentially progressive although much needed revenue is allowed to be dissipated. This reform alone, whether it is a total revamping of the tax structure, or a reform of the current code has the potential of producing huge increases in the amount of revenue available to federal and state governments. This could be accomplished without the need for increasing tax rates, or even in some cases lowering tax rates. If the current problems that are facing the US are to be settled within the current governmental institutions over the long term then these steps must be taken.

When it comes to the problem of lack of bi-partisan cooperation in American politics the solution is at hand. The public must not only demand that its representatives act in a manner that produces bi-partisan cooperation they must punish all of those who do not heed the warning at the ballot box. The representatives must be made accountable to the public and must be punished if they do not adhere to the demands of their constituency. This can only be accomplished by making the actions of interest groups, lobbyists and other political power brokers transparent in relation to their activities with individual representatives. On the other hand, it is the duty of the public in respect to this transparency to take the time to find out what their representatives have been doing.

In addition every vote taken in the House of Representatives and the Senate should be electronically recorded rather than by a voice- or hand-vote. These records should be made easily available to the public at no cost to the individual. The public must take responsibility for making sure that the representatives who serve them actually serve in the manner requested by the constituency. Because of the nature of democracy it is to be expected that a certain amount of uncivil debate will arise when emotional chords are struck. It is also to be expected that at times there will be stalemates and gridlock over legislation sponsored by opposing parties. What has made the US successful as a democracy over the last two centuries, however, is the ability to compromise. Compromises on important legislation has kept the occasional sense of gridlock and stalemate from becoming permanent. Over the last two decades it appears that the ability to compromise has become a lost art. It will be necessary for the public to take responsibility for electing representatives with a political philosophy that doesn't produce ideological stalemate or gridlock of such a nature as to prevent compromise.

Lastly, over the short term a start must be made to reform the American health care system. There is so much to be done and the problem is so large that little can be expected in the short term beyond a beginning. Over the long term, however, the health system must be reformed to bring it back into line regarding cost, quality and availability. The finest health care in the world can be found currently in America however the problem is that only a very small percentage of the population can afford this care. An equally large percentage of the population would not have the finest care available to them even if they could afford it. Most health care is currently paid for by means of insurance, either privately or publically provided. Many of the people who are able to afford health care can do so only because payment is provided by the insurance provided through their employer or by public agencies, such as Medicare and state health programs. The problem is that the employers are now beginning to realize that they cannot afford the rapidly escalating cost of health insurance, and the public programs are equally unsustainable. Those who are not employed have already been to a large degree priced out of the private health insurance market. In the US this has led to an estimated forty million people, roughly 13 percent of the population having no health insurance. Another significant number of people, especially those who are employed in the private sector, are required to pay for a substantial portion of their health insurance. Those who are not still in the work force but have reached the age of 65 or more are likely to be receiving their sole health care insurance through Medicare and Medicaid. This today represents some 58 million people or another 19 percent of the population. Thus if Medicare and Medicaid were to fail, or be eliminated, then about a third of the population would be without any resources to pay for health care beyond their own personal finances. Even with the private and public insurance programs in place a very significant number of people cannot cover the cost of their portion of the health care. This cost represents the payment of deductibles (the amount the individual must pay before insurance kicks in) and co-payments (the amount the insured must pay as his portion of health care covered by the insurance). With Medicare this normally amounts to twenty percent of the bill and the same is about the average for private insurance. In order to qualify for Medicaid an individual must demonstrate that he or she does not have assets above a certain dollar amount. Currently this amount is about $5,000.

The cost of private insurance to cover the co-payments or deductibles not paid by the primary insurance coverage is beyond the ability of many to pay and is a real burden to most of those who can pay, especially if it is a Medicare supplement. For a husband and wife, a good Medicare supplement policy will cost in the range of 200–300 dollars a month. The same would probably be true of supplemental policies to cover charges not paid by employer insurance programs. In addition, the insurance companies routinely rule illnesses and disabilities as pre-existing conditions and will not pay for treatment related to them. As might be expected by the time a person reaches 65 there may be several such preexisting conditions. Many insurance policies include clauses that allow the insurance company to cancel the policy in mid-treatment when costs exceed a certain stated amount. All of these add to the cost of covering health care both for the private employer and the private individual. This industry must be looked at in depth concerning the cost, availability and contents of the contracts.

Lastly the pharmaceutical industry must be looked at in detail regarding the drugs that have come to the market, the duplication of drugs on the market under different trademarks, the cost of producing the drugs, and the availability of these drugs to those who need them. There are many regulations in place concerning the approval of new drugs, the distribution of the drugs, and the manner which these drugs can be produced but very little concerning their use and cost. Some of these factors are under the control of the federal and state governments others are solely the responsibility of the drug industry. All these factors contribute to the cost of these drugs to the consumer. This industry is a prime example of the need for reform at not only the national level but on the international level.

The health industry must also be reevaluated in relation to the amount of fraud, misrepresentation and illegal activity that is assigned to it. The Medicare system is under high levels of fraud not only from the medical profession, but also by individuals and companies that are eligible for benefits. Private insurance companies are subject to medical providers willing to misrepresent their patients and to commit fraud to garner larger payments. The legal profession is equally guilty of filing frivolous lawsuits related to health and medical negligence and jury's are guilty of awarding outrageous settlements in cases of little or no value. Steps must be taken, whenever possible, to reduce this type of activity. The reduction they would bring to spending in the medical field would undoubtedly be enormous.

All of these steps must be started in the short term and brought to a solution in the mid-term and long term. There will be no solutions in the long term if what can be done in the short term continues to be postponed as it has over the last few decades. The steps that need to be taken in the short term will be both unpopular in certain segments of the population and painful in other areas of the population. The time has come for the American people to step up to bat and demand that their congressional and executive branch representatives begin to fix the problems that face the nation.

Up to this point the discussion has centered on two distinct points of view. The first involves the prediction that the individual nations can effectively do nothing to resolve the economic malaise that confronts them. The individual nations are also powerless to amend the same problems that face the global market system on a supranational basis. These facts will result in the continued implosion of the national and global economies, and the only remaining question will be whether this implosion occurs in the short or long term. If this implosion occurs, it may result in the total abandonment of the current reliance on nationalism, liberal democracy, liberal economics and modern science as supports for the current political and social structures. These four- or five-century-old mainstays of "Western civilization" are likely to be replaced by two or maybe three regional economic "empires" based on non-democratic forms of government, that is, an intergovermentalism similar to what exists in the current European Union. These empires are likely to be operated on the basis of a rather Machiavellian political outlook with a rather high degree of economic regulation. Modern science, of course, would remain but its role would be reduced to that of a tool for the creation of technology. The world would survive but might be nearly unrecognizable to those living today. This is the prediction that is attached to the gloom and doom scenario.

The second prediction revolves around the belief that the individual nations need do little if anything in a positive way in relation to the current problems. It is important under this scenario that the individual nations do nothing more than make a show for their public indicating they are attempting to address these problems. Any positive action might actually disrupt the natural processes that will over the short term resolve the problems. Within a couple of years the market forces now in play will bring the national and global economies from a mild recessionary trend into a robust period of boom. This will resolve the budgetary issues and allow for the financial bailouts necessary to resolve the fiscal crisis. Some restructuring of the national and global economies may be necessary but the current reliance on nationalism, liberal democracy, liberal economics and modern science will remain just as it is today. In the long term the manner in which the world operates will change very little from what exists today under this prediction.

This latter scenario at this time appears to be the more realistic and it should be adopted, especially by the highly developed nations. If this prediction turns out to be accurate and the gloom and doom scenarios are avoided the pain and suffering expected will also be minimal and of short duration. In that case the conditions would arise as needed to implement Mr. Friedman's geopolitical ideas. There will be little improvement however in the status of the third and fourth world nations. There also will be little change in the current levels of unemployment because of the continued marginalization of labor. The lesson of the current economic setbacks will make it clear that the various nations must control both budget deficits and long-term debt within manageable levels.

Under the second prediction one factor that can be expected in the long term is a continuation of the cycles of boom and bust that have occurred throughout history. This may in the long run create circumstances in which some weaker nations, such as those in parts of Africa and Latin America, will fail as nations. It is likely that the wealthier nations will in most cases be able to easily absorb the failure of these weak nations and will be willing to allow it to happen. This prediction assumes that in the long run conditions will be produced that require a nation to reach a certain size in terms of economic activity and social stability in order to be able to maintain a position in the global marketplace. If this prediction is correct the current over-extension of nationalism will play itself out and there will be considerable reorganization in Africa, Latin America and other areas of the globe. As the people of the world slowly become better educated, enjoy noticeably higher standards of living and witness the creation of new middle classes within the various nations, liberal democracy will reach its maximum influence across the globe. Whether or not this will result in the development of different forms of democracy remains to be seen. There is also some question as to whether or not this second prediction would also lead in the long run to a series of economic free markets, or economic empires. It is not hard to imagine a world of national democracies being capable of developing regional economic empires; but it is equally easy to imagine a true global market open to participation at some level by every nation then in existence.

This brings us to the opportunity to attempt to set forth a description of the existing world order and to determine, if possible, whether this existing order is in a real state of crisis.

CHAPTER 6. A LOOK AT THE WORLD ORDER AS IT EXISTS TODAY

There is one prediction that allows us to go back and determine what conditions exist currently and to make a guess as to how they will play out in the future. This is the prediction made by George Friedman set forth above. He first dismisses the current national and global financial crisis, the high unemployment problems, and the national and global debt crisis as irrelevant to the future. They are seen as merely the aftereffects of the continual boom and bust economic cycles that have occurred with some regularity throughout history. He assumes without much ado that the next decade will begin with a return of economic boom conditions that will alleviate, if not eliminate, the current problems. As these conditions are either pushed into the background or eliminated until the next bust cycle, he sets forth his vision of how the world will develop. His approach is based largely upon geopolitical rather than geo-economic factors. Each of his geopolitical assumptions will be judged by what appear to be the current economic conditions. He begins by stating that the US is currently a global empire, at least economically and militarily, although this fact is not publicly recognized by the American leadership. This empire has arisen in a rather organic fashion since the end of World War II, especially since the fall of the Soviet Union in 1992. He speculates that it is the historical conditions, especially since the end of World War II, that have forced the US into this position just as historical conditions earlier forced Great Britain and Rome into their positions as empires. Regardless, the fact that the US has become a global empire requires that its foreign policy be adapted to this reality.

This adaptation will require a new emphasis for US foreign policy including some rather unusual commitments to new alliances. American foreign policy must be based upon the creation of regional balances of power and their maintenance. This would include the use of these regional power balances to fight whatever wars were necessary rather than committing US troops. This envisions that wars will no longer be global in nature but rather limited to very specific regions; and that the conflicts will be small enough to be handled by the local power structure created by the United States. Because of the unusual nature of some of these alliances, the conduct of foreign policy will need to be Machiavellian in nature, at least initially. Although the president of the US will need to be overall a "moral" person, he or she will also need to be capable of the lie, deception and ruse of the Machiavellian politician. It is the economic and military hegemony currently exercised by the US that represents the basis of the American empire or Pax Americana, and it is this hegemony that the US must protect. As stated earlier, the overall goal of the US is to establish regional balances of power. They have been laid out in some detail earlier but for a different reason. Here an attempt will be made to use them to show the state of the world order as it exists today.

Friedman first approaches the Middle East. This area, he contends, is the most critical over the short term and will, therefore, involve the highest amount of policy investment by the US executive branch over the next decade. The establishment of a balance of power in this region requires that several factors be taken into account. The former balance of power in the region was based upon the fact that Iraq and Iran offset each other's ambitions to become the premier regional power in the Persian Gulf. In addition, Pakistan stood as a balance to the power of India in its desire to exert naval influence in the Indian Ocean and Persian Gulf. Israel by means of its treaty with Egypt was a balance to the power of Syria, Lebanon and Jordan in the western Middle East, and Turkey stood as a counter-balance to the power of Russia in its designs on the Middle East. With the fall of the Soviet Union, several new nations were created on the perimeter of the Middle East, that is, Armenia, Georgia and the nations of Western Central Asia. The former balance of power has been disturbed since 2001 by the US decision to wage a war against "terrorism", leading to the invasion of both Iraq and Afghanistan as part of a generalized war. As a result, the nation of Iraq has been completely removed as a counter to the power of Iran. Pakistan, because of its involvement in the war in Afghanistan, has also been weakened to the point where it cannot stand as a counter to India's ambitions in the Indian Ocean and Persian

Gulf. Israel, because of the treaty with Egypt and the American presence in Iraq and Afghanistan, is independent of American aid at this point. Israel without pressure from Egypt and Iran is more than a match militarily for Syria, Lebanon, Jordan and the Arabian Peninsula nations. The only real difficulty facing Israel is its reluctance to establish a Palestinian homeland in the short term. Thus, as the US honors its commitment to withdraw its forces from Iraq by the end of 2011 the main outcome will be to give Iran the unrestricted ability to become the premier power in the Persian Gulf. There is little doubt in Friedman's view that Iraq and the Arabian Peninsula nations will fall under the influence of Iran. Then Iran would be in a position to block the flow of oil out of the Middle East by mining of the Strait of Hormuz or through control of OPEC.

The same claim is being made in relation to the war in Afghanistan. No matter who runs the country, whether it be the US or a NATO coalition or the Taliban and Al Qaeda, what matters to US interests is the fact that Pakistan has already been so weakened that it cannot deter Indian ambitions.

In order to correct this loss of the balance of power the US must adjust its alliances in the Middle East. First, the US must accept the fact that it must withdraw its forces and end the wars in both Iraq and Afghanistan. Second, the US must accept that under current conditions it does not matter much who is ruling either Iraq or Afghanistan. Third, the US must withdraw its unconditional support of Israel and allow itself the flexibility to establish new alliances. Fourth, the US must attempt to create normal political relations with the nation of Iran. Fifth, the US must do everything in its power to promote the continued development of the economic and military sectors in Turkey.

This being said, current conditions in the US bring the following into focus. Clearly, the withdrawal of unconditional support from Israel and the establishment of normal relations with Iran cannot be conducted in the open. The Jewish political lobby in the US is much too powerful to be so antagonized. That would be a form of political suicide. Similarly an open attempt to repair relations with Iran would make a mockery of the current US position in both Iraq and Afghanistan and would result in a loss of credibility in the Persian Gulf and in Eastern Europe. This too would be a form of political suicide. As a reference point one must remember that under the US system the President is solely responsible for the conduct of foreign policy and it is this office that suffers the consequences of failure or success in foreign policy.

The proposed withdrawal of the US commitment to Israel is premised on the above mentioned fact that Israel no longer needs US military or economic support. Our attempt to stay engaged with Israel should be solely on the basis of aiming to help establish a Palestinian nation in the short term. The US needs to establish relations with Iran, given that we can no longer prevent that nation from becoming the premier power in the Persian Gulf. Our primary interest here is the continued free flow of oil from the Middle East. The US should be able to establish such a relationship because Iran needs to reenter the global community and it needs to stimulate economic growth. This can best be promoted by US support for removal of all economic sanctions now in place. These sanctions are only partially successful anyway, and their removal would clearly denote our concern for the economic development of Iran. The removal of sanctions would also allow the reentry of Iranian oil into the world market, necessitating the continued free use of the Strait of Hormuz. This may be as far as the US can go to promote its relationship with the current regime in Iran; but as Iran is opened to the world marketplace, there will also be an opening for wider resistance to develop against the current regime.

Turkey is becoming a regional power regardless of the position taken by the United States. Turkey has the largest, best trained and best equipped military in the Middle East. It also already has the strongest, most diversified economy in the Middle East. It will play a role in the balance of power in the Middle East and the US can only benefit by closer relations with Turkey, including support for Turkey to be admitted to the EU in the short term.

Under the system advocated by Mr. Friedman the US interest is best served by the creation of this new balance of power. This would be to offset the power of Iran with that of Turkey and Israel, as well as maintaining the independence of the Arabian Peninsula. In addition the US will need to promote the rebuilding of the economic and military strength of Pakistan to stand as a balance against India. This policy too will require a very Machiavellian approach. In connection with all of this Mr. Friedman in a general way requires that the American public accept the fact that the war on terrorism is an exercise in futility. Nothing can be done in such a war to make the US homeland any safer against the determined individual terrorist. We must, he says, do what we can do to protect ourselves from individual acts of terrorism and promote international efforts to do the same. What we cannot continue to do is to fight a war where the costs outweigh the benefits obtained. Later, we will take a look at the feasibility of this approach under current conditions especially within the time frame of the next decade.

The second area of concern for Friedman is found in Eurasia. In this case the term is used to denote the area contained in the European continent in total plus Western Central Asia and Turkey. American foreign policy in this area is based on two basic factors. One is the current American commitment to the Western Central Asian nations created after the fall of the Soviet Union, and in particular the European nation of Georgia. The Western Central Asian nations are presently furnishing very important military bases for the US operation in Afghanistan. Our commitment to Georgia is minimal at this point, but it is creating tension in the area and distrust of US ambitions. The most important factor is Russia's ambition to reconstitute its status as a world power, beginning with reestablishing its influence in Western Central Asia and finding a means of entering into a more influential position in relation to Europe. The current US commitment to the nations of Western Central Asia is impractical, according to Mr. Friedman. It is impractical in the first instance because the whole area is naturally within Russia's sphere of influence. All of these nations will see that their primary interest is to not antagonize Russia. It is also very apparent that, should Russia decide at some point to reincorporate these nations back into a closer relation to itself by force, the US would be powerless to prevent it. Therefore a commitment to these nations, although interesting in terms of US philosophical principles, is a negative factor in US foreign policy. Friedman, therefore, recommends that the US end its implicit commitment to Georgia, in particular, and to any thought of extending it to Western Central Asian nations. Once again this will require some Machiavellian discipline to keep from reducing our credibility in the eyes of the new Eastern European nations who are in our positive foreign policy interests.

The Russian ambition for closer ties with Europe is, according to Friedman, being fueled by the current discontent of Germany with the European Union. German discontent is based largely on the fact that she has been the financial mainstay of the EU, including the bailout of the weaker members' economies. Germany also appears to be quite upset over the immigration policies of the European Union. On the other hand, Germany appears to have been cultivating closer economic ties with Russia over the last decade or two (ostpolitik). There is some clear evidence of this attempt to create a so-called German–Russian entente. The Russians are in great need of technology and investment capital, both of which Germany has in abundance. Germany, on the other hand, is in great need of the abundant natural resources found in Russia and the manpower represented by the excess labor position found in Russia. If an entente is concluded, which Friedman fears it will be in the next decade, if it materializes at all, will result in the growth of a regional power that will replace US influence in the Eastern European nations and weaken US influence with the European Union. Friedman also sees a possibility that if the entente is not blocked the nations of Eastern Europe will find it in their interest to become closely associated with the entente. This would result in the creation of a global power capable of competing or surpassing the US militarily also. Therefore, it is in the interest of the US to prevent the formation of this entente or at least make it very difficult to obtain.

In doing so the US must, in Friedman's view, establish a firm buffer zone between Russia and Germany. This would be accomplished by promoting the economic and military independence of a string of nations (Intermarium) reaching from Poland to Turkey. These nations would primarily consist of Poland, Romania, Hungary, Moldova and Turkey. It might also include Slovakia and Bulgaria, but not necessarily. The purpose of this buffer zone would be to block the direct flow of natural resources, especially oil and gas, into Germany from Russia; and to prevent the free flow of German technology and industry into Russia. The buffer zone would also provide the US with the time necessary to launch a response to any Russian or Russian–German attempt to include these nations into the entente by force. Turkey would be incorporated into the buffer zone to block Russian naval power from access to the Mediterranean Sea. Turkey and Iran could also act as a buffer against the advance of Russian or Russian–German influence into the Middle East. Once again, this foreign policy initiative will require that the US clearly understand the current state of affairs. First, our relationship with Georgia has led directly to a Russian distrust of American intentions in Eurasia. Second, the current US relation with the EU and Western European nations in particular, is already in a rather serious state of decay. In order to combat this decay the US must focus on its "special relationship" with Great Britain and its commitment to NATO, even though militarily NATO might be almost useless to the US at this point. The latter commitment will go a long way to shoring up our credibility in Eastern Europe and will help in setting up the buffer zone. Third, the US must continue to repair its relationship with Russia although many of our interests are in competition with theirs. At the very least the US must do nothing in the short term to antagonize the Russians into accelerating the growth of ties between Germany and Russia. On the same line of thought the US should do what it can in the international market to relieve Germany's financial burden in relation to the bailout of weaker members of the union. As noted earlier, this might be accomplished by using the offices of the IMF and World Bank for US contributions as a sort of modified Marshall Plan. This set of foreign policy requirements will also be looked at in terms of feasibility later on as we review the current state of world affairs.

A third region is Asia, which in this case constitutes India, Southeast Asia, China, the two Koreas, Japan and the Pacific Islands including New Zealand and Australia. As presented by Friedman, US policy in this region is less about the creation of power balances and more about the maintaining of the current US naval superiority in the area. Currently the US has a monopoly of both military naval power and commercial naval power in the Indian Ocean, the Sea of Japan, the South China Sea and the Pacific Ocean. The main interest of the US in Asia is to maintain this hegemony. In relation to the Indian Ocean our most likely competitor for commercial naval control is India. Thus it is in our interest to thwart India's development of commercial naval power in the Indian Ocean by promoting its concerns over its conflict of interest with Pakistan. As long as India must concentrate on its military and the resulting competition with Pakistan, it will be prevented from developing its commercial naval power. Friedman believes, however, that this is a long term consideration and that in the short term India will be most concerned with the problems created by the slowdown of its economic growth. This Friedman expects to occur near the beginning of the next decade. With nearly a billion Indians living in abject poverty, the slowdown in the economy can be expected to create serious social problems and a threat to the Indian regime. It is likely that widespread civil unrest, possibly violent revolt, will occur in regions of India. At any rate, the short term interest of the US in relation to India is to delay the buildup of Indian commercial naval power which could challenge the US hegemony in the area.

China is another nation over which the US has very little influence. We, of course, must not antagonize China as she represents the largest creditor holding US national debt — China currently owns about 900 billion dollars worth. She also represents a very significant portion of US trade in Asia. Without a doubt, China is the premier land-based military power in Asia and can be expected to remain so for the foreseeable future. The status of China, however, like that of India, will be somewhat weakened by the expected slowdown of its economy in the early years of the next decade. Once again the fact that nearly a billion people are living in abject poverty raises the specter of large scale social unrest and violent revolt. Further, the effect of the economic slowdown on the growing middle class in China is unknown, but it can be expected to lead to demands that their current position in Chinese society be maintained. Regardless China will remain an economic and military power in the region for some time to come. The US policy should be based upon maintaining its current naval superiority in the region through a promotion of the Japanese and South Korean economic systems. Both of these nations are currently capable of offsetting Chinese economic power. The biggest threat to the US in this area, according to Friedman, is the expansion of the already considerable commercial naval power of the Japanese into a military naval power that challenges US control in this area. The best policy for the US in its attempts to prevent the growth of Japanese naval power is to promote the alliances it already has in the area. This would include expanding access to US markets for South Korean and Japanese manufactured products, the promotion of the existing trade agreements between New Zealand and Australia with Japan, and the promotion of a united Korea to reduce tensions in the area. In addition, the US must strengthen its ties with Southeast Asia, in particular with Indonesia, if it is to maintain naval control of the Strait of Malacca. This would, in Friedman's view, make it unnecessary for Japan to expend assets to unseat the US as the leading local military naval power. The only other threat to US naval control in the area would be found in Russia. While Russia's current economic woes keep it from building the necessary naval presence in the area, an entente with Germany could change this picture completely. Here the main obstacle is the distrust of Japan, China and South Korea of Russian ambitions in the area.

The fifth area of concern for the US is Canada and Latin America. The US and Canada are each other's greatest trading partners. The two nations also have many areas of common interest, in particular sharing the tight alliance with Great Britain known as the "special relationship". At any rate, no great investment in foreign policy will be needed in relation to Canada during the next decade. The US has only to retain its current relationship with this nation. Much the same can be said about Latin America, that is, Latin America is essentially outside of US foreign policy interest — with the exception of Cuba and Mexico, whose geographical proximity makes them very important to the United States. During the next decade it is likely that the Castro brothers will both pass on, leaving the US the opportunity to open normal relations with Cuba. This is in the interest of both Cuba and the US and would rapidly lead to an overwhelming US influence in Cuba. Our relations with Mexico, outside of maintaining the North America Free Trade Agreement (NAFTA) that is already in place with Mexico, center on drugs and immigration. The drug traffic in Mexico has led to serious violence along the Mexican and US border, albeit mostly on the Mexican side of the border. The long border with the US has also facilitated the massive influx of both legal and illegal immigration into the United States. One point that should be emphasized here is that the further from the border immigration moves the more likely those immigrating will seek legal status in the United States. It is only the border areas where the back-and-forth traffic largely makes it unnecessary to obtain legal status. According to Friedman, however, Mexico has no real interest in stopping either the drug traffic or illegal immigration due to the massive amount of revenue (approximately 25% of its total GDP) produced for the Mexican economy. The US also, in Friedman's view, has no interest in stopping either the drug traffic or illegal immigration. The US cannot effectively halt the drug traffic, or the illegal immigrations for that matter, due to the massive amount of commercial traffic between the two nations under NAFTA. The US also has a real need of unskilled labor, especially in the field of care for the elderly, and cannot expect to find this labor in any other way. Therefore, as long as the violence remains on the Mexican side of the border and the illegal immigrants remain important to both nations, neither will be curtailed. Because of the political ramifications, however, both nations are in a position where they must convince their citizens that everything within their power is being done to curtail the drug traffic and to prevent illegal immigration; while at the same time making sure that neither is accomplished.

The rest of Latin America will become important only if Brazil continues to develop and becomes a regional power. This, according to Friedman, is not likely to happen in the next decade, but the US should be aware that it will happen in the relatively near future. As a preemptive measure, the US should cultivate relations both with Venezuela and Argentina as possible balances to the growing power of Brazil. In the case of Argentina, this would be made easier if both Paraguay and Uruguay could be brought into some type of free trade agreement with Argentina. The primary US interest, however, in Friedman's view, is to maintain the long standing tradition of the Monroe Doctrine and block any other power from becoming influential in Latin America. As with Canada, it does not appear that serious foreign policy commitments need to be made in Latin America during the next decade.

The last area considered by Friedman is Africa. In Friedman's view, Africa is not within the US foreign policy interests and we should walk away from the whole continent. Any commitment in Africa beyond whatever trade interests can be promoted would result in much more cost than could be repaid. However, so far the Obama administration seems to take a different approach, and Mr. Friedman feels that that position should be reversed.

This is a brief synopsis of Mr. Friedman's perspective on the direction that US foreign policy should take in the next decade in response to the current world order. The main driver for these policies is the fact that the US has attained the status of an empire. Friedman's only real concern about the US adopting a stance acknowledging the fact of empire is whether or not the US republic could be saved at the same time. In the case of Rome, for example, the realization of empire destroyed the Republic. In Mr. Friedman's prediction, four things are essential to the US being able to maintain its status as a republic. The first is that the executive branch of government accepts the fact that the US has become an empire. The second is that the President of the US be capable of leading foreign policy in a Machiavellian manner while still maintaining a moral vision (a Republican vision). The third would be a president who understands what power is and also understands how it should be used. The fourth requirement is that the American public becomes mature enough to accept the responsibilities of a global American empire and be willing to sacrifice to meet those responsibilities. (What exactly Friedman means in his reference to the concept of Republic in relation to the US and just what it is that he wishes to save is not detailed in the book.)

The last step in our look at Friedman's prediction for the next decade is to attempt to analyze whether it is feasible, and if feasible, whether it is also probable. President Barack Obama may only be in office until the next election, but it will be at least another year before we know who his likely successor might be. Friedman's prediction seems to require a high level of consistency in US foreign policy. The eight years maximum presidential service may be too short a time to promote such consistency. The other factor is the rather large variance in the political philosophy of the two major parties as concerns international relations. The current Republican stance seems to lean towards a neo-isolationist policy coupled with unilateral action. This would not bode well for the type of foreign policy leadership that is needed under an empire scenario. The Democrats, on the other hand, seem to be much more open to the concept of active participation in international relations and might better provide the type of leadership expected under conditions of empire although this is far from proven. In any case, for the next decade it is possible that we could have as many as four presidents, each of a different party affiliation. This would make it impossible to implement a consistent foreign policy as called for in Friedman's vision for the nation. It is also possible, of course, that we would have only two presidents during the next decade and they could both be of the same party affiliation, which would make the discipline required in foreign policy more likely. However, even this does not guarantee that all the individual presidents will be equally adept at Machiavellian diplomacy. It is possible, too, that the foreign policy bureaucracy rather than the president will take the lead in providing the needed consistency. In conclusion, under current political conditions in the US it does not seem feasible that the President will be able to provide the type of consistency needed.

In addition, it is very likely that the American public will remain focused on domestic issues, at least through the election in 2012. As stated earlier, this focus includes a call for the federal government to withdraw into isolation from international involvement, a call which will continue at least until the US economy recovers from the recession, headway is made in reducing unemployment, and the financial crisis is substantially resolved. The American public will continue to be focused on domestic issues, preventing them from achieving the type of maturity in foreign policy required under Friedman's scenario. This suggests that one factor needed, in Friedman's opinion, to retain the Republic, will be missing. In other words, his vision seems to be based in part on a condition that cannot be met: a continuation of the US concern for international affairs. The mid-term elections of 2010, and the aftermath, certainly indicate that the public's attention has been withdrawn from foreign affairs. This in fact may be the basis of Friedman's conclusion that the American public currently lacks the maturity he is seeking.

Friedman suggests that a return to a focus on domestic issues over the next decade will have the following results. First, if the US withdraws from Iraq without making adjustments in the regional balance of power, this will automatically result in Iran becoming the premier power in the Persian Gulf. Then Iran could bring the industrialized nations to their knees by cutting off or disrupting the flow of oil. That could only be avoided by instituting a war against Iran and its allies. Second, US focus on domestic affairs for the next decade would allow the development of the German–Russian entente, which would automatically draw Eastern Europe into its orbit. This would produce a global power capable of equaling or surpassing the US in economic and military power. Third, our exclusive focus on domestic issues would force the Japanese to build up their naval power in order to be capable of replacing the US in the South China Sea and Pacific Islands. Then Japan could take control of trade with South Korea, China, Indonesia and probably New Zealand and Australia. This would, in the short term, lead to the loss of the American empire and return the US to regional power status. The current world order, in other words, would be overthrown.

Mr. Friedman's model politician is found in Abraham Lincoln, FDR and Ronald Reagan, all of whom he claims were, overall, moral men, but capable of a rather ruthless execution of foreign policy when needed. One might also add George H.W. Bush to this list in consideration of the job he accomplished in executing the first Gulf War. A leader of this type, however, does not appear to be now in office or waiting in the wings for the presidential election of 2012.

Although one can hope and wish that the American public will mature, essentially overnight, as Mr. Friedman clearly hopes, foreign policy cannot be executed upon wishes and hope. In reality it seems more likely that the US public remains immature, and if that is true then foreign policy will be tailored to that fact rather than to the fact that America has become an empire. It appears that the most rational policy to accomplish the foreign relations goals indicated by Friedman would be to plan a change in the domestic structure of the US to allow the establishment of a centralized executive government at the federal level. This would allow the continuation in power of the president that is needed to guide a consistent foreign policy. However, this is the scenario that Friedman hopes to avoid, in other words the loss of the Republic.

With President Obama ignoring the demands for spending reductions, the next decade will likely see at least two presidents, each from a different party. It is difficult to select from the probable candidates for the Republican race in 2012 one that would fit the needs suggested by Mr. Friedman. On the other hand, if the current administration is, through some unforeseen alteration in policies, able to convince the public that they have the right programs and that these programs will succeed in fulfilling the voters' demands, they may get reelected. The first six years of the next decade would then see Obama as the leader of foreign policy. While this offers some hope for the type of leadership required by Friedman, that is, Obama's stated willingness to carry on diplomatic discourse with Iran, to withdraw from both Iraq and Iran, to withdraw unconditional support from Israel, etc., Obama would nevertheless spend most of his time trying to deliver on his domestic promises.

If the Obama administration serves for only one term, a new president will take office with the opportunity to serve out the remainder of the decade; that president would be domestically focused from the beginning. This does not mean that he or she would not be adept at foreign affairs, but again foreign policy cannot be conducted on the basis of hope. The worst case scenario, if Friedman's predictions are well-founded, would be for a Republican president to be elected in 2012 along with a solid majority for the Democrats in both houses of Congress. This would only increase the gridlock in Washington and probably make it impossible for the president to act boldly in foreign affairs.

If the Obama administration is unlikely to stir the public in its favor with its current domestic policies, could such favor be curried in the international arena? A successful withdrawal from Iraq could possibly produce such a reaction. This would require a withdrawal that left Iraq capable of stable government and capable of playing a significant role in Persian Gulf politics. But if, as is expected, the withdrawal leads to a growing instability in the Iraqi government through the influence of Iran, and insurrectionist elements, Iraq will descend into a Shia system of government in close alliance with Iran. This is not a result that the US public would easily accept after nearly a decade of involvement coupled with the expense and loss of life involved in the war. As already pointed out, the most promising scenario for supporting the independence of Iraq and the Arabian Peninsula is to establish normal diplomatic relations with Iran. To achieve that, the US would need to push for the removal of all UN sanctions against Iran, it would have to remove its own sanctions, and it would have to ensure that Iranian oil re-entered the world market. The current mood in the US would not support such a policy if it was conducted openly; therefore, that policy would have to be conducted while giving the impression that our policy was the exact opposite. The Obama administration shows no sign of having the type of savvy, or the experience, to carry that out.

If for some unknown reason Obama should win another term, he would have the same chance upon withdrawal from Afghanistan in 2014. This country, however, even more than Iraq, presents a Viet Nam-type picture. It is unlikely that the US will make much progress in creating a stable nation-wide government there in the next couple of years to replace the power of the various warlords and tribal leaders. That being the case, a withdrawal of US and NATO troops would result in an almost immediate takeover by the Taliban and Al Qaeda. This result too would be unacceptable to the public after a decade of fighting. In order to prevent this, the US would need to rely on the influence of Pakistan in Afghanistan to control the redevelopment of Afghanistan as a haven for the training of terrorists. This policy may or may not be realistic and is at least as likely to produce negative as positive results. Convincing the American electorate to go along with open acceptance of Pakistan also appears unlikely to be possible.

It is equally unlikely that the US will be able to effectively intervene in the development of a German–Russian entente, should one develop. The US is viewed with a great deal of distrust by both the Germans and the Russians in regard to our policies in Eurasia. The Russians resent US attempts to exert influence in Georgia, Armenia, and Western Central Asia, as well as in Ukraine. The Germans resent our exertion of influence in Eastern Europe, especially in Poland, Slovakia and the Czech Republic. In addition, our standing with the leading members of the EU, with the exception of Great Britain, has slipped to an all-time low. Without very expensive and long term commitments in Eastern Europe and the Middle East the US will have little to offer as a means of controlling events in Eurasia. It is hard to see what events on the international scene could lead the American public to take a favorable view of the Obama administration before the 2012 election. This in turn defeats the process of effective American action in regard to the concept of a Russian-German détente.

For all the above reasons it can be surmised that at least the next six years will be spent with the executive branch focused on domestic issues. It is also most likely that withdrawal from Iraq will, over that same period of time, allow Iran to consolidate its power in the Persian Gulf and to establish its influence in Iraq, which for all practical purposes will be a puppet of Iran. This being true, all advantage found in the Iran's current openness to creating an entente with the US would be dissipated. If Egypt as a result of the fall of the Mubarak regime should develop an anti-Israeli stance, and other moderate Arab regimes begin to fall to Shia style regimes, Israel may well feel trapped by her neighbors. This might provoke her into launching a preemptive attack against Iranian nuclear facilities to delay the growth of Iranian power. If this provoked a military response that included Egypt, Iran, Syria, Lebanon and Jordan, then Israel would be unlikely to sustain its existence without direct help from the United States. Such a situation could easily escalate into a global conflict. The only saving grace is that the whole of the Middle East is dependent on the free flow of oil for their existence. The Middle Eastern nations not involved in the oil trade are equally dependent on their trade with the US and the EU for their existence. It would, therefore, be suicide for any one nation to arbitrarily cut off the flow of oil or to do anything that would make it so expensive that it would prod the users into finding alternative sources of energy in the short term. Regardless of what happens in Egypt, Yemen, Bahrain, Iraq, and Afghanistan, it is unlikely that any significant changes in the flow of oil and other trade would occur. The worst that could happen would be the destruction of Israel, and its replacement by a Palestinian state and the possibility of increased ability on the part of terrorists to train and launch attacks on the US and other Western nations. As Mr. Friedman pointed out, there is nothing we could do to control such attacks, and what we have tried to do up to this point is, in the long run, costly in relation to the benefits.

The civil unrest that began in Tunisia in 2011 and spread to Egypt, Syria, Bahrain, Yemen and other Arabic nations is a third scenario to those drawn by Friedman. In this case there is the real possibility of movement towards the creation of democratic systems to replace the existing long term dictatorships in the region. If this movement continues and is successful, Iran is less likely to be established as the premier power in the Persian Gulf. Iran will be replaced by a regional power which might include the whole of the Middle East in a political structure similar to the one found in the European Union. This would without a doubt include a much tighter control of oil supplies and prices, a guaranteed delivery of oil throughout the global market, and stronger Arabic influence on the global political and economic scenes, and, of course, would include Iran as a major power. If the "Arab Spring" continues, the next decade will show many changes. This scenario may develop even if the insurrections result in the establishment of Islamic regimes rather than democratically orientated regimes.

If the recession and financial crisis continue to bring about the failure of the weaker members of the EU over the next six years, two things are likely. First, the Germans and Russians will see their opportunity to put together an entente with the possibility of including the nations of Eastern Europe. Second, the EU may be forced to demand the withdrawal of some of the weaker members; or, alternatively, some of the wealthier nations such as Great Britain, France, Luxemburg, the Netherlands, etc. may voluntarily withdraw especially if they are saddled with the burden of the bailouts Germany refuses to fund. In either case this would improve the chances of a German–Russian alliance and decrease the ability of Western Europe to play a significant role in international affairs either economically or militarily. It would also clearly keep the US from barring these options through the promotion of the buffer zone desired by Friedman.

The result of our rather hasty review of current conditions in the US and around the world seems to indicate that it is highly unlikely that the type of foreign policy sought by Mr. Friedman will be feasible. It is possible, however, that he is right and instead that the position taken here is the one that is not feasible or probable. It is more likely, however, that the current US policy in the Middle East will be replaced with the "soft" power approach sought by the European Union. Under this approach the US should do whatever is necessary to help institute stable governments in both Iraq and Afghanistan with the effort being towards the establishment of democratic administrations and the establishment of diplomatic relations with those best suited to reach that goal. The US should do all that it can to establish diplomatic relations with both Iran and Turkey, at least, to the extent that we are viewed by world opinion as being their enemies. The best way to establish a balance of power in the Middle East is to promote the natural growth of Iran, Turkey, Egypt and the Arabian Peninsula in relation to one another.

Trouble spots in the next decade are most likely to be found in the Kurdish people and the Palestinians. In both these cases the US should push as hard as possible — without totally antagonizing Israel, Turkey, and Iran, for independent Kurdish and Palestinian states. This effort should be promoted in connection with the nations of the Middle East calling for and monitoring the disarmament of Al Qaeda, Hamas, Hezbollah and other insurrectionist organizations. The US may have little influence on the events that occur in Middle East although in the long run the US will more likely be able to engage in beneficial relations in the Middle East through cooperation with the EU rather than unilaterally. This will be particularly true if strong democratically orientated regimes replace the existing regimes in the area. This will be more likely to allow the inclusion of the Middle East in some form of free trade system which would include the EU and possibly the United States.

The same may be true in the case of Eurasia. I believe that Mr. Friedman's policy recommendations are very much to the point. It is most likely true that Russia does covet a return to not only regional but global power. It is equally likely that over the long run there is nothing that the US can do to prevent this from happening. The US response must be built upon a realistic recognition of what is in the power of the US to accomplish and what is not. A determined Russian military attack, for example, on the Ukraine, Georgia or the Western Central Asian nations, could not be stopped by the US even under the most favorable circumstances. In the short run it is definitely in the US interest to withdraw from any large scale commitments to Georgia, the Ukraine or the Western Central Asian nations, among others. For this reason it is equally in the interest of the US to do whatever can be done in Eastern Europe to insure the independence and stability economically and militarily of Poland, Hungary, Romania and Slovakia as a buffer to Russian ambitions. The US must do all that is within its power to insure that Germany remains a viable partner in the EU, assuming the EU survives the current crisis.

Even if the EU only survives on a reduced scale, or Germany pulls out, it is certainly in the interest of the US to insure a buffer zone to obstruct German and Russian ambitions. This corridor for many reasons can be none other than that of Poland, Romania, Hungary and Slovakia. All of these nations are members of the EU and also members of NATO and the US should use its influence to maintain that status. This is true even with the slow deterioration of US influence within the EU and the fact that NATO is now essentially useless to the United States. Both commitments, if handled openly and transparently, will boost the credibility of the US in Europe, especially Eastern Europe, in terms of our seriousness in keeping those commitments.

In light of this goal, that is, the segregation of German and Russian interests, it will also behoove the US to promote the economic and military well-being of Turkey, including support for its desire to join the European Union. As pointed out by Friedman, this will place a block to the Russian naval presence in the Mediterranean Sea. In the end the policies called for by Mr. Friedman in relation to Eurasia are the same, whichever prediction is used.

The worst case scenario would be the Russian entry into the European Union. This would place the continent of Europe in a position to become the premier global power both economically and militarily. There isn't much the US could do to prevent such an eventuality if it happened the US empire will be replaced by a new European Empire.

It would then not only be in the interest of the US to establish a free trade agreement or at the very least a customs union with the expanded European Union. The only reasonable response to the creation of such a European Union would be to attempt to create blocs of nations that could compete with the EU both economically and militarily. For example, the creation of an American Union composed of all the nations of North, Central, and South America could be created to build a single market capable of competing with the European Union. The same type of union might be put together by Japan, South Korea, Southeast Asia and the Pacific Islands, including New Zealand and Australia. The latter, however, might be more comfortable joined to the American Union, as long as the US maintained is naval superiority in the Pacific.

India and China are wild cards in this scheme. They are so vast in both territory and population, and so uniquely placed geographically, that they might be single markets on their own capable of competing in the world being envisioned here. Together they represent about 40 percent of the total world population and something like 33 percent of the total global land area. They are contiguous on the northeast frontier however the Himalayas are an impenetrable barrier. At any rate, there can be no question that an Indian–Chinese trade agreement could, if the world enters into another economic boom period, compete with the other blocs both economically and militarily.

Africa, of course, remains African. Until this continent finds a way to open up the natural resources hidden in its inaccessible jungles and deserts and develop a political system that would foster a Pan-African Union it will not be able to compete either economically or militarily. Even if these two requirements were fulfilled, it is doubtful that Africa would ever truly become a global military power.

For these reasons the foreign policy of the US, as seen in either the Friedman scenario or one of the other alternatives, would tend to be in agreement in the case of Asia and Africa. The US must continue to maintain its naval superiority as long as possible in the Indian Ocean and the South China Sea, as well as the smaller bodies of water made up of the Sea of Japan and the Yellow Sea. While this is unlikely to last forever, the US must do what it can to continue its naval superiority in the Atlantic and Pacific Oceans for many decades. A challenge may be offered by Russia, or by an EU that contains Russia. In order to insure our naval superiority in the minor water bodies, it is absolutely necessary for the US to promote access to the American market for South Korea, Japan and Indonesia, with preferential benefits being given in relation to our ability to carry and protect that trade. The same guarantees should continue to be given to New Zealand and Australia, with an attempt to promote even closer trading contacts between them and Japan, South Korea and Indonesia. This essentially, as is pointed out by Friedman, entails little more than a constant promotion of the alliances we already have in the area and a closer tie with Southeast Asia. Our growing relationship with Southeast Asian nations bodes well in this regard.

The US can probably accomplish most of the goals required under the predictions offered by Mr. Friedman without the promotion of an American Empire by Machiavellian means. With the sole exception of the Middle East, the goals can be obtained using an aggressive, open and transparent foreign policy. In the Middle East the same goals may be obtained, but regardless of what strategy is used the US will have to pay the price for the destruction of Iraq, Afghanistan and Pakistan. These mistakes, made under the misguided belief that terrorism could be defeated in a conventional war, cannot be reversed.

The best that can be hoped for is that in the natural course of events the market forces involved in the global market economy will induce the nations of the Middle East to take a position where their cooperation cannot be withheld.

Even with all this said it is unlikely that either the foreign policy advocated by Mr. Friedman will appear within the next decade or the foreign policy measures advocated under the counter predictions will develop. The political environment in the US, probably for the next several years, appears likely to foster a relative isolation from foreign involvement and a further weakening of international influence in regard to the United States. It can be suspected that the US will neither pay attention nor clearly recognize its status as an empire if it exists; or will it pay attention to the growth of the EU as a premier global power until it is too late.

As an aside an EU that included all the nations of Europe, including the Russian Federation and Turkey, would almost certainly result in some form of federal political structure. This would appear to be essential for two reasons, first, to prevent the overwhelming of the current EU by the size and scope of the Russian economy and military; and second, too absorb the vast differences in culture, religion, and background that would be found in the inclusion of Russia and Turkey in the Union. This structure might continue the current federalism of the EU under its intergovernmental form or it might develop into a more closely knit political structure. The size and responsibilities of such a union would be very difficult to manage under the system currently in use. The ability of members to withdraw without penalty, the failure of the EU institutions to enforce their laws and regulations, etc., become almost impossible to imagine on the scale we are talking about at this point. In addition there are economic predictions that call for a more thorough political integration of the existing EU to deal with the fiscal crisis. The added historical, cultural and religious differences that would accompany the addition of Russia and Turkey also add an unknown dimension to the political dynamics of such an expanded European Union. Should this come about in the long run, it may be under circumstances that require all nations to take a look at the possibility of a world government. Such a development, however, is beyond the scope of this work.

Regardless of how the world develops over the next decade, i.e., whether it is an American empire, EU Empire, or a series of regional power balances, it still remains to be determined if the US will weather the effects of the recent depression and current financial crisis. If we assume, like Friedman, that during the coming decade, that is, by 2021, the US will enjoy a very robust economic boom, can we determine how this might come about? Just what would have to occur over the next two years? It is difficult to imagine any combination of circumstances that could bring us to such a positive economic situation. There is such a lack of confidence in the business community that both the lending institutions and the corporations themselves are hanging onto a huge cash position. The lending institutions will not lend and the corporations will not invest. The stock market is slowly returning to a somewhat normal appearance of moderate gains and losses, but can the stock market at this point be trusted as a weather vane of economic conditions? American consumers do not appear to have enough confidence in the economy that will allow them to open their wallets either. If small businesses cannot borrow money to continue or expand their businesses, big corporations refuse to fund further research and development, the housing crisis continues to deepen, and the level of unemployment remains high, what is left to stimulate the economy into robust growth? One answer over the last two years has been the infusion of huge sums of tax payer dollars into the economy in an attempt to stabilize the housing market, to bailout the largest corporations and investment concerns, and to promote infrastructure development, etc. This to date appears to have been an unmitigated failure and can't even be pointed too as responsible for the slow growth that has suddenly appeared in the economic picture. Now the government is calling for increased spending on research and development, in particular in the bio-medical and alternative energy areas, to stimulate innovative new industries and jobs; coupled with spending on education (science and math) to support this research and development and high speed trains to support the movement of people to these new jobs; or to the sources of the new educational opportunities. Even if these programs were successful the effects of their success probably would not be evident for several decades maybe even a couple of genera-tions. Another answer rests on reducing government spending. This ap-proach calls for no new spending programs such as those set forth above coupled with an across the board spending reduction. All government programs, both at the federal and state level, would be reduced signifi-cantly and many of the programs would be eliminated totally. So far this approach has not been tried on a scale large enough to indicate how ef-fective it would be as a policy. To date it hasn't even been applied to the amount of money spent within Congress itself. Without serious at-tempts to find compromise on spending bills there is not even a chance of reaching a balanced budget during the next decade. If unemployment remains high, the foreclosure rate on homes remains high, and there is a continued failure to produce new jobs the revenue available to both the federal and state governments will also decrease. This is exactly what some economic forecasters are saying will happen in the next two to five years. From what has been said it does not appear that any real evidence for confidence in the prediction that the US will enter into a period of robust economic growth can be found for the short term. If some experts are to be believed, and there is no evidence that can be found showing that economic cycles of bust and boom just happen again and again, then little can be done to force the issue. The best that can be done, therefore, is to concentrate on what can reasonably be done in the next two years.

Let's assume the US enters into a robust period of growth economi-cally and remains in this boom cycle for a significant number of years; what will we be likely to see if we look closely at the US under these conditions? It is likely that we will see several things that should give us great pause. First, we are likely to see that the US politicians (whether Republican or Democrat, whether in the legislative or executive branch or the federal or state government) will not have maintained the disci-pline to balance the budget or to reduce the national debt. They will have, as they always have done, submitted to the constant pressure from the various pressure groups for money to be increased for their pet projects or the creation of new projects. This is a matter of course in a country in which your chances of election to political office are based upon the amount of money you are able to raise for your campaign. They will also have caved in to the always insatiable demand of the American public for greater social welfare programs. The politicians will, as they always do, tend to forget all about the past recession and financial crisis and fail to correct the procedures which led to them. Second, we will find that the politicians, especially in the executive branch, have not been able to make the tough decisions necessary to protect our interests in international affairs. This will be true whether the foreign policy needed is that predicted by Mr. Friedman or any of the alternatives presented. The US will have failed to take the necessary steps to protect itself from the economic muscle of a rejuvenated EU and will find itself faced with a real challenge to our economic superiority in the global market. This will also be true whether that challenge comes from a German–Russian entente as predicted by Mr. Friedman or an expanded EU that includes Russia and Turkey. There is no doubt that this level of economic power could seriously limit our influence in India, China and Southeast Asia. In retaliation we would see Japan, S. Korea and the Pacific Islands attempting to offset the economic power of both the US and the European Union. The influence that the US currently wields in the Middle East would be replaced by that exercised by the EU with much different results. As we have seen it is unlikely that the US will be able to develop a consistent focused foreign policy within the next couple of years or even within the next decade. Third, we will see that the effects of the 2010 election have come to fruit over the first couple of years of the next decade. The Republicans and Democrats will still be locked tightly into their ideological positions incapable of real compromise. As Paul Ricoeur said a few years ago, when ideology loses its ability to explain reality, it becomes frozen and repressive. The ideological gridlock that will appear in the next two years in the US will clearly show this statement to be accurate. There will have been little or no action taken on the core issues that face the US and what little that has been done will be merely of token value. There will have been much effort and time spent on placing the blame for the gridlock on each other with no time left for bi-partisanship (what used to be known as the ability to find compromise). This brings us to the election of 2012. Can the American people do anything through this election to alter the predictions made above? Some believe that the answer is yes they can. The first step would be to make a full sweep of both the legislative and executive branches at both the federal and state level. Then the American Public will have to make an effort to find candidates that meet their qualifications rather than the candidates looking for a public to defend the qualifications they wish to display. The only real way for this to happen is through a grass-roots movement such as the Tea Party and a serious increase in the level of voting.

It appears obvious to those who watch election results, without trying to interpret them in a way that fits a preconceived notion, that the 2010 mid-term election manifested a mandate by the public for bi-partisanship.

At the very least that is the manner in which the major media wished to interpret the election results and in this case it appears the media got it right. Enough time has not elapsed since the election to determine if this mandate is going to be acted upon. However, early signs would indicate that it has not been heard at the federal level, although there is evidence that it was heard at the state and local level. During the lame duck Congress which came to an end in December 2010 the Congress voted to extend the Bush Era tax cuts and to reduce payroll deductions for one year on Medicare. Both of these votes were conducted along strict party lines. There was no bi-partisanship in either of these acts. Since the inauguration of the new Congress in January 2011 the Congress has passed several other bills and in all cases the votes were nearly on straight party lines, and along the line of the majorities in the two houses. That is to say, the Republican majority in the House of Representatives was able to carry the vote in opposition to the Democrats, and the Democratic majority in the Senate was able to carry the vote against the Republicans. Again the votes in each house were split essentially along party lines. The lack of bi-partisan action was so strong, in fact, that there was a threat that the Congress would fail to act on the appropriation bill necessary to fund the remaining seven months of the fiscal year 2010 which ended in September 2011. If this bill had not passed the government would have shut down as of September 30, 2011 or shortly thereafter. This happened back in 1995 for several weeks and turned out to be a total disaster for the party perceived to be responsible. The "new" Republicans in the House of Representatives set this scenario up by requiring spending cuts equal to the appropriation bill which the Democratic Senate said it would not pass and the executive branch claims it would veto. Once again there was a significant amount of posturing going on between the parties with the intention of placing the blame for the shut down, if it occurred, on the opposite party rather than focusing on some type of compromise that would fund the rest of the fiscal year. The arguments over spending reductions, methods for reducing the national debt, the National Health Care Act, and many others are currently being debated mainly along strict party lines. The above gridlock has resulted in a further loss of confidence in the US economy, a downgrade in the US credit rating from AAA to AA+, and severe losses on the world's stock exchanges. However there appears to be a split developing in the Republican Party between the long term Republicans and the "new" Republicans. This only seems to intensify the fear that Washington will once again sink into a serious ideological gridlock at least until the 2012 election.

At any rate, it seems very likely that the political environment in the US will change very little over the next two years and possibly for the next decade. The elections will remain unclear in the sense of determining what the American public really wants. As a result the elections will essentially be unpredictable as to the changes in personnel that are likely to take place. In fact, we have already seen a number of incumbents declare that they would not seek reelection in 2012. It is almost as if they see some negative handwriting on the wall. There seems to be little doubt that gridlock and stalemate will become even more entrenched and bitter. It would seem equally unlikely that the US will develop a foreign policy as consistent or focused as Mr. Friedman would like to see. It would seem equally assured that the government will not develop the fiscal discipline necessary to avoid a recurrence of both recession and financial meltdown. The corporations, investment industry, and banks are already back to promoting the same procedures that brought the last recession and financial meltdown, that is, huge bonuses, shaky investment documents, and bad managerial decisions. Regulation to bar such practices does not appear to be on the way any time in the future so the US will live by the consequences that follow such lack of regulatory insight.

The one aspect of the 2010 mid-term election that is not given much attention is its ideological demands. At the base of this demand is the desire of the American public to return to the politics of a century ago. The call is for a return to a new isolationism, a new nativism and a new consumerism. These tenets have been an ideological underpinning of the American system throughout its history. Isolationism essentially consists of the idea that the US maintains a stance towards the rest of the world that is based on non-involvement. Non-involvement can be political, economic or military. In some cases isolation was limited to military involvement in the wars of other nations around the globe; but did not affect our interest in maintaining commercial activities with the rest of the world. In other cases isolation was limited to political non-involvement in international affairs while still remaining active in both the commercial and military activities of international affairs. Today isolation seems to be concentrated on undoing the consequences of the globalization of the market place. The call is for the US to bring home its manufacturing concerns, to withdraw from all free trade agreements, and to commit ourselves to the development of the internal economic market. Nativism is a reliance on one aspect of the domestic culture to the exclusion of all the rest. At one time this was expressed as using the white Anglo-Saxon male as the archetype of the American soul. This nativism is normally attached very strongly to the idea of patriotism or love of country. To-day this element or ideology is most clearly visible in the reaction of the public to the immigration of Latin Americans into the border areas between the US and Mexico. This concern is expressed in the belief that 'American jobs should be for Americans'. Protectionism today is associated with the stimulation of the internal economy and the reduction of unemployment. This is normally associated with the establishment of high tariffs and other barriers to free trade. This type of response to the recent recession and the fiscal crisis is rather common throughout the industrialized world. It would, however, entail a substantial undoing of the current conditions found in the global market.

The weariness of the American public with ten years involvement in two wars in the Middle East, coupled with the constant warnings of new terrorist attacks on the homeland, have led to a call for the withdrawal of America from the political affairs of the rest of the world. Nativism has been stoked to a red hot level in the case of illegal immigrants, but has also spilled over into thoughts of ending even legal immigration into the United States. Protectionism has been brought to the front burner by the knowledge of just how many jobs have left the US with the exit of manufacturing concerns overseas. Recently, for example, it was pointed out that a major corporation had created 70,000 new jobs, but that only 30,000 of them were located in the United States. It is these ideological concerns that should garner our attention and they should be addressed in a way that points out their likely repercussions to the public.

First, the concept of isolation as it seems to be most often expressed in public debate is based on response to globalization of the market place. It was the decision of American industry that the manufacturing facilities could be moved overseas not only to obtain cheaper labor, but also to avoid the cost of pollution control and other safety regulations. This movement was allowed by the development of a global market place that opened these markets to American industry. This globalization of the market place also allowed the US companies to shift the best paying, most secure employment to the domestic market while at the same time shifting the low skilled, low paying employment overseas allowing the avoidance of union interference. The result was a significant marginalization of a large segment of the American work force and the institution of high levels of unemployment and under employment. In addition it made it imperative that the US military hegemony that existed in relation to the global market was used to maintain the peace and freedom of trade. This in turn became the source of the need to combat terrorism by invading both Iraq and Afghanistan although the official reason was to assure the safety of the public at home. In this area the public seems to want to enjoy the benefits that come with control of the global market but is unwilling to pay the price of keeping it.

As mentioned above, nativism is closely associated with patriotism in the debate offered by today's public. The issue has arisen due to the public's perception that illegal immigration, especially along the border with Mexico, has not only cost Americans jobs but also has increased the cost of medical and education costs in the United States. The call is no longer about keeping the American culture pure in the sense of religion, race, or ethnicity, but rather that American jobs are filled by American workers. The problem being that the US needs the additional workers willing to take the menial, low paying and less than attractive jobs, such as the care of the elderly. This latter need is going to increase dramatically over the next decade due to the population bulge of the "baby boomers" who are rapidly reaching elderly status. These jobs, if not taken by immigrants, will remain vacant as a result of the level of social welfare which makes it possible for those unemployed not to take them. In addition, as stated above, neither Mexico nor the US has any interest in blocking the flow of illegal immigrants even if they could. This is equally a problem for the EU and it is also having great difficulty in finding a solution.

Protectionism is an ideology which rises to the forefront whenever there are economic problems that seem to be based outside of the control of the nation affected. The tendency in this case is to withdraw from the international or global market into the national market. In addition, each nation will erect whatever barriers it feels are necessary to protect its home market from competition abroad. There have been many recent examples of methods by which protectionism could be operated other than through import and export tariffs. Some of these are specialized financial documents which give unfair trading advantages to the nation using them; privileged trading status (preferential trade agreements with ex-colonial nations, etc.); foreign aid tied to exclusive trading privileges either in natural resources or imported goods. International organizations are also used to insure trading privileges for the core industrial countries, that is, such organizations as the IMF, the World Bank, and WTO. These organizations, in fact, represent the core of the global market system. The EU was formed as a method by which the European market generally could be protected against foreign competition while still allowing its member nations to compete in the global market on the same level as the US and Japan. As a result the EU is now the largest single market on earth with some 450 million consumers and controlling roughly 18% of the total global goods traded. The euro has also become the second largest reserve currency in the world behind only the dollar. The EU is now beginning to be accused of restricting free trade by the US and Japan. This is in response to the EU instituting some aspects of protectionism in response to the recent recession and economic turn-down. Many nations today are unilaterally turning to the institution of protectionist measures to avoid the austerity measures they feel must be instituted to combat the current financial crisis. It is likely, however, that the level of economic integration that has already been reached in the global market will make these policies ineffective. The international conglomerates (most of the top 100 companies in the US, for example) would find it very difficult to survive if these ideologies were put in place by the leading industrial nations.

From what has gone before one might suggest that the most likely result would be the following for the next decade.

1. The failure of the US to accept its role as an empire and to initiate the necessary foreign policy to establish that empire.

2. The continuation of the effects of the current economic crisis until the reemergence of a "boom" economy, if one truly is to be expected.

3. The development of widespread social unrest in the highly developed nations coupled with starvation, famine and pandemic disease in the third and fourth world nations should the current economic crisis worsen for any reason.

4. That the highly developed nations will fail to institute the austerity measures needed to end the current budgetary and national debt problems facing them. This may lead directly to the worsening of the economic conditions now in place.

5. The beginnings of a significant reshuffling of the current power structures on a global scale. This reshuffling might include the following changes.

    a. The rise of Iran as the premier regional power in the Persian Gulf without any balance to her power being created.

    b. The destabilization of both Afghanistan and Pakistan as the Taliban and Al Qaeda regain control after the withdrawal of the US troops.

    c. The development of a global power based upon the integration of German, East European and Russian technology, natural resources, manpower and military capability.

    d. The slow decay of economic growth in both India and China and the rise of very significant social unrest in both countries.

    e. The emergence of Japan, South Korea and Southeast Asia as the dominant economic powers in Asia.

    f. The growth of Brazil and Venezuela as regional powers in South America and the possible establishment of a free trade zone, or customs union, between North America and all of Latin America.

    g. The continued marginalization of Africa below the Sahara and some of the Pacific Island nations.

    h. The possible destabilization of the EU with some select members withdrawing from the union and the possible retreat of the euro from international prominence.

    i. The continued social unrest in the Middle East as the private sector seeks to overthrow the long term regimes now serving in North Africa and the Middle East; with a possible push towards the Democratization of the now moderate Arab nations in both Africa and the Middle East.

6. The end result would seem to be the development of two global powers, i.e., the US and either an expanded EU or a German–Russian alliance; and a series of regional powers as outlined above. This would all be in accordance with a further globalization of the world market place pursuing free trade such as is now found in the European Union.

Whether the above developments would lead to a more peaceful stable world is at least debatable. In some ways it would seem that a more stable situation could not help but be established, for example, in the Middle East. In some areas, however, it might bring about greater instability and violence, such as in Sub-Saharan Africa, India and China. Most important, under this kind of prediction, is that the major problems currently facing the world's nations such as economic cycles of boom and bust; financial irresponsibility; poverty; high unemployment; massive migrations of people; pollution; and pandemic disease among others, will remain unresolved. In addition, the resources for the solutions to these problems will be no greater than they are currently and the motivation for solving the problems may be less than is apparent today.

The above predictions, although the most likely to happen under current conditions, may be significantly altered by two major changes in the expected conditions. First, should this alteration see the end of the current economic crisis brought about by the rapid default of a series of nation-states the following might happen; first, within the next two years almost all of the conditions set forth above could either not develop or develop in a different way due to these defaults. The current recession could become a depression under these conditions (on the scale of, or greater than, that of the 1930') and all of the conditions set forth above would either be enhanced (poverty, famine, etc) or eliminated completely (an expanded EU or a German–Russian détente). Second, on the other hand, if the robust economic recovery becomes a reality the same conditions set forth would be affected in a much different manner. The EU might be able to expand much faster than is currently expected. The fear of nation-state default might be avoided altogether and fiscal responsibility might be restored without any of the dire consequences. As set forth above, however, there currently is no prediction that sees this happening within the next two years, and probably within the next five years. Even under the most optimistic projections the economic conditions are likely to get worse before they get better. The need for International cooperation has never been more apparent than it is at the current time although it appears to be even less likely to be realized than it was during the early 1990,s with the fall of the Soviet Union.

In addition the turmoil in the Middle East and Northern Africa has, as was feared, begun to spread from its original beginnings in Tunisia and Egypt. It has now spread to Libya, Yemen, Iran, Lebanon and Syria among other nations. It may spread even farther if these public revolts lead to success in any significant way. At the very least they have the potential for seriously altering the current conditions in the Middle East and therefore the predictions made above concerning the next decade. It is still too early to tell what will happen in either Tunisia or Egypt concerning the final government that will be established in these nations. Currently it looks as if there is a real possibility that a more democratic regime will be set up in both nations, but it cannot be expected to happen for something approaching a year. The question, of course, is whether the US will be worse off in the Middle East than it is today or as well off as it would be under either of the two predictions made above. The answer is based on the price that the US, or anyone else, would have to pay for oil. The worst case would be for the oil to be in the actual control of the nations where it is found. Currently international conglomerates control the extraction, processing and shipping of the crude oil. They have through this control the ability to manipulate the supply and thereby the price of oil to a large degree. Should the control of oil be taken from these companies and put into the hands of the producing nations what would be the result? First, all of these countries depend almost totally on the sale of oil for the support of their economies. In many of these nations having the ability to produce more oil would result in more oil being produced. The increased supply of oil hitting the market would under normal conditions translate into lower oil prices for all consumers. This is not always what happens on today's market as the international conglomerates are to some degree able to manipulate both the supply and the timing on when the oil hits the market producing artificial rises in price. Even if they lost their direct control over oil supplies they would still control the refining process in the consumer nations including the stockpiling of oil reserves. In this way they also can control both the supply and the price of gasoline and other oil based products. In the long run then the effect of a takeover by the producing nations would tend to be the cause of an insignificant change in consumer habits. If for some reason the producing nations decided to interrupt the flow of oil, for example, to teach the "West" a lesson the result would likely be a quick innovative surge bringing alternative fuel sources on line making oil obsolete. This is certainly not in the interest of the oil producing nations. No matter how you look at the problem the solution is to bring alternative energy on line. The days of cheap oil are gone forever and so is the opportunity to support economic growth or recovery on the use of fossil fuels. Even though little is made of this possibility it is likely that everyone would be amazed at just how fast a safe, cheap, abundant source of energy could be put on the market to replace oil if necessity was driving the research. Unfortunately neither the US nor any other highly developed nation is likely to do anything to bring alternative energy online until it is forced to do so.

In the short term, regardless of whether the economic bust turns into an economic boom no real alteration in the global political trends seems possible. Those nations that already represent what is known as the core nations (some twenty eight or so nations out of the 200 plus in existence) will continue to do so. This includes such nations as the US, Canada, Japan, S. Korea and, of course, the regional unit known as the European Union. Over the next decade a few more nations may work their way into the exclusive club, such as Brazil, Australia and Indonesia. During the short term, however, it is unlikely that any regional political organizations will come into existence outside of the one that already exists, that is, the European Union. Even the exclusive club of core nations, although continuing to operate within the loose structure known as the global market, will not during the next decade move much closer to economic integration let alone political integration. The EU, of course, will make its own decisions just as all national entities will make theirs, however, the EU may expand the tasks that it allows its supranational institutions in the international arena, although the overall decisions will remain with the member nations. The only time that the core nations will show any type of unity is when a nation, whether a member of the club or not, breaks one of the rules by which the global market operates. This is essentially what happened in 1992 when Iraq invaded Kuwait and the club joined together in the expulsion of Iraq. This would also happen if Iran, for whatever reason, decided to attempt to disrupt the flow of oil out of the Persian Gulf. This is essentially an unwritten agreement between the core nations to maintain peace and control violent social unrest as bad for business. In this vein "poor relief" will continue during the next decade and may even increase in the amount of funds expended. In relation to international politics it may become necessary during the next decade for a uniform policy to be established by the core nations to react to the peaceful revolutions that may pop up during the next decade. One such revolution is the one just concluded in Egypt. What has not yet been determined is the core nation's reaction if a non-democratic government is established in Egypt. At this point the core nations are waiting to see how the military in Egypt handles the transition to a new regime. The core nations might accept another authoritarian government established by the military along the same lines as the old Mubarak regime, but it is unlikely that they will accept a Shia regime if it can be avoided without military action. For example, the core nation's reaction to the violence in Libya has been a united stand condemning the existing regime for using violence and support for the establishment of a new regime. What the core deplores is the rise in the price of oil across the board to a short stay at $100 or above a barrel. Therefore, the continued unification, at least in the loose sense of the global market, will continue with the core nations, supported by those nations that qualify as second tier nations, such as Indonesia, Brazil, Venezuela and others in control; coupled with the further marginalization of the third and fourth world nations. This status quo will be accompanied by a continued deregulation of the global market and the need to maintain continued rates of high unemployment.

One problem that is facing the core nations currently will intensify over the next decade. All the core nations, with the exception of the US, are facing a declining birth rate and a slow decline in population. This has resulted in a rather rapidly growing bulge in the population on the side of the aged. The problem is acute in Japan and Germany, and is even evident in the US although not at the same level as in the other two nations. This problem creates two levels of concern, one it results in a deficit in the amount of domestic labor needed, and two, it creates a social problem related to the care of the elderly, that is, welfare budgets that are unsustainable. On the other hand, the fastest growing populations are found in the Middle East, Northern Africa, Southeast Asia and Latin America. This has already resulted in a rather extensive migration of peoples from East to West and from South to North. This migration of peoples will continue to grow as the problem of the labor deficit grows in the core nations. All of the core nations will be faced during the next decade with establishing a workable domestic policy in relation to the needs of this labor deficit and filling it with legal immigration. Currently all of the nations experiencing rapid immigration growth are faced with growing discontent on the part of its native population. Immigration is to a large extent blamed by the people for the high levels of unemployment within the domestic market. Immigration, however, is not really the culprit as this lies at the feet of the industrial concerns decision to move jobs overseas and slow domestic economic growth. The people who have lost their jobs because of these factors are still attempting to replace them with equal jobs in relation to benefits and compensation. This has turned out to be impossible under the current conditions and many of these people would rather accept welfare than the "shame" of taking a menial job. A large number of these "menial" jobs are filled by the incoming immigrants and cannot be filled in any other way. During the next decade it does not seem likely that the "core" jobs will increase significantly while at the same time the service sector jobs (menial labor jobs) will increase significantly, that is, the domestic economy will continue to be "McDonaldized".

In the end therefore the conclusion that should be drawn is that under any set of predictions, either in relation to the economy or in relation to international relations is that the attempt to maintain the status quo will be made, at least, to the greatest extent possible. The cost of change is always very high in comparison with remaining locked in the status quo. If, for example, the US approaches the problem facing the EU with a promotion of international bailouts of the weaker members the need for Germany to move out of the EU is eliminated. Under these conditions the German considerations will likely be that it is more cost efficient to remain in the Union than to develop an entente with Russia. On the same calculation the US will find that it is less costly to promote a unified response to the response to terrorist threats than to attempt the unilateral solution currently being used. This will support the continued attempt by the US to extricate itself from its commitments in Iraq and Afghanistan. Likewise the core nations will find that it is less costly to provide "poor relief" than it is to attempt to actually resolve the issues that make such aid necessary in the first place. In short, everything tends to point to the maintenance of the status quo.

What would the maintenance of the status quo mean for the US in particular? First, barring a rapid return to a boom economy the American public will face the necessity of accepting some rather mild austerity programs. These programs will be instituted at both the federal and state level as the various governments attempt to contain spending within reasonable limits. This would probably over the next decade mean the elimination of such social welfare programs as food stamps, farm subsidies, urban transit and housing subsidies, subsidies for research and development and other entitlement programs. It would also include significant reforms in the benefits received from Social Security, Medicare and Medicaid. This, if spread out over the next couple of decades, might be accomplished by increasing the age of qualification and by reforming the system to allow the elimination of benefits to those who don't need them. Regardless, however, reductions in the benefits paid at both the federal and state level will be made. It would also include a significant cut in the size and scope of the military and other government employment. The people would also continue to see a slow erosion of the housing market with a significant decline in used housing values and a sharp increase in the number of foreclosures. The middle class would also continue to see a slow decline in the real value of their income. This would be accompanied by a sharp rise in the amount of wealth accumulating in the hands of the top five percent of the population. As a result there would also probably be rather dramatic increases in the use of illegal drugs and the rate of crime. Lastly, it would also probably result in a rather noticeable increase in the level of grass roots activity like that experienced in 2010 with the Tea Party.

CHAPTER 7. THE CREATION OF A NEW WORLD ORDER

Looking at the results of our survey of current economic and political conditions around the globe a rather universal list can be attempted concerning the most pressing of these issues. It is fair to say, at least in the case of the core nations and those on the immediate periphery, that the list is common to them all. Third and Fourth world nations, of course, although faced with the results of these issues have other issues of their own that are either relieved or aggravated by the response of the core to its issues. It seems likely that the third and fourth world nations will remain relatively dependent on the decisions of the core (and core candidate) nations for their existence, at least, over the short and mid-term. The following represents the major sources of the problems that currently are challenging the core and near core nations.

1. The highly industrialized nations are faced with a continuing level of high unemployment, slow or stagnant economic growth, and increasingly unsustainable social welfare systems.

2. The above factors when combined with fiscal mismanagement, risky financial investment and profit taking, and uncontrolled spending have created a fiscal crisis that is most evident in increasingly high budget deficits and national debts.

3. The resulting recession/depression conditions do not any longer appear to be controlled by the normal bust and boom cycles and their solution. Today the economic recessions/depressions are controlled by the artificial creation of "bubble" conditions, such as the hi-tech

bubble, the housing bubble, and the financial bubble. These bubbles have been brought into existence through the intentional use of faulty investment vehicles that create artificial valuation of underlying assets, hence the charge of financial mismanagement.

4. As a result of the conditions set forth above the various governments have taken the approach that their financial institutions are too big to fail and that weaker economies cannot be allowed to fail. Attempts are therefore being made to "bail out" these institutions and governments by writing off the debts through tax-payer revenues. In short, many feel that the decision is one in which throwing good money after bad is now a sound economic procedure.

5. Many are beginning to believe that these conditions have arisen largely through the failure of the national governments to regulate the financial and industrial communities as well as continuing to allow the global market to deregulate its operations.

6. The growing awareness that there may not be any solutions to the existing fiscal crisis outside of allowing the weak nations and offending financial institutions to go into default. This in turn would undoubtedly require serious reorganization of existing economic and political structures without knowing what the unforeseen consequences might be. The known, or believed to be known consequences, include civil unrest, violent protest, famine, pandemic disease, etc. Such reactions may be violent enough in some cases as to require the institution of some form of martial law.

If the worst case scenario was to occur can a prediction of what type of world order would ensue be made? Here one must emphasize that the future cannot be predicted accurately under any conditions. As the old saw goes, 'the best laid plans of mice and men oft go awry'. There are, however, a couple of global trends that have developed since 1945, and especially since the fall of the Soviet Union, that give some hope for what could be possible under the worst conditions. These will be looked at in the next chapters. This chapter will begin with a look at the existing EU as a possible guide to a new world order.

One most important issue that was overlooked in the book *World Government: Utopian Dream or Current Reality* is confederalism. It was assumed in the above book that the democracy represented by the early United States and supported by 19th century liberalism was the most appropriate for a world union. In the second volume of the work a look was taken at the confederal system represented by the European Union and its strong and weak points. In the end the assumption made in Volume I was confirmed in Volume II as the most appropriate for the purpose of creating an effective world government. Here we have earlier suggested that even though a world government might be the overall best answer it cannot be implemented soon enough to be expected to solve the issues set forth above.

The European Union (EU) presents a different picture in relation to democratic structure. The format for the creation of the EU was confederal from the beginning. The decision making powers were delegated to a limited transnational organization while most sovereign power remained with the member nations. The EU public was isolated from direct influence both in relation to EU policies and to the EU governing elite that manned the transnational or supranational organizations that were created. Until 1979 none of the people who manned the EU institutions were elected by the citizens of the European Union. Indeed the EU was intended not to be a sovereign government but rather a union of nations. As a result the EU was treated by European political parties as if it was a second tier of national policy making and concerned them only in relation to national issues. The public either did not know of the EU or did not feel any connection to the institutions and how they operated. This has historically been the main criticism of confederal organizations, that is to say, that they are not governments but rather an opportunity to reach communal decisions on matters of common interest to a group of member nations.

Any attempt to establish a system of world governance based upon a federal model, regardless of the number of levels of government, will be forced to face the same issues that have faced the European Union. As we saw in the above referenced book it is very difficult to imagine a global government based on the Presidential model in relation to mass elections of the executive branch. This is, of course, the model used currently in the United States. In the US experience presidential elections have become to a significant extent personality contests. The two political parties have a strong, if not total, control over the selection of the candidates that will run for executive office at both the federal and state level. They also have the same control over the issues that will be discussed during the election campaign and how those issues will be presented to the voting public. Within these parameters the public has full latitude to determine the issues and personality that best suits their interests. The trend in relation to executive elections in the US over the last few decades has been one of growing apathy on the part of the voting public. The number of registered voters actually voting has fallen in increments to a low of about 45%, a number which might allow for the possibility of electoral manipulation. The trend seems to reflect the fact that the voting public no longer believes that voting is effective.

The lack of access to influence over EU policies and EU politicians has led to the same type of apathy on the part of the EU public in relation to EU parliamentary elections. EU wide issues are not discussed during the parliamentary election campaign but only in relation to their effect on national issues of the same type. Those chosen to run for parliament are not selected by the public but by the national parties on the basis of national identity. In 2004 this led to a voter turnout of less than 49%. This trend has also been expressed in the concept of democratic deficit and lack of transparency. Indeed the elections of Members of Parliament are conducted on a reward/punishment basis in relation to the job being done by the party in power at the national level at the time of the election.

In a world governmental environment the diversity of national, cultural and religious interests would be even more diverse than is true of the European Union. Even so, however, there would still be the same positioning of national interests along a left/right dichotomy, as well as along pro/anti integration issues. In the latter case this would revolve around the powers to be delegated to the highest level and the powers to be retained at the lower levels. It could be envisioned that the structure of the government would be multi-level, that is, transnational, national, and sub-national. Under any reasonable outlook the machinery necessary to carry out mass elections for transnational office would be cumbersome to a significant degree. Currently it is not possible to project in just what manner this type of election would be conducted, but it is at least likely that some other system for selecting office holders would be used. In the above referenced book a combination of mass elections and appointment by national legislatures was suggested. Whatever process is chosen it will face not two or several party structures but several hundred; issues will be framed in reference to not only national interests, but to regional interests; non-governmental interests (environmental interests, military interests, business interests, etc.); ethnic interests; religious interests and many others. Such massive, and probably multi-level elections, would appear to be inefficient and non-cost effective. The Presidential model as currently being used in the US would appear to be improbable when transferred to a global level.

One alternative offered was to use the "electoral" system first used in the early US The men who wrote the constitution were facing the same problems back in 1789 that would face us in a world union situation today. That is to say, the use of mass elections in the early US were just as cumbersome and difficult to manage as they would be on a global level today. Therefore, the electoral system was created. This allowed the candidates for the executive offices of President and Vice-President to be chosen by a limited election. Each state legislature nominated a group of electoral representatives based on state population who would then vote for the candidates running for President and Vice-President. The vote would be taken in each state on the same day and the votes would then be forwarded to the House of Representatives where they were counted at a full session of congress. The two top vote getters would then be President and Vice-President. There were procedures set out to handle tie votes, a lack of majority votes and other technicalities. The candidates for office were nominated by the federal congress, usually from among their own members or at least from the two parties. The Senate was directly appointed by the state legislatures. The House of Representatives were the only members of the federal government elected by mass election. Each state held elections based on the candidates selected by the state legislature and then voted in each state on the same day. The citizens are indirectly responsible for both the electors and the candidates through their election of the state legislatures and the House of Representatives at the federal level. They are directly involved in the selection of federal representatives only.

In the EU the only members that are elected for European level office are the members of Parliament. The candidates are chosen by the political parties based on national interests, and the election is conducted at the national level for national reasons. The people again are only indirectly involved in the appointment of executive officials and Judges through their control of national legislatures and parties. The chief executive officer in the EU is the President of the Commission. The President of the Commission is chosen by the national members of the European Council and approved by the Parliament. The choice made by the Council is normally rubber stamped by the Parliament. Therefore the executive branch is appointed rather than being elected even indirectly by the people. The same is true of the judicial branch. This has led to recent complaints concerning a "democratic deficit" in the accountability of EU level officials. It is also the reason that the EU is not considered to be a sovereign government but rather an intergovernmental organization. Because the European Council operates without access by the public and in secret there has also arisen a concern with transparency. To date the EU has been able to do little to defuse these complaints. In 2005 a draft constitution was offered to correct the democratic deficit and lack of transparency issues but it failed to pass referendums in France and the Netherlands and fell by the wayside. It would not appear that any additional effort will be made to add a constitution in the near future. A treaty reform movement may end up getting some of the key points offered in the constitution into force through restructuring the existing treaties.

The fear that a world government, if established, would be both unrepresentative and undemocratic is legitimate. First, the concept of world-wide elections based on something other than national issues, cultural concerns, or religion is almost incomprehensible. Second, even the issues of how the selection of candidates for office would be conducted; how the campaigns for office would be carried out; or how the legislature would be made representative of not only national members, but regional interests at sub-national levels present almost indeterminable logistical problems. Third, any proposed system of world government that prevents any significant section of the world's population from being capable of representation must be avoided. Within the limits of liberal democracy it is difficult to determine how this might be accomplished. The EU offers the alternative of a global system of governance that is something less than a government but which operates in much the same manner as a government. Currently twenty-seven sovereign nations are successfully cooperating on many common issues; however, they are faced with the problems of a perceived democratic deficit and lack of transparency. There does not appear to be a reason to automatically rule out the possibility of accomplishing much the same type of governance with some two hundred nations. It will be necessary then to now look at the EU model in some detail.

The EU Model

My initial approach to world government was conducted under three basic assumptions. First, that world government would be initiated as a true government as understood within the system of nationalism. Second, the concept that the world government established would be a federal system. This would include both supranational and national governments with a third layer containing sub-national government. The government, in essence, would be established using the US Constitution as a guide. The use of a written constitution allows for the specification of powers that will be delegated to the supranational level, which powers will be retained by either the national or sub-national governments and by the people. Within the supranational government (herein called the federal government) a written constitution also allows for the specification of the powers, duties and qualifications of those who serve in the executive, legislative and judicial branches of the government. Third, it was initially expected that all the existing nations would become members of the union at the time of its ratification; and that all the nations as members would have a representative democratic structure. This again was based on the US Constitution being used as a guide.

The use of these basic assumptions did not allow the experience of the EU to be incorporated directly into the new government, but in some cases the EU could provide a guideline for setting up operating procedures. If, in fact, a system of global governance is established that is something less than a true government in the nationalistic sense, then it is easily conceivable that the EU would be the guide rather than the US Constitution. The current EU system of governance is usually referred to as either confederal or intergovernmental. It has some features of a federal system, that is, the European level institutions have been delegated a degree of sovereign power through the series of treaties that established the EU; but the national states that are members of the union have retained a large share of the political sovereignty. The union also has some resemblance to a parliamentary democracy with the parliament being elected to five year terms, while the judges and executive members are appointed by the national governments. The appointments are usually made by the chief executive of the national government from the candidates provided by the political party in power. As integration of the union has grown in the economic field with the creation of the single market and single currency the union looks more like a government but is still truly intergovernmental in operation.

It might be of value to start with the factors that under the current system of nationalism make up a definition of true government. The most important factors are the two main security functions. A government is expected to provide its citizens security from attack by external forces, such as other nations, and to provide security against internal insurrection. In order to provide the security expected the general government normally has the exclusive use of force within the society. The general government is also expected to enforce obedience to the laws which it passes on behalf of the citizens. The US under its constitution was given all three of these powers from the beginning. In the EU the general government does not have any of these three powers. Each nation is maintaining whatever military force it deems necessary to repel external invasion and quell internal insurrection. The general government is capable of passing laws, regulations, etc. but must rely on the member nations to enact the laws into the national legal system and to enforce them. Although the lack of these powers is part of the reason that the EU is not considered a government it has been relatively effective over the last sixty years, particularly in the economic sphere. Recently there has been a renewal of interest in future integration within the EU especially in the social arena. Sovereign powers have been delegated to the general government in the areas of general security and defense. This has led to the establishment of what is known as a rapid deployment force of fifty thousand men that operates outside the auspices of NATO. It is specifically intended to respond to natural disasters and attacks by terrorists. In one case, the Bosnian crisis, the force was intended to be used to quell a civil war, but was not effective in doing so. This was somewhat embarrassing to the union, but did show the willingness to provide peacekeeping forces when needed.

Lastly the EU also lacks a fourth power which identifies a true government under the system of nationalism, that is to say, the control of international relations. The US federal government was delegated this power exclusively by the constitution, but the treaties creating the EU leaves this power in the hands of the member nations, except in the case of economic relations. For example, the EU has recently been given the sovereign control of speaking for "Europe" in international trade and financial organizations, such as the International Monetary Fund, the World Bank, and WTO. In the case of treaties the general government of the EU has little independent power. It does, however, have the power to open diplomatic offices in third party nations and many third party nations have opened diplomatic offices in Brussels. With the institution of the euro the EU has also become a unified voice for Europe in relation to financial issues, but once again most policy making decisions in this area are still made at the national level.

It is also part of the ideological substructure of nationalism that a state is indivisible in relation to its sovereignty. The US, of course, fought a civil war over this issue as have many other nation-states. In the case of the EU, however, any one of the members can voluntarily withdraw from the union for any reason that it sees fit. It is this power reserved to the nation-states that makes the EU in many eyes a confederal system.

This power of absolute sovereignty in the nation-state has come under serious scrutiny since World War II. The establishment of the United Nations was intended to be a small delegation of sovereign power to a supranational organization with the intent of maintaining global peace. Indeed, one of the main attractions behind the idea of the "EU" was the maintaining of peace in Europe. There are now literally thousands of international organizations that have been given some degree of sovereign power, normally limited to the specific function for which the organization was created, but not governmental powers per se. There have also been treaties signed by any number of nation-states that delegate some degree of sovereign power to the treaty organization, such as the Kyoto agreement over pollution. The EU, however, is consistently seen to be something greater than an ordinary international organization such as those described above.

It is important to remember that even though the EU does not represent a true government within the system of nationalism this does not prevent it from being a democratic system of governance. This would require that the EU qualify on two different levels. First, the citizens of the EU would have the power to elect or appoint through their representatives those who would serve in the general government. Second, that the operation of the institutions of the general government would be open to the scrutiny of the citizens (transparent) and that these institutions would be open to access by the individual citizen. Currently the Parliament is the only European level institution in which its members are directly elected by the citizens of the European Union. The members of the executive and judicial branches of the general government are appointed by the national governments with the Parliament having a right of approval only. The citizens of the EU have indirect selection of these members of the general government through their right of electing the legislative branch of the national government. This power, however, is remote in the sense that in most of the member nations the executive branch is appointed by the legislature which is controlled by a coalition of political parties. It is the remoteness of the members of the general level government, its ability to meet in secret, and its right to not publish the results of its operations that has led to the complaint that the EU lacks transparency and has a democratic deficit.

The lack of transparency and the democratic deficit have led over the last several decades to a general lack of trust or interest in the EU and its operations within the general public. As knowledge about the EU institutions; the manner in which they operate; and the effect they have on the daily lives of EU citizens have grown this distrust or lack of interest has grown into demands for greater transparency and democracy. This led to the drafting of a proposed constitution that was intended to provide the transparency and democratic control that was being demanded by the public. The constitution was put up for ratification in 2005 but the referendums in two countries, one of which was France, defeated the effort. It is not likely that another attempt will be made along this line in the near future. The EU has, however, started to slowly incorporate the most important elements of the proposed constitution into the EU treaties through a reform process. This has not yet resulted in many concrete results due to the difficulty of reforming the treaties which requires a unanimous vote of all twenty-seven members.

These issues, that is, the confederal nature of the EU coupled with the lack of transparency and the democratic deficit, allow one to question whether the EU is an adequate model to use as a guide in the establishment of a global system of governance. In relation to just these issues, the US model would seem to offer more feasibility, probability and actuality to the establishment of an effective world government. By feasibility, I mean a system that would allow the general system of governance to demand the cooperation of two hundred plus nation-states and political entities. By probability, I mean a process whereby these nation-states and political entities can agree upon the powers that are to be given and retained by the global system of governance and the nation-states and other entities. When I speak of actuality I mean the creation of a contract (constitution or treaty) that would put the system of global governance in action.

Over the last four hundred years these issues have normally been resolved through the creation of the nation-state, but that is not necessarily the only solution. There have been many examples of governing entities that were not truly nation-states, for example, various empires the latest being the Soviet Union. There have also been various confederal polities such as that formed by the Articles of Confederation which created the United States of America. The growing use of international organizations, limited in power to the operation of a specific purpose, also shows that global cooperation can be obtained with something even less than a confederation. Indeed the EU takes the concepts of international organization and confederal systems to a higher level than anything yet found in history. Although it is usually denied, the EU may in fact be a form of true government that is merely not recognized under the concepts of nationalism. That would, of course, make sense, considering that the EU is not attempting to become a nation-state.

At the very least the EU has conjoined twenty-seven independent nations in a cooperative endeavor verging on a true government, and it clearly indicates that a worldwide organization of at least equal complexity is feasible. The ability to draft an ongoing series of treaties to adapt the EU to both foreseen and unforeseen consequences clearly shows that a global system probably could be instituted along the same lines. Initially the global system might, like the EU, be limited to the economic and social arenas, but this does not reduce the probability that a global system could be created. Whether or not such an organization is both feasible and probable is a different question.

Over the last sixty years the EU has not had much success in the area of political integration. This has directly restricted the amount of power that the EU projects in relation to third party concerns. It is at least questionable whether such delicate problems as the regulation of the global market, the regulation of the use of outer space, and the regulation of environmental pollution among others can be handled without political integration on the global level. The experience of the EU leads one to believe that nation-states can and will delay the implementation of global laws that affect their national interests; or that they will evade the enforcement of such laws if possible. There have been cases of both types of behavior on the part of various members of the European Union. In most cases, however, the obstacle has been overcome and the laws, regulations and edicts of the general government have been incorporated into national law and enforced. This may be even more difficult to accomplish on a global level with the vastly more varied interests involved, but there is no need to write off the effort before it is tried.

The EU is currently under a serious strain due to the latest recession and financial crisis. Several member governments have reached a default stage and the EU has had to detach itself from its stand against governmental bailouts. Even the wealthier members are having considerable difficulty in satisfying their citizens' demands for higher rates of employment and less immigration, not to mention the problems of sustaining an extensive system of social welfare. These problems have tended to make some members retreat into a protectionist mode rather than a multilateral mode. There is a fear that a deepening of the recession or a deepening of the financial crisis will lead eventually to the collapse of the euro as a single currency and the withdrawal of some of the weaker members from the union. George Friedman, author of *The Next Decade*, has taken the approach that the key member, that is Germany, may seek to establish a close relationship with the Russian Federation to relieve the pressure it feels in relation to the European Union. Whatever the result of these speculations, however, the very possibility that they could happen is important to any discussion about establishing a system of global governance.

Many hope that the trend towards future integration will continue within the EU until the stage is reached where the EU becomes a true government. In this sense, the EU would then be a giant nation-state in direct competition with other giant nation-states such as the US, China, India and Indonesia. If this were to occur during the next two decades, one of the major questions that would be raised is whether or not the Russian Federation will become a member. It appears from polls that have been taken that a significant portion of the Russian population is in favor of joining such a union. It is likely that if Russia is not included as an actual member, it would be brought into a close relationship with the EU through a treaty.

It would also seem to be favorable, especially if the Russian Federation is included in the short term, that further expansions would continue to draw in the remaining sixteen nations of the European continent that are currently outside the union. There are also predictions that the EU may go beyond the continent for either extensions of free trade agreements or actual members. The French, for example, still maintain close contact with Morocco, Libya, Tunisia and Egypt, while the British still maintain close relations with India, Egypt, Lebanon, Syria and Turkey. Turkey is, of course, already connected to the EU as a candidate member. Most likely within the near term membership will be restricted due to the effects of the recession and fiscal crisis, but in the medium term membership could again become desirable. Should the EU grow to include the Ukraine, Moldova, Bulgaria, the former nations of Yugoslavia and Turkey during the medium term, the EU will surpass the US, Japan and China in economic, political, social, and if it wishes, military power. Given the proclivity of the citizens of the EU for peaceful co-existence it is likely that such power would be used to enforce some type of global disarmament procedure.

There can be no doubt that the continued success of the EU and the possible expansion of the EU are causing some power balance realignments outside the European Continent. The US, for example, has reacted to the single European market by creating a North American Free Trade Area (NAFTA). A similar free trade zone has been established by the

Latin American nations (MERCOSUR). This trend, however, does not seem to extend to Africa and Asia. Here the nations involved are so diverse culturally and historically that cooperation is difficult at the very best. One approach sees the US as currently being an empire in the 19th century sense of liberalism (George Friedman). He claims that the US is unaware of its empire status and has yet to take into consideration the consequences of this status. He calls for the US executive branch, in particular the president, to accept the foreign policy implications of this status. Friedman returns to the concept of the balance of power as it was used historically in Europe, with the caveat that the US will extend this on a global scale.

The incorporation of the remaining European nations into the EU, and the possible incorporation of Russia into the union, or initially into a free trade agreement, would end all aspects of the envisioned American empire as a balance to the power in this area. It is equally likely that the withdrawal from Iraq and Afghanistan will have unexpected consequences which will lead to results the opposite of those expected by Friedman. It is in the interest of Iran to have the embargos under which it exists removed and for the oil which it produces to enter the world market. The EU is currently making diplomatic efforts to become instrumental in negotiating this outcome. It is also likely that Pakistan will not long be able to contain India's growth, but it is equally likely that a slowdown in the Indian economic growth will result in stronger regional autonomy demands within the Indian state. If this is so, India will be unable to prosecute its desire to develop a strong regional navy. This concept is set forth to indicate that alternatives exist to Friedman's geopolitical ideas, or that when operative that modifications are likely to be made to his system.

Based on the above conjectures, the establishment of a global system of governance is not as farfetched as one might imagine. At the base of feasibility is a redefinition of the concept of government a redefinition not based on the concept of nationalism but on current global political conditions. The definition of government included in nationalism is based upon the retention of absolute sovereign power in the nation-state. Sovereign power is seen as absolute in relation to all third parties, that is, other nation-states. Sub-national governments, however, have only limited sovereignty, in the sense that whatever powers they have are directly delegated to them by the general government and can be retracted by that government. Both the US and the EU are exceptions to the rule of absolute sovereignty. The general government (federal) of the US theoretically has only the powers delegated to it by the constitution. The powers retained by the member states are also independent of delegation by the federal government. The EU level government has obtained its power through delegation by treaty and reform of the treaties entered into by the member nations. It is in this case true that the member nations have not given up most of their sovereign power, but have only agreed to delegate sovereign power to the European level in specific areas and for specific purposes. The US is, however, still considered to be a true government under the concepts of nationalism. The US federal government while not absolutely sovereign does fulfill all the other requirements of a government under the system. The EU, on the other hand, is not considered to be a true government although it is considered to be something more than an international organization. It is proposed that the redefinition of government be expanded to include the European Union. This would make sense when one considers that any system of global governance is not attempting to become a nation-state but rather a supranational institution.

By redefining government to include the current system of the EU, we can be more flexible in our concept of world government. It would, in fact, allow us to study the institutions of the EU with a mind to establishing their importance in an extension to global government. It is imperative in this sense that we begin by setting forth what the EU has become within the system of nationalism. The EU has as its basic structure what all international organizations contain, that is, a limited degree of sovereign power that has been delegated to it by its members. This limited sovereignty is further limited to action within a specified arena, for example, the financial powers granted to the International Monetary Fund. The EU began as an institution empowered to have exclusive control of policy making decisions — involving the coal and steel industries of six nation-states. Its powers were sovereign in this arena but were limited solely to action within that industry. The result was quickly seen as an enhancement of each of the six nation's efficiency within that industry and the consequent enhancement of their competition with third parties. From this beginning, additional sovereign powers have been delegated to the European level, largely economic and financial in nature, but also including some social goals of the members. At this point, the EU is greater in the extent of the sovereign powers that it exercises than any other international body in existence; however, it has less sovereign power than most existing nation-states.

The redefinition of government suggested above insures that there is no need to assign any particular status to the EU in terms of governance. The EU could be adopted as a guide for the establishment of a global system without any further ado. All that would be necessary is to set forth the structure of its institutions, to delineate how these institutions operate, and to set forth the manner in which they are staffed. Once this has been accomplished, adjustments can be made in order to forestall any problems that have arisen from the operation and staffing of the EU institutions. Lastly, the institutions can be used as the model for setting up the system of global governance by treaty or constitution.

The most significant resistance to a global system of governance lies in the question of sovereign power. This question has plagued the EU since its inception, that is to say, how much sovereign power is needed by the European level institutions to accomplish the goals of the member nations. There are questions as to how much sovereign power should be delegated, or pooled, and also whether the delegation or pooling of such powers should be permanent. The feasibility index of a world governing system will be directly related to what powers are considered necessary, how they are to be delegated or pooled, and whether the power given is permanent or temporary. The fewer powers delegated or pooled and the more restricted the policy areas affected, the easier it will be to find agreement among nations interested in becoming members of the larger community.

The EU began with the agreement of six nations to delegate or pool some of their sovereign control over the coal and steel industry. A limited set of powers was delegated or pooled, and they were strictly limited in the area in which they could be used. From the very beginning the delegation or pooling of such powers was temporary in nature, as any one of the six nations could withdraw from the agreement for any reason — or for no reason at all. A further limitation on the delegated power was made through the requirement that any action taken at the European level had to have the unanimous consent of all six nations. Even with these restrictions, as we have stated before, the community saw a definite boost in the overall efficiency and competitiveness in the affected industry. In short, the experiment proved to be a success in both the operation aspects of the industry and was taken as a proof that cooperation between sovereign states was possible and profitable. This success resulted in the rather quick expansion of the EU, first to nine nations and shortly afterwards to twelve nations. Expansion has continued; today there are twenty-seven nations in the EU and three existing candidate nations.

With the establishment of the European Economic Community (EEC) originally involving only the six nations involved in the Coal and Steel Community the EU expanded to nine members in 1973 and twelve members in 1983. The EEC brought a further delegation of sovereign powers to act in expanded arenas. It is during this period that the concept of European integration took root. By 1992, the concept of a single European market welded together with the free trade concepts of a free movement of goods, services, capital and people was adopted. The EEC was renamed the European Union, and three new members were added, bringing the total to fifteen. By 2002, the single European market had been established and was joined to a unified currency system, known as the Euro zone, consisting of seventeen of the now twenty-seven members. The result was an almost total integration of the twenty-seven members' economic and financial systems.

It also brought forth further attempts at integration in the social and military arenas. The social arena included the delegation or pooling of some sovereign powers in the areas of the institution and enforcement of European level laws, regulations and edicts; and in the area of environmental issues. In the military arena, a rapid deployment force of fifty thousand men was created to shore up the security and defense issues and to stand outside the auspices of NATO. This latter has to date been something of both an embarrassment and failure on the part of the European Union.

To date, major shortcomings in the EU system are that the integration of Europe has failed to move forward significantly in terms of political issues; and second it has failed to operate in a democratic manner. As we will see, the structure and operation of the European level institutions is such that the citizens of the EU for all practical purposes have no access to the EU or any direct control over its operation. This has led to demands by the citizens that the EU become more transparent in its operation and more democratic in its structure. These issues were approached by the EU through the drafting of a proposed constitution, but this attempt failed to garner ratification. The recent recession and financial crisis has also caused many of the members to become more concerned about national issues than Europe-wide issues, preventing effective political union. Much more will be said concerning these issues later.

To be successful and efficient, the global system will have to be both democratic in its structure and transparent in its actions. Success of such a system is very likely to relate directly to the extent of support it can garner from the citizens it will incorporate. All large governments face the problem of how to engage their citizens in the policy processes, the obedience to laws, regulations, and edicts passed and the ease of access granted to their citizens. In this sphere, the EU may not be as good a guide as the United States. If this is true and the success of eventual global governance is predicated on these issues, the EU may not be the best guide, at least in relation to these issues.

In both the US and the EU, however, the public is slowly becoming aware of the amount of power that has drifted to the general government and how that affects their daily lives. As this growth in knowledge appeared the lack transparency became very apparent. Closer scrutiny by the public has also brought to light episodes of corruption, leaving a definite negative feeling about the operation of the general government. Whether or not this is an attribute of government based upon the definition of nationalism remains to be seen. It is possible that the size of government based on absolute sovereignty puts limits on the effective operation of transparency and democracy. Regardless, it is now time to look at the EU as a possible guide to the establishment of an effective system of world governance.

EU as a Guide

The EU is definitely one model for establishing a world union. The first step is to determine one limited area in which all signatory nations can agree to pool sovereign power for a joint goal. There are many such areas that could be purposed; any area that is now composed of a number of nations as members who have pooled a limited sovereign power could be the basis of such an agreement. The EU started with the coal and steel industry, for several reasons, but one of the most important reasons was the desire to address the competitive impulses in these industries that had in the past contributed to the inception of war. Several conflicts in Europe had begun with the competition between Germany and France over the coal industry. Modern war could not, it was hoped, be waged if there was no national control over coal and the manufacture of steel. It was seen as necessary to tie Germany into the interests of the other Western European nations to prevent German aggression. Essentially, however, the decision boiled down to the idea that joint control of these industries would guarantee peace on the continent. It is a fact that the European Continent has been more peaceful in the last sixty years than it has been for centuries.

If the same rationale is used to choose the area of agreement to begin the process of global governance, the choice would appear to be either nuclear proliferation or environmental pollution. The goal, of course, in the former case would be to lead to a general global disarmament and in the latter case to a substantial reduction of environmental pollution.

It should, however, be expected that regardless of the area chosen, not all nations are going to be interested in becoming signatories. For example, perhaps only those nations that are currently in the nuclear club, or close to becoming members of the club, would initially be interested in accomplishing the goal of non-proliferation. The initial goal of an agreement to ban nuclear proliferation would be to pool enough sovereign power to enforce the ban on proliferation. If the organization created was successful in preventing the further spread of nuclear weapons, and possibly achieve the opening of discussion on complete nuclear disarmament, then the goal would have been obtained. It is likely, as with the EU that success in this one area would lead to further cooperation in other areas and also attract other nations to join the group, especially if part of the spillover was discussion of complete global disarmament. The growing integration of the global market system is another area where one might expect a desire for coordinated action.

What institutions would be needed to accomplish the ban on nuclear proliferation? At the very least, a verifiable system of inspection would have to be instituted along with the power needed to enforce the ban in cases where it was being circumvented. The verification systems used by the United Nations might be used as a model. Currently there are no effective ways of enforcing the concept of non-proliferation in the nuclear field. This has led to much uneasiness in relation to the rapidly growing number of nations with nuclear capability, in particular those nations that are seen as also capable of using them. This alone means it should be in the interest of those nations that already belong to the club to stop further expansion of nuclear capability. The only method used so far for enforcing the prevention of nuclear proliferation is diplomatic and economic pressure in the form of sanctions. These have been ineffective in stopping the proliferation into nations considered to be rogues in the international community, that is, Iran and North Korea.

Regardless of the specific area chosen, if that choice is to act as the Coal and Steel Community did in Europe, there must be a common cause for cooperation. It is likely that the choice will be made by only a few nations, initially, in the same fashion as in Europe. A few influential nations (probably the leaders of these nations) will meet and come to agreement on a path to be taken. These individuals will then use their national influence to bring the plan to the attention of a wider circle of national leaders that may have the same common interest. If a rather general and widespread agreement can be obtained, then a treaty will be drafted and signed by those interested, leaving it open for others to join later. As with the treaties upon which the EU is founded, this treaty will attempt to set forth the goal to be obtained, the institutions needed to obtain the goal, the method of selecting those who will serve in the institution and the powers that will be pooled in favor of the institution created. This treaty will then need to be ratified by the signatory nations on the basis of a unanimous vote. Any of the treaties used in the EU could stand as a model for this process. The Treaty of Paris is the most likely to stand as the model since it delegated a very limited amount of sovereign power and the actions that could be taken under it were severely limited.

The European Coal and Steel Community (ECSC) did not accomplish many of its stated goals, even the main goal of integrating the coal and steel industries of the signatory nations. The ECSC did, however, accomplish the goal of showing the feasibility of regional confederation in Europe. The same question of feasibility will need to be answered on the global level as well. Some would argue that the growth of international organizations from 8,400 in 1984 to over 25,000 in 2007 already shows the feasibility of international cooperation. The growth of international organizations, when coupled to the continued economic integration of national economies into the world market, appears to indicate that the world may be ready to test this feasibility on a limited scale.

The Treaty of Paris consisted of the following elements. There were six initial signatories, that is, West Germany, France, Italy, Belgium, The Netherlands and Luxembourg. They all had diverse and separate reasons for joining in the treaty, but the main actors were the French and Germans, particularly the French. The main goal was to integrate the coal and steel industries in such a fashion as to prevent their consolidation into another attempt to militarize the French or German society. In order to accomplish these goals, the signatories created a supranational institution that contained the forerunners of the later institutions that compose the European Union. It is likely that the same procedure could be followed in establishing a global institution with limited sovereignty and a limited realm of action. It would also, however, as did its European counterpart contain the seeds of later institutional evolution.

The EU contains the following institutions, all of which have been delegated some sovereign power and who are routinely capable of instituting Europe-wide policies:

1. The European Commission. The commission is arguably the most important of the EU level institutions. The commission has both executive (implementation and enforcement) powers and legislative (initiates all EU legislation) powers. The commission is composed of a college of commissioners consisting of 27 members (one from each member nation) holding five-year terms. The commissioners are appointed by the head of each member nation. There are also twenty-six Directorates-General who are again appointed by the various member nations and are responsible for initiating legislation in their field of expertise. There are eight service departments for technical services and advice attached to the Directorates. There is also a Secretariat-General with several hundred employees who are responsible for the day to day activities of the Commission. Lastly, the commission has hundreds of committees spread out over the EU gathering information, overseeing implementation of laws, rules and regulations and acting as enforcement agents.

2. The Council of Ministers. The Council of Ministers is the forum in which national governments, through their ministers, meet to make decisions on EU law and policy. In some ways, although this comparison is limited, the council operates in a fashion similar to the US Senate. The Council is supported by a large bureaucracy known as the Committee of Permanent Representatives (COREPER). The Council's official name is the Council of the European Union.

The Council is composed of four main elements, the council of ministers; the Committee of Permanent Representatives (COREPER I AND COREPER II); the Presidency; and the General Secretariat. The councils are nine in number and include the following: agriculture and fisheries; competitiveness; economic and financial affairs (ECO-FIN); education, youth and cultural affairs; employment; social policy, health and constitutional affairs; general affairs and external relations, justice and home affairs; environment; and lastly, transport, telecommunications and energy. COREPER is the most powerful bureaucratic force within the EU — as well as being the most secretive and misunderstood. COREPER was not officially recognized as part of the EU until the Merger Treaty of 1965. The Council also has hundreds of committees that gather information, give technical advice and provide all the support needed by COREPER. COREPER due to the increase in its workload has been divided into two separate organizations. COREPER I handle the preparation of the final work to be viewed by the Council in its six month summit meetings. COREPER II does all of the preliminary work in the initial preparation for the meetings of the Council. The Council in its six-month meetings operates on the basis of three voting systems. On some issues it can vote on the basis of a simple majority (usually only routine matters), a qualified majority or QMV which is actually a triple majority consisting of 255 votes (74% of the total votes available), the 74% must also qualify as representing the majority of the member states and 62% of the total population of the EU (this usually applies to any issue that is expected to affect national interests) and lastly a unanimous vote which is used on any reform of treaty obligations or other issues that affect all members. The voting system although somewhat complicated is intended to protect the interests of the smaller member states (majority). The presidency is held not by a person but by a member state subject to a six-month rotation system. The presidency has several duties: it prepares and coordinates the work of the European Council and the Council of Ministers; it arranges and chairs the meetings of the Council of Ministers and COREPER and the represents the Council in relations with other EU institutions; it mediates and bargains and is responsible for promoting cooperation among member states. In this aspect the presidency is rated on its ability to promote compromise and consensus among EU members; it oversees EU foreign policy for six months; acts as the EU's main voice on the global stage; and aids members in their international meeting obligations, such as the G8 meetings and it chairs the summits of the European Council. The rotation system is currently under review as the system only allows repeat presidencies among members every 14 years since membership has grown to twenty-seven. The General Secretariat, and its staff, handles the day to day affairs of the Council and the work of COREPER. The Council of Ministers is the most important of the European level institutions that have been created and most of the work done at the European level is done by the Council of Ministers in cooperation with the Commission.

3. The European Parliament. The Parliament is a quasi-legislative body. It cannot initiate legislation although the members do debate, amend and accept or reject the proposals offered by the Commission

in conjunction with the Council of Ministers. The EP is, however, the only European level institution in which its members are subject to direct election by the citizens of the European Union.

The EP consists of 785 members elected for five year terms, which number is divided with half elected on years ending in 4 and half in years ending in 9. The Parliament is broken down into a Presidency, 14 Vice-Presidencies, twenty parliamentary standing committees (permanent in standing) and a large number of temporary committees and agencies of inquiry. There is also a conciliation committee consisting of members of Parliament (MEPS) and members of the Council of Ministers charged with producing compromise when stalemates are reached.

The Parliament, although the only democratically elected body has never been trusted with a lot of independent power. This makes sense in light of the fact that the founders of the EU were all heads of national governments and somewhat guarded about transfer of sovereignty. Over the history of the EU, however, the EP has slowly accumulated power, if not sovereign, at least capable of standing as a check on the power of the Commission and the EC. The defeated constitution would have extended the powers of the EP into a real legislative organization.

4. The European Court of Justice and the Court of First Instance. Although this court system does not have the same level of power as the US Supreme Court and lower federal courts, they operate in much the same manner. The Court of Justice has twenty-seven members appointed to six year terms with half of them coming up for appointment every three years. Appointments, therefore, tend to be much more frequent and less political in nature than in a life time tenure system such as the one in the US.

The court consists of a president who is selected by a secret ballot of the twenty-seven members. In the US system, the chief justice is appointed by the president with the approval of the Senate. The court is allowed to meet in sessions containing all twenty-seven members but normally sits in sessions containing thirteen, seven or five members. In some circumstances sessions are held with only one member of the court sitting in judgment. The court also has eight advocates general who initially review the new cases that come in, study the arguments presented by the parties (legal briefs) and render preliminary verdicts for the courts review. The Court of First Instance was established to handle the growing overflow of cases being heard by the Court of Justice. It operates in the same manner as the Court of Justice. Even so, however, the work load has become so large that it can take two years or more to obtain a final verdict in a case.

5. Outside of the EUCJ system, an EU Civil Service tribunal has been created to hear cases involving EU institutions and their staffs. The Tribunal contains seven judges and their staff. The jurisdiction of the tribunal is limited to cases affecting the work environment within EU institutions.

6. The European Council. This council is composed of the leaders of all twenty-seven members (prime ministers, etc.). It acts in essence as a board of directors of the EU and does not have any direct executive, legislative or judicial role. The EC was created in 1974 but was not officially recognized by treaty until the Single European Act of 1986. The European Council contains a president which is in fact a member state serving on the basis of an established rotation system. The Council meets every six months (summits) and is intended to settle the broad outlines of policy matters to be handled by the European Union. It is in fact the major policy making institution within the European Union.

The major attributes of the council are its flexibility (no bureaucratic opposition); no rules or regulations (operates beyond any formally accepted organization); informality (most of the work is done before the actual meeting by COREPER and others in relation to their duties with the Council of Ministers); the ability to meet in small casual lunches and other circumstances; and the delegation of decisions (all decisions made by the Council are enacted and enforced by the Commission, the EP, or the Court of Justice). This allows the Council to act in its role as the major policy making body for decisions involving further European integration and to act as a brake on the growth of power within the EU institutions. It is also probably the most visible of the EU institutions in relation to the European public, but due to its closed meetings and secret ballots maybe also the most responsible for the criticisms involving the democratic deficit and lack of transparency.

In addition to the European Council, a number of other European-level organizations have been created that are essentially outside the official EU institutional system. The most important is the European banking system, consisting of the European Central Bank (ECB) and a system of National Central Banks intended to establish European monetary policy in connection with the administration of the Euro zone and to advise both the EU and the national members of this policy. This system was established with the intention of allowing the banking system to operate independently of both the EU institutions and the member nations; however, the national members have retained a significant amount of influence within the system. There are also a number of other independent and more specialized agencies, such as Europol (a Europe-wide criminal information gathering and sharing body); Economic and Social Committee and Committee of Regions (COR). These latter two being established to allow contact points for organizations (interest groups), individuals and others with the EU institutions.

Several agencies operate more like international organizations while still maintaining close contact with EU institutions. They include the European Investment Bank (EIB); the Court of Auditors; the European Environmental Agency (EEA) and the European Bank for Reconstruction and Development (EBRD). All of these agencies are dual funded by the EU (structural funds) and by the member nations (direct contributions). The membership of these agencies includes some who are not also members of the European Union.

The EU, through the evolution of both its mainstream institutions and the above cooperative agencies, has resulted in the following remarkable successes: one, and by far the most important if measured by the American experience, is the evolution of a Europe-wide legal system which stands as supreme over the laws of the members, including any of the members' constitutions. As we clearly saw in *World Government: Utopian Dream or Current Reality*, this same development in the US system has been the basis of the drift of power from the states to the federal government. It can be expected that the integrative power of this process will continue to have an extensive effect on the continued growth of power within the European Union. Second, and probably the most basic to the practical goal of European integration, is the creation of a true single market among all twenty-seven members. Within the concept of the single market can be included the development of a unified monetary system through the euro. There is nothing from a practical point of view that brings the fact of integration to the public better or more thoroughly than the effect on his or her wallet in regards to a single currency. The single market (in the sense of free trade), the euro and the discretionary powers allowed the EU in international economic meetings has brought the EU in direct contact with the daily lives of all of Europe's peoples, as well as with the political elites of most other nations. Third, and probably most significant for our purposes, is the development of a European level social and security policy. This policy decision is an attempt to co-ordinate European cultural identity, that is, to foster a real commitment on the part of citizens to the EU; as well as to allow a single European voice in relation to international affairs. It is in many ways the recognition of the fact that since the demise of the Soviet Union "soft", or economic power, has become as important as "hard", or military power in the globalization process.

A world union based on the current EU would raise the following questions (among others of equal importance). First, on the basis of the concept of intergovermentalism, could two hundred plus nation-states (through heads of state) act as effectively as the twenty-seven nation-states of the EU and the EC? Second, would a world Commission, a world Council of Ministers and world Parliament be as effective as their European counterparts? Third, would the citizens of the world union be even more remote in terms of the concepts of democratic deficit and transparency than their EU counterparts? It is likely that the answer to these questions will be found by looking closely at the operation of the European Union.

Even with only twenty-seven members the structure and operation of the EC has had to change to accommodate these numbers. The Presidency of the European Council and the Council of Ministers, for example, was originally set to revolve every six months which allowed each member the presidency on a regular basis at a relatively short term time frame. With twenty-seven members, however, leaving the system unchanged would result in each member sitting as president of the council only once every thirteen years. Under a world union set up under the same system each member would sit as president only once in every century. Therefore under a world union the system will need to be structured in a different way, possibly with the presidency being set up as a committee rather than a sole member position to effectively give a voice to each member on a regular and relatively frequent basis. How this restructuring would take place and how it would affect the operation of the World Council (WC) cannot be predicted in advance. All that can be stated is that the EC was established to give the small members (both in terms of size and economic wealth) a significant role in policy making. This role would also have to be incorporated into any restructuring of the WC. The EU has not yet resolved this issue and cannot act as a guide for the construction of a world union on this issue. The resolution of this first issue would contain within it the answers to the second and third questions. The role and operation of the Commission, the Council of Ministers and the Parliament could remain much the same as they now are within the European Union. However, here again the question will arise as to how the structure of such bodies must change to accommodate the increase in the size of the world level bodies. In this sense the structure of the WC will probably also determine any restructuring needed in the Commission, Council of Ministers and Parliament at the world level. If the world union is constructed along lines identical with the existing EU then the answer to question three would clearly be that the world citizens would be even more remote than the citizens of the European Union. However, if the restructuring of the WC is done in a manner which allows a more democratic method of selecting representatives to the Commission and Parliament this could change.

A more generalized answer to the three questions posed above might be found in the concept of power drift. During the evolution of the EU, two major types of power drift have occurred. First, the EU, mainly through the efforts of the EC, has developed its supranational control of international policy (external and mainly in the economic field) and its security policy (internal security issues of self-defense and control of terrorism, etc). Both of these power drifts became possible with the fall of the Soviet Union and the decreasing need for an umbrella defense system (NATO) and the continued integration of the global market. The US tendency towards unilateral policy decision became apparent after the shock of 9/11, coupled with a growing internal financial crisis. These factors appear to have dampened US interest in continued control of the global market, that is, hegemonic control of the world marketplace ("empire", in Friedman's terms). The financial crisis has led to an internal debate within the US over what has been termed an uncontrolled budget deficit problem coupled to an unsustainable national debt. One side of the argument (conservative) holds that the budget deficit and national debt are the result of spending on the part of the federal government, primarily in the area of social entitlement or welfare programs. This includes Social Security, Medicare, and Medicaid as the main culprits, but also includes all social programs. Related to the spending on entitlement is a call for tax reform, including cuts for the business and wealthy sectors of the society and a real reduction of the regulation burden on business. Both of these latter areas are needed to stimulate the economy into robust growth and to reduce the high levels of unemployment from the conservative point of view. The other side of the argument (liberal) would rather emphasis the non-social aspects of spending, including military expenditures, consumer spending, and further regulation and taxation, especially of the wealthy and the business sector. To date the internal debate has resulted in no concrete measures being taken. It does appear certain, however, that in the short term the US will be forced to face up to its increasing budget deficits, growing national debt, and imbalance in trade. The only reaction so far has been a neo-isolationism on the part of the current administration, that is to say, a recall of international businesses back to the domestic market and measures to increase the productivity and employability of the American labor force. This, in turn, has been seen as an increase of US unilateralism in the international arena and a further sign of the decline of the American hegemony over globalization. The same issues are currently facing the EU and have caused some to predict that the same process will be found there, that is, that the members of the EU will become more national minded and that the Germans may tire of footing the bill for member bailouts. Some even predict that a number of members will exercise their ability to voluntarily withdraw from the union, or even the total collapse of the union and the Euro zone. Speculation along these lines is a common reaction to economic recessions and large scale financial crisis.

On the other hand, there are many predictions that the EU will solve these problems with a move towards greater integration, especially on the political front. If so the EU will certainly be in a position to inherit the current US hegemony in relation to globalization if such a takeover is desired. In the mid to long term it seems quite possible that both the US and the EU will recover their balance and return to leadership in the continuing globalization of the world economy. This seems to be true, largely due to the fact that both seem to be willing to do what needs to be done to correct the problems that led to the financial crisis; and the economies of both are beginning to grow, even if slowly. It will, however, be interesting to see the details as these adjustments are made to both systems of governance.

This completes our brief explanation of how the EU could act as a guide to a global system of governance. It is now necessary to see how the growing divergence in political ideology between the US and the EU can be addressed. If the EU is to be used as the guide to a system of world governance, the EU and the US will have to be the major actors in its creation.

There are two areas that seem to share most of the responsibility for the growing divergence in the political positions of the US and the European Union. These have resulted both in the trend towards greater integration in the EU (on the social and security levels) and in relation to a single voice in international affairs. The first was the US opposition to and control of the Suez Canal invasion orchestrated by Great Britain, France and Israel. The US, in essence, ended the invasion without consulting any of the involved parties and clearly left the impression that when US interests were predominate Europe could not depend on the US security umbrella. In relation to this, the EU attempted to develop its own security forces outside the NATO organization, which has always been mainly controlled by the United States. The US encouraged this movement, to a degree, as a way of reducing its own defense expenditures in Europe. The Bosnian crisis, however, clearly brought to the worlds' attention that the EU was not ready for even internal peacekeeping missions, and the US stepped in. Second was the invasion of the sovereign state of Iraq by the US and its allies, again expressing the US dependence on unilateral action of a military type.

As a result of this growing dislocation, the EU determined to strengthen its diplomatic position in international affairs through the use of "soft" or economic power. This EU approach had two results, first, the EU was reluctant to provide financial support for the US position in Iraq and Afghanistan, resulting in a substantial share of the 2010 US budget deficit of 1.5 trillion dollars and the 15 trillion dollar national debt, and second, the US was reluctant to contribute to the international bailout of EU members going into default.

In addition, the US has been unable to conduct a foreign policy that is in sync with its international position. Since the early 1990s the US has been without question the premier military power. The first Bush administration, the Clinton administration and the second Bush administration were unable to develop a consistent policy concerning military primacy. The biggest problem appears to be the international perception that the US has adopted a military policy based solely on unilateralism. The US, so far, has involved itself in two very unpopular or misunderstood wars, that is, the war on terrorism with an invasion of Afghanistan, and the war in Iraq as an adjunct to the war on terrorism. There have also been several incidents of saber rattling that brought the US under criticism, such as the Bush administration designation of an axis of evil (the approach taken in relation to the Iranian and North Korean nuclear programs among others). In short, the US struggle to find a consistent policy for the use of its military predominance has caused some to question the adequacy of military power as a measure of international capability. As a result the US has also adopted some confusion concerning its continued role in the international field in relation to the economic and political arenas. The former has led to a clear recognition that its former economic hegemony, if it existed, has been substantially reduced by the growth of Japan and the EU in this area. It has also led to the realization the US is no longer politically dominant in either Asia or Europe. The US has allowed its political influence in the EU to recede mainly due to its lack of interest in addressing the demands made by the EU for sharing policy making decisions that involve both. In Asia the US has come to the realization that not Japan, but also China and India, have growing strength in the international political arena, which the US is having problems adapting too.

This has not, however, all been on the plus side for the European Union. The union has also suffered severely from the recent economic recession in the form of national bankruptcies. Greece, Portugal and Ireland have all had to sustain an extensive bailout from the pressure of their budget deficits and national debts. This has put a strain on the entire economic outlook of the EU including the outlook for the wealthier economies, such as Germany and France. Both of these nations had to seek, and obtained, relieve from fines that should have been assessed in relation to their keeping their budget below the 3% of GDP required under the Growth and Stability Act of the Euro zone members. The Germans, in particular, have shown growing reluctance to contribute to any further bailouts. Indeed by treaty the EU is prohibited from executing governmental bailouts. As a result the euro, like the dollar, has been under considerable pressure towards devaluation. Japan, however, which recently endured a decade-long recovery from the same financial and economic pressures facing the EU and US, is now facing economic devastation due to a record-breaking earthquake and damage to its nuclear reactors. The yen is also not in a position to take over as the international reserve currency of choice. For the short term, Japan seems to be losing economic influence in favor of China, Indonesia and South Korea along with the increased political influence that goes with it. In the long run, however, it is predicted that China and Indonesia will suffer a significant economic slowdown which will result in a growing civil unrest within their borders.

There is currently a great deal of uncertainty as to the direction of economic, political and military power in connection with the integrative effects of globalization. The four powerhouses of the last several decades, that is, the US, the Soviet Union, the EU and Japan, have either disappeared or are reeling from economic and political shocks. This has led to a perception that there has been a wholesale withdrawal from internationalism (seen as intergovernmental cooperation) to a revived concept of balance of power (similar to the 19th and 20th century concept in regard to the European Continent, but regional or global today). This neo-nationalism seems to hinge on the actions taken in Asia, in particular in China, India, Indonesia and the Korean Peninsula. It is likely to be a couple of decades before the economic problems facing the US, the EU and Japan will be brought to a satisfactory conclusion. During this period of time several major events could transpire. The US could fail to meet the obligations of its budget deficits and national debt and find a way to force the issue through its military superiority. The EU could suffer such setbacks that a major state such as Germany would withdraw. Such a withdrawal would probably be dependent upon a successful entente between Germany and the Russian Federation as outlined above. Whether or not this would include the Balkans and all of Eastern Europe would depend on circumstances. Japan might decide that its protection, that is its very existence, depends upon its revitalization of its military power in relation to Korea, China and Southeast Asia. On the other hand, the same circumstances could result in the construction of several regional power balances as outlined and discussed earlier. In this case the neo-nationalism now so evident would be concentrated into regional free trade zones that would include unified economic and military agreements.

In any case the various individual nation-states would still be left facing rather intractable problems such as high unemployment, the increasing number of unsatisfactory jobs (low-wage service sector jobs, temporary employment, part-time labor, and others), an aging population in industrialized areas or over-population and immigration from poorer areas. In all of these cases the solutions seem to rely on the ability to restructure the social welfare systems in the wealthier industrialized nations coupled with the need to encourage immigration to care for the aging population and to take the other undesirable jobs. Whatever restructuring is done in the industrialized nations to resolve these issues must at the same time allow room for the growing competition from the Russian Federation, China, India and Southeast Asia. This competition may become most acute in the control or access to natural resources such as oil and gas.

The poorer regions or nations will also have to face up to the fact that globalization as it is conducted today is not conducive to their survival. They will by most accounts need to concentrate first on the reconstitution of internal agricultural until food self-sufficiency is obtained. Secondly, they will need to develop internal consumer industries rather than export industries to eliminate their intractable poverty. In the short and mid-term this may mean their withdrawal from the globalization process and the "poor relief" of the wealthier nations. In the context of regional balances of power, they will benefit only if they are advantageously approached by one or another of the regional powers.

They may find that time to accomplish these changes is provided by the predicted failure of economic growth in China, India, South Korea and Southeast Asia along with the apparently improbable repair of the economy of the Russian Federation over the short term. India and China both have nearly one billion people living at the poverty level, but who are expecting to see relative economic prosperity relatively soon. Should this not occur, due to a slowdown in economic growth, it is expected that large scale civil unrest will result, both in the form of individual civil unrest and demands for local autonomy. In the case of the Russian Federation the ability to recover from decades of economic devastation is restricted to say the least. The need for technology and capital investment is almost unlimited, and the only source for obtaining it is the vast reservoir of natural resources and large workforce found in Russia. If significant recovery is likely to be several decades down the road, then the US and EU could use this time to resolve their major internal problems and resume their full power vis-à-vis the rest of the world.

The prognosticators are equally divided in relation to the European Union. Some see a worsening national debt crisis forcing either the break-up of the EU or a voluntary withdrawal of a number of members from the union, perhaps including a German entente with the Russian Federation. Others see a continued series of internal problems, in particular the aging population and unsustainable levels of social welfare and immigration as contributors to the slow emergence of neo-nationalism forcing the EU institutions to concentrate on economic aspects alone. This would entail the survival of the EU but without any emphasis on further integration, or possibly a lessening of some of the already existing trends towards integration, such as the social and security aspects of the European Union. Indeed, the UK is already attempting to regain some of the powers it earlier granted to the EU. Lastly, there are others who see a return during the next decade of robust economic growth throughout the global system. This forecast would portend the further expansion of the EU and a growing political integration to resolve the issues that would arise from increased membership. Under current circumstances, additional expansion is not expected to take place until the last portion of the next decade or the following decade, and integration of a political nature is also expected to extend over a considerable period of time.

In relation to China and India, even the most promising predictions see a reduction in economic growth rates accompanied by growing levels of social unrest. India is already experiencing a growing demand for more autonomy for its various regional divisions. Such pressure for autonomy has put a strain on India's federal structure and the growing centralization of the federal government. A slowdown in economic growth and the suffering it would cause are expected to create additional civil unrest and fragmentation of the federal system. The same process is also already occurring in China; but the Chinese have allowed substantial autonomy to the various regions in regard to the local economy and social relations. The Communist Party, however, has maintained a tight control over the overall economic and social environment through the continuance of centralized planning system at the top level of government. A significant slowdown of economic growth, however, will have a much stronger effect upon the general population's expectations than in India. The middle class in China is much larger than that in India and its expectations for a future standard of living are much higher. The billion or so people in China who live at the poverty level or below also have high expectations for improvement. The net result is expected to be more widespread social unrest and for a longer duration; with much of the stress being placed on regional autonomy from the central party structure (similar to what happened in the Soviet case). The most optimistic commentators see the concessions being made to demands for local autonomy as a positive indication of a growth of democracy accompanying a further incorporation of China into the globalization process. The more negative see it as provoking a severe response from the Party accompanied by brutal repression. Repression would be aimed at preventing any movement towards a multi-party system and a probable withdrawal back into political isolation from the world community, at least temporarily. There is no easy prediction to be made in the case of China's hybrid system, but all predictions clearly forecast that neither China nor India will be able to obtain the economic or political power now residing in the US, the EU or Japan for at least a decade or two.

Southeast Asia, on the other hand, has already met the expectations predicted by futurists' early warnings. The area generally suffered the expected economic slowdown and needed adjustments during the last decade, as did Japan. They experienced the widespread social unrest that was predicted as a result of the slowdown in economic growth and appear to have adjusted to those demands and are currently entering into full recovery. It is expected, however, that Southeast Asia will experience the same slow economic growth rates as the global economy and will be plagued by the consequent high levels of unemployment and growing demands for the institution of social welfare programs. The continued economic growth of Indonesia, Thailand, Vietnam, South Korea and a few others may lead to a loose federation of the Pacific economic arena including New Zealand and Australia into some type of free trade or customs union association. This may be particularly relevant in the event that Japan is unable to quickly recover from its recent natural disaster and China begins to suffer from social unrest and withdraws into itself. Under the best conditions, however, the rise of Southeast Asia to political and economic power in the international arena is decades away.

The above exercise has made it possible to set forth two propositions concerning the current political environment. First, the global market has brought with it several rather intractable problems; that is, financial instability; slow economic growth rates, high global unemployment, and a marginalization of both poor nations and a portion of the working population within the highly industrialized nations. Second, there is a growing realization that some of the problems that face the existing nation-states have grown beyond the ability of individual nation-states to cope. A growing number of nation-states, including the US, the weaker members of the EU and Japan are suffering from supposedly unsustainable budget deficits and national debts. The generalized slowdown of economic growth globally has resulted in high levels of unemployment that are beyond the ability of most nations to remedy. The solution has been found below the governmental level through the willingness of people to migrate to areas where they might expect to find work. The growing realization that the polarization of rich versus poor, not only between nation-states but also among the populations in the nation-states, has led to growing social unrest that is in some cases beyond the capacity of the government to control (the occupy Wall street movement, for example). All of these problems have been initially met by a conscious retreat back into nationalistic solutions, that is, protectionism, authoritarian type regime structures and a willingness to withdraw from the globalization process. The institution of "poor relief" and other such programs has been ineffective in controlling social unrest to date, although that was one of its main duties.

The growing interest in regional confederations of free trade or custom unions has also been rather ineffective in relieving the pressure of the above problems. Even the most successful free trade and custom unions, such as the EU, NAFTA and MERCOSUR, have been limited in their success at controlling high unemployment, immigration issues, and financial instability (trade balances, monetary exchange, etc.). The EU has taken a stance against the deregulation currently established in relation to the globalization process, and this may in fact be the right approach. This view sees the above problems as stemming from the existing global market ideological tenets, that is to say, the US hegemonic dominance. The US hegemony has been used to enforce the US stand on how the global market should be constructed and evolve. The US vision of a global market sees a market that is essentially unregulated (free of governmental interference) and open to the free play of market forces (economic liberalism). The institution of these two goals require that the national players in this market institute procedures to insure low levels of inflation which in turn require the maintenance of high levels of unemployment and fiscal discipline in relation to budget deficits and national debts. In return the players will see a return in terms of high rates of economic growth and capital investment opportunities. In contrast the EU position takes the approach that the deregulation of the global market has led to large scale fiscal mismanagement resulting in global financial crisis in both the investment and housing industries. This in turn has led to slow rates of economic growth that resulted in the onset of a global economic recession and the perceived need to bail out the large corporations (especially in the investment sector) and national regimes (Greece, Portugal, etc.). The spending required to sustain the large welfare sectors of the highly industrialized economies has led directly to growth of budget deficits and ballooning national debts. So far individual nation-states have been unsuccessful at resolving these issues on their own.

In addition, international economic organizations, such as the International Monetary Fund, the World Bank, World Trade Organization and others have also been unsuccessful in finding operating procedures within the existing global market system that will relieve or solve them. The IMF and World Bank are reliant on the contributions of the highly industrialized wealthy nations for their wealth redistribution functions. Even the current levels of contributions fall far short of what would be needed to "bail-out" from the financial crisis. WTO has been unable to control, through its function as an intergovernmental agency, the leadership in relation to the adjustment of the global market to these conditions. In particular the US has been a major violator of its own market rules in relation to budget deficits, national debt and fiscal discipline generally. Exceptions have also been made in the case of Japan; and more recently Germany and France mainly because no viable system of enforcement is in place. The enforcement that was on hand, that is, the US hegemony has essentially failed to exercise its enforcement role.

Assuming for the sake of argument that the EU position is the correct one and that the global market needs to adapt to a different set of ideological tenets, we can attempt to determine what that would entail. In all likelihood it would entail the institution of some type of regulatory power to control the global market at the global level. This could be an institution similar to the European Council acting in a strictly intergovernmental capacity or a true world system of governance. The regulation of the global market might be accomplished in much the same fashion as national markets are controlled, that is, a centralized control of internal trade, control of tariffs and customs, tax laws, monetary policy and all the other regulatory apparatus. It would, of course, require that whatever rules and regulations were put in place could be adequately monitored and enforced.

The last reason for confederal institutions to be considered as the new world order is that using the EU as a guide allows for a rapid installation of at least the institutions needed to resolve the most pressing problems facing the world. An EU type of global governance would under the conditions involved in the construction of the EU allow for a controlled and limited amount of sovereignty transfer, a limitation on the scope and operation of supranational powers and a direct focusing of these limited powers on the problems most in need of solution.

There is, however one additional level of organization in place currently that also could be used as a guide to effective global governance, that is, the existing system of international organizations. In this respect, it might be worthwhile to spend some time on the analysis of Robert Cox and the collection of essays he published under the title *Approaches To World Order*.

CHAPTER 8. A LOOK AT A NEW WORLD ORDER BASED ON INTERNATIONAL INSTITUTIONS

Robert Cox is concerned with both the global economic climate and the global political climate, seeing them as essentially incapable of separation. He is mainly interested in the concept of using the system of international organizations as the stepping stone to world governance both economically and politically. Cox clearly indicates that global governance does not necessarily directly equate with global government. His system would require the pooling of limited sovereign powers for limited specific purposes, possibly on a temporary basis. Cox contends that all existing international organizations already are structured in that way. The overall supervision of the international organizations could be handled within the current US global hegemony, if the US were willing to make concessions to the non-hegemonic actors to maintain its hegemony. Cox also contends that regional or global intergovermentalism could just as easily provide overall supervision if a global hegemonic system failed. Under this latter system, only issues on a global scale, such as conservation of natural resources, pollution, pandemic disease, regulation of the global market, the use of outer space and others would be subject to handling at the global level. All other issues would be handled at the national level or through lesser international agencies, even in some cases at sub-national levels of government.

What remains to be answered is the question of whether any form of global supervision or governance is necessary. If necessary for the operation of a global market, then the question becomes what type of governance will bring about the greatest efficiency in solving these large issues. In writing the collections of essays, Mr. Cox has an opportunity to express the many thoughts that his experience has triggered. Mr. Cox, a confirmed socialist, approaches the world order problem from the point of view of a reconstituted socialism. He certainly does not question the failure of "real socialism" or the difficulty in reconstituting a mostly dead theoretical socialism.

Looking at the use of such terms as "post-Westphalian", "post-Fordism", "post-hegemonic", etc., allows us to firmly place his views in the intellectual realm rather than that of the world of action. All of the above terms are used by Mr. Cox to fix the position from which the current world order has grown. Post-Fordism fixes the point (1970s) at which the globalization of labor (production) replaced the system based upon national economies protected by the state (protectionism). Fordism represents the stage where large corporations placed large numbers of workers in a single factory to produce homogenized consumer items for a mass national market. This required the close cooperation of big business, labor unions and government. The state protected the business sector from the competition of external businesses through the restraint of free trade, e.g., tariffs, etc. The state also protected the disadvantaged within the state that is, the unemployed, disabled, aged, etc. This was done through the institution of direct transfer payments known generally as social welfare (today known as wealth redistribution generally).

The Post-Fordism system, on the other hand, is based on the marriage of capital and a group of "core" employees who produce for a highly competitive global market and are supported by a highly segmented transnational labor force promoting flexible production methods. This system has led to a globalization movement which calls for a deregulated global financial and economic structure supported by the military power of the United States. Globalization has led to the decline in the strength of labor organizations as well as the ability of the state to intervene in economic and financial matters. All nation-states are required to conduct domestic policies that support high levels of unemployment, fiscal discipline and flexibility in labor policies. The latter includes the acceptance of high levels of immigration. The US has largely been allowed exemption from these rules due to its role as the hegemonic power source and the source of the currency that stands as the international reserve currency of choice.

The hegemony spoken of in interrelation theories is essentially the military power of the US, used in conjunction with its support of the premier economic and political position the US found itself in after World War II. It is the *Pax Americana* which replaced the earlier *Pax Britannica*. Post-hegemonism fixes the point at which the US is supposed to have lost its role as a hegemonic power (1990s) and its replacement with a different world order. Currently the debate is yet unsettled as to what type of world order has replaced, or will replace, the US hegemonic position. The increasingly unilateral use of military power by the US (in Iraq, for example), coupled with its loss of sole control of international economic and political leadership, has led to the concept of post-hegemonism.

To date it is not so much the hegemonic system that is breaking down but rather the concept of a truly global market. As we have stated earlier, several alternatives to hegemony appear to be at least theoretically viable. One would be the recognition by the US of its position as a global empire, as suggested by George Friedman. This would consist of the US maintaining a series of balances of regional power through the overarching military power it exhibits. A second would be the creation of a series of regional economic-political blocs that would together enforce the new world order. This system would be part of a post-Westphalian system, that is, the replacement of individual nation-states with regional systems of government. A third would consist of the establishment of a world system of governance, either by intergovernmental or global government.

As an aside, a unique way of looking at Islam in relation to multi-level global federalism was brought in focus by Mr. Cox. The thought consists of seeing Islam, in particular what Western journalism likes to refer to as fundamentalist Islam, as a replacement for "real socialism" as the voice of the disadvantaged. Islam can be seen as a rejection of the role of capitalism in peripheral nations, especially in North Africa, the Middle East and parts of Asia. Aspects of this rejection of capitalism can be seen in the Islamic penal code, the position of women in Islamic society and the concept of jihad. These are all aspects of Islam that are essentially incomprehensible to the peoples of capitalistic systems. As social unrest unfolds in North Africa and the Middle East, it is clear that the disadvantaged (unemployed, women, students and the urban displaced) are being used by Islam as a tool for organizing against the autocrats that have controlled as the tools of capitalism for decades, or so the argument concludes. As will be seen later, this fits well with the goals of an earlier movement to establish a new world order (NEIC) sponsored by third world nations.

In the same vein, another attempt to debunk the existing world order can be found in the idea of democratic ungovernability. The argument again retreats to socialistic metaphor. Ralf Dahrendorf criticizes the conservative (status quo) approach in its call for "...a little more unemployment, a little less education, a little more deliberate discipline, and a little less freedom of expression [that] would make the world a better place, in which it is possible to govern effectively." (*Crisis of Democracy*, 194)

Under the existing world order, as envisioned by Mr. Cox, the US represents the core of the core at the first level of power, that is, the few nations that are entering into the post-industrial era. They represent about 15% of the world's population. The second level is made up of those nations that have become somewhat peripheral to the core but still might win the struggle to become part of the core. This level also represents about 15% of the world's population. A third level of power is represented by nations who are capitalist dependent, that is, they are not capable of entering the core group but are still relatively speaking wealthy and maintain a somewhat articulate voice in the world order. They represent another 15 to 20% of the world's population. The first three levels, therefore, represent approximately half of the world's population and to a large extent have an interest in maintaining the status quo or existing world order. The fourth level represents another 25% of the world's population and consists of the nations that have been truly marginalized. They are seen by the top three levels as candidates for poor relief and possibly riot control. They have no hope of entering the core or peripheral core and are to a large extent inarticulate, with the possible exception of the social unrest exhibited by the Islamic revolutions, rogue nuclear states and terrorism. The fifth and last category represents another 25% or so of the world's population and consists solely of the nation of China (the People's Republic of China). It does not fit anywhere into the structure set forth above and represents a real x-factor in the current world order. Some fear that China will upset the current world order precipitating the creation of a new world order (post-hegemonic era). Others see China as capable of being co-opted into the current world order through a sort of reversed "favored nation" status. Only time will tell whether China has the capacity to organize the disadvantaged; especially the third and fourth levels, into action against the status quo. If so, even the more marginalized segments of the first and second levels could join in the issue. The result, of course, would be a world order that cannot be envisioned at this time.

The above analysis assumes that the current world order is in some form of crisis and that there is no real chance of that crisis being resolved. However, Mr. Cox admits that co-option may be the most viable of all courses available for maintaining the status quo. Under the co-option alternative, the first two categories adapt their policies in accordance with the perceived needs of the other categories. In doing so, they persuade the other categories to acquiesce to the status quo without changing the status of the first two levels within that order. On the national level, this alternative was presented by Howard Zinn in his *People's History of the United States* as the normal operating procedure of the political elite. In short, most power structures are routinely forced into co-opting, or adapting to, the needs of the public to hold onto the power to maintain the status quo or their own power base in the existing system.

In some ways, this type of analysis seems simplistic. It is, of course, natural to assume that compromise will be used as a tool whenever feasible to resolve problems. However, the status quo cannot be maintained, or at least it has never in history been maintained, through a consistent use of small scale co-option of resistance to the first level of power within a given society. In most cases the status quo has been changed either through violence or internal death when the gap between those with power and those without power spreads too wide. Such was the demise of Athens, the Roman Empire, the Pax Britannica, and possibly the Pax Americana.

Since the beginning of the 21st century, some of the predictions made by Mr. Cox concerning signs of the decay of the existing world order have come to life. First, a global financial crisis became apparent in 2007. The crisis has several causative factors, two of which were a failure of financial discipline on the part of investors and uncontrolled spending on the part of governments. The US led the world in its addiction to consumption beyond the ability of production to pay for it. This blind impetus to spend was fueled by the greed and mismanagement of the financial industry, evidenced by that industry's short-sighted emphasis on short term profit maximization. This replaced the older investment strategy of emphasizing long term security. Second, as Mr. Cox predicted, the remedy chosen by the global economy to repair this crisis was to withdraw spending in the social sector, that is, to reduce spending on welfare programs.

From the perspective of the ideological underpinnings of the global economic elite spending on welfare restrained the natural growth of national economies, thereby slowing down global economic growth. The free trade philosophy which dominates the global market requires the free flow of goods, services, capital and people without the interference of any governmental agency. The global economic elite stresses the view that this free flow is hindered by welfare spending in the following ways: first, welfare spending locked capital within national borders and lowered the amount of capital available for productive use in the global economy. Second, welfare transfer payments restricted the free flow of labor through immigration and acceptance of low paying employment. Third, welfare spending tends to focus economic attention on the domestic economy rather than the global economy. As we see in the latter case, the US has seriously turned its attention to the reduction of unemployment and domestic economic growth. This is seen as a lack of willingness on the part of the US to exercise its hegemonic role in relation to the global market. Therefore, the global elite, and the economic elites within the national markets, stand firmly against the use of transfer payments as a method of wealth redistribution. The same is true of spending on the global level in relation to transfer payments used in the poor relief system. The use of capital for government bailouts, developmental aid, and other welfare payments as a redistribution of wealth from the core to the periphery is discouraged as much as possible. The aid, if given, should be given for only two reasons: to facilitate the cost effective production of homogenous consumer goods for export to the core nations, or to prevent the mobilization of social unrest. The global social policies, however, that were intended to contain social unrest have, in fact, led to the unrest now being seen in Africa and the Middle East. This unrest is a result of the failure of the autocratic governments supported by international welfare on one important front. They failed to allow the welfare to trickle down to the disadvantaged in amounts large enough to sedate the population. In short, the elites within the peripheral nations confiscated the welfare payments rather than using them for riot control. Whether the current unrest will lead to democratic reform of some type in the periphery or will merely result in a new autocratic regime remains to be seen.

The concept of a new international economic order (NIEC) that arose in 1973 under the auspices of the G-77 points in a different direction. Under this concept the periphery nations would reject the economic order presented above. They would replace it with a concentration on the development of domestic industries (rather than export industries) and self-sufficiency in the agricultural arena. This could be done either overtly, as the Chinese have done, or indirectly through the institution of anti-capitalistic institutions such as those mentioned earlier in relation to Islam and socialism. The collapse of socialism, both real and theoretical, during the 1990s, leaves this option dead in its tracks. The growth of Islamic unrest in Africa, the Middle East and portions of Asia is basic, as we have seen above. Islam rejects the liberal economic ideology and attempts to replace it with Islamic culture, including the ideas of the NIEC. In most cases the latter consists of local control of natural resources such as oil in the attempt to provide stable independence from the existing world order and its programs of poor relief. The independence seen growing from this policy will allow the development first of an independent internal food source and secondly the opportunity to develop a true consumer economy.

The case of China is unique. While China's aim is the same as that of the G-77, i.e., self sufficiency, China has approached this goal by decentralizing both economic control and social control to the various semi-autonomous regions. Although autonomy has been granted to a significant degree, China has maintained overall political control through the continuing use of centralized planning on the macro-level. Currently the Chinese are one of the strongest creditor nations in existence; for example, they currently hold about $1 trillion of the US debt. They have been successful in obtaining Western technology, capital investment and commercial techniques without becoming dependent on the donor nations. The Chinese also have, at least in terms of argument, the most effective military on earth. This for many observers is directly attributable to the creation of a mixed economy. As we have seen, some predict that this will all change when the expected slowdown in economic growth hits China. The prediction, however, is based upon the cycles of boom and bust that have repeatedly plagued the industrial economies of the West. Since the Chinese system is clearly a hybrid, the same cycles may not become apparent. If those cycles are indeed averted, the fourth and fifth level nations will be keen to follow the Chinese system, and China may be able to lead them into a new world order. However, one must consider the possibility that any large scale restructuring of the world order might be resisted through the use of military force by the core nations; as was the case in Iraq. Regardless, it does seem certain that China will not be a candidate for use of the co-option alternative if she remains independent of the existing world order. Whatever role China is able to maintain will eventually alter the world order in ways that are largely unforeseen today. Even under the system advocated by Mr. Cox, the Chinese development is forecast for several decades into the future.

All of this, however, is predicated upon the idea that the current world order is in crisis. In some segments this is portrayed as a failure of the US hegemony that has been in place since 1945. Under this scenario the global system is seen as a result of conscious efforts by the US to establish its own economic system as the basis of the global market, replacing the former Pax Britannica. The system established by the US in 1945 has evolved into a fourfold system in which the first level consists of the core nations — in which the US has the role of primary actor. This core is established around the liberal economic theories of the US system. A second fold is made up of a socially oriented group of nations, called by Mr. Cox the "social democratic". This group accepts the liberal economic system but emphasizes its social goals rather than its purely economic goals. A third fold is represented by the third world in the most inclusive use of the term. This level expresses a much segmented version of the original NIEC ideology. The fourth fold again consists only of China.

There can be no doubt that the first two folds are facing serious financial and economic problems. These problems have led the elite in these two levels to institute an ideological reality check. So far, the debate at this level has concentrated on the question of instituting regulation at the global level, the growing disparity between rich and poor, and the continued marginalization of nations and labor. The two levels under discussion here are still in the midst of the problems created by the recent recession, but the global economy has begun a slow economic recovery and this is also being felt at the national level. There is still internal opposition to emphasis on the global economy, but efforts are being made to at least appear actively engaged in reducing unemployment and uncontrolled spending. In relation to the last issue, the main problem revolves around the huge commitments that have been made to social welfare, especially at the second fold level. Support for these commitments appears to be financially unsustainable over the long term, or even sooner, but the possibility of a quick fix is also elusive. The populations of the first and second level nations have, to an increasing degree, become dependent upon these social entitlement programs. The political elite has shown little heart for making the tough decisions needed to make the programs sustainable due to the risk of losing their constituency (their power). So far, no readily acceptable solution to this problem has been advanced.

The initial reaction of the first and second levels has been to drastically reduce the welfare offered to the third level, resulting in increased social unrest. International organizations, such as the IMF, the World Bank, the OECD, etc, have been restricted not only in the amount of funding they receive but in the rules to be applied in granting the aid that is given. This has resulted in a stronger emphasis at the third level on the tenets of NIEC and social unrest (hypothetical democratic demands).

There is, however, a growing school of thought within the core and social democratic level that the storm can be weathered without any significant change to the existing world order. In both the US and the EU, there has been a growing willingness on the part of the citizens to accept the need to restrict social welfare programs and the consequent spending required. This revolves around the recognition that an aging population will need to be serviced by shrinking revenues. The goal of the restructuring in the long term is the reduction of budget deficits to the point that they become surpluses and the reduction of national debts to truly sustainable levels, if not to zero. As the case of Japan clearly shows, unforeseen circumstances such as natural disasters can easily knock even the wealthiest of nations off track. In general, however, if the will of the people remains strong enough and consistent enough, there does not appear to be any reason these problems cannot be resolved without changing the existing world order.

In addition, it is likely that large segments of the third level will eventually be co-opted into the existing world order without disturbing the status quo. In the long run, this latter policy will probably require that the nations of the third level be made to emphasize agricultural self-sufficiency and domestic consumer industries rather than export industries and international food imports.

The most immediate need is to co-opt that portion of the third world that controls most of the available supply of oil and natural gas. Even under this alternative, however, China still remains the x-factor. Most likely, China will eventually be co-opted into the system as an independent actor on the favored nation basis or something similar to it. The importance of China to the existing world order could be reduced both by the gaining control of the budget deficits and national debts of the first two levels and by a failure of China to meet the growing consumer demand of its internal market. Assuming that the current world order revives as expected, it will not fail if China remains outside the system but continues to work closely with the system.

Even more intriguing is the concept of the status quo changing from within, without necessarily causing the creation of a new world order. For example, it can be expected that the revival of the world order will also entail a renewed interest in expanding the European Union. Currently sixteen nations on the European continent are not members of the union. They are: Albania, Armenia, Azerbaijan, Belarus, Bosnia, Croatia, Georgia, Iceland, Macedonia, Moldova, Montenegro, Norway, Serbia, Switzerland, Turkey, and the Ukraine. Today only Croatia, Macedonia and Turkey have the status of candidate nations. This does not include the Russian Federation, although the Russian public has indicated that they would accept membership in the European Union. In the longer term some of the former colonial possessions of the EU members may be solicited for membership. These might include Algeria, Cyprus, Egypt, Israel, Jordan, Lebanon, Malta, Morocco, Syria, Tunisia and the PLO. This is part of the purpose of the Barcelona process that was launched in 1995.

The difficulty in accommodating the last group of Eastern European nations most recently admitted to the EU points to a long term process for incorporation of the nations mentioned above. Indeed, such a process might extend over a half century or more. A shorter term project might emphasize the projection of a free market or customs union relationship with the Russian Federation and the nations of the Middle East and North Africa.

The stability of the Russian Federation both economically and politically is crucial to the European Union. As of 2011, the EU has been slowly lowering its dependence on oil from the Persian Gulf by developing more dependence on Russian oil. Most instrumental in this movement is Germany, who has recognized and acted upon the Federation's need for technology and capital investment. There is some question whether each can reach its goal without becoming dependent on the other, i.e., can the Federation remain independent of the donor nations in terms of technology and capital, and can the EU remain independent of the Federation's natural resources. The easiest solution, of course, is for the Federation to either join the EU or negotiate a type of free trade or custom union arrangement with the European Union.

It might also be expected that a few select nations will be able to change their status from third world to core or social democratic status. The leading candidates currently for that type of status change are Indonesia, Brazil, Argentina and India. This might leave the core group of nations split into a tripartite system incorporating the existing core, social democratic split and adding a third group of nations identified by national or religious earmarks (Catholic/Latin American, Islamic/African, Hindu/Asian). This development could lead to a deepening of the understanding of the cultures represented by this split.

Mr. Cox envisions the development of a new world order, either arising from the third and fourth levels and violent revolt or internally through peaceful means such as the expansion of the European Union. In either case the governance of this new world order will be developed from the existing international institutions. The United Nations, for example, has over its history become the forum for the expression of the ideas contained in the NIEC program begun in 1973. In the opinion of Mr. Cox the EU can be viewed as one of the most powerful and effective of international organizations. Developing complementary global institutions comparable to those of the EU in scope and function would be a matter of restructuring existing international institutions such as the IMF, the World Bank, the WTO, and the OECD among others. This, in his view, would become a necessity should the EU begin to expand, even if only to the point where the Russian Federation was accepted. In this case a system of governance broader than the existing intergovernmental system of the EU would be needed. The x-factor is China, that is, at some point China may be capable of leading the third and fourth level nations (the majority of existing nations) into a NIEC type of governance. This may or may not include the use of existing international organizations, but it may well be due precisely to the increasing use of these organs to state alternatives to the current world order.

Whether global governance takes the form of a confederal government, an intergovernmental form such as is currently found in the EU, or a form involving the expanded use of existing international institutions, the call is loud and clear. The post-Westphalian system has come upon us and is creating a situation in which the facts of its existence can no longer be ignored. In this writer's opinion, regardless whether something less than a true global government is used to begin the process, it should end with the establishment of a true world government based upon liberal democracy (in this case a multi-level federalism), liberal economics (a modified free market system, which would retain as much of the 19th century vision of free enterprise as possible), and modern science (in this case technological advances for the benefit of mankind). The model for this type of world government has been set forth in earlier publications.